THE BATTLE FOR CONGRESS

Consultants, Candidates, and Voters

JAMES A. THURBER
Editor

BROOKINGS INSTITUTION PRESS
Washington, D.C.

ABOUT BROOKINGS

The Brookings Institution is a private nonprofit organization devoted to research, education, and publication on important issues of domestic and foreign policy. Its principal purpose is to bring knowledge to bear on current and emerging policy problems. The Institution maintains a position of neutrality on issues of public policy. Interpretations or conclusions in Brookings publications should be understood to be solely those of the authors.

1775 Massachusetts Avenue, N.W., Washington, D.C. 20036
www.brookings.edu

Library of Congress Cataloging-in-Publication data

The battle for Congress : consultants, candidates, and voters / James A. Thurber, editor.
p. cm.
Includes bibliographical references and index.
ISBN 0-8157-8464-3 (cloth : alk. paper)—ISBN 0-8157-8463-5 (pbk. : alk. paper)
1. Political campaigns—United States-Case studies. 2. Political consultants—United States—Case studies. 3. Campaign management—United States—Case studies. 4. United States. Congress. House—Elections, 1998—Case studies. I. Thurber, James A., 1943–
JK2281.B35 2000 00-011825
324.973'0929-dc21 CIP

9 8 7 6 5 4 3 2 1

The paper used in this publication meets minimum requirements of the American National Standard for Information Sciences—Permanence of Paper for Printed Library Materials: ANSI Z39.48-1992.

Typeset in Sabon

Composition by R. Lynn Rivenbark
Macon, Georgia

Printed by R. R. Donnelley and Sons
Harrisonburg, Virginia

Contents

For

Claudia, Mark, Kathryn,
Greg, Tristan, and Bryan

Acknowledgments

FUNDING FROM The Pew Charitable Trusts for the Improving Campaign Conduct project at American University's Center for Congressional and Presidential Studies is gratefully acknowledged. Sean Treglia and Michael Delli Carpini, of The Pew Charitable Trusts, provided direction, sound judgment, and support for the project's research, and Rebecca Rimel, president, has offered continued support in the effort to understand and improve the quality of elections, campaigning, and governance in thc United States.

I am especially indebted to Neil Kerwin, provost of American University, for his strong support of this research and of the Center for Congressional and Presidential Studies. Thanks also go to Walter Broadnax, dean of the School of Public Affairs, who has been an active supporter of the center.

American University's School of Public Affairs, the Department of Government, the Center for Congressional and Presidential Studies, the Robert J. Dole Institute for Public Service and Public Policy at the University of Kansas, the Open University of the United Kingdom, and the British Broadcasting Corporation also deserve special recognition. Richard Maidment of the Open University was instrumental in gaining support for the production of two BBC documentaries: on the Capps-Bordinaro contest in California and on the Moore-Snowbarger race in Kansas. The BBC directors, editors, film crews, and production staff spent hours with the candidates and campaign professionals filming the inside of these two campaigns. Both of these excellent documentaries are being given to those interested in them as a supplement to the case studies in this book.

Besides the case study authors, participants in the Money, Media, and Madness conference in December 1998 at the National Press Club in Washington, D.C., added to our knowledge about the relationship among voters, candidates, and consultants for these case studies. They include Rep. Brian Baird, Martin Hamburger, Nancy Johnson, Lou Kitchin, Sheila Krumholz, Dawn Laguens, Mark Lotwis, David Magelby, Joe McCormick, Paige Richardson, Paul Taylor, David Welch, David White, Fred Yang, and Norman Ornstein.

The Center for Congressional and Presidential Studies faculty and staff who helped to coordinate the research activities of these six case studies and to assist in the production of the book include Katherine Creecy, David Dulio, Jennifer Dyjak, Michael Kaiser, Leslie McNaugher, John McPhillips, Lindsay Musser, Candice Nelson, Erin O'Brien, Faith Passy, Christine Pollak, and Scott Sherwin.

At the Brookings Institution Press, I thank Robert Faherty, director, Christopher Kelaher and Nancy Davidson, acquisition editors, and Janet Walker, managing editor. Theresa Walker edited the manuscript, Eloise Stinger proofread it, and Julia Petrakis prepared the index.

THE BATTLE FOR CONGRESS

CHAPTER ONE

Introduction

JAMES A. THURBER

CAMPAIGNS AND ELECTIONS are central to our democracy. These battles are often the single most important event in American democratic life, as they tie citizens to their government and offer Americans an opportunity to give their consent to be governed. Congressional election campaigns also provide a mechanism by which Americans can choose and hold members of Congress accountable for their past performance. In a representative democracy, these campaigns become a mechanism by which the people choose who makes public policy and sets the congressional policy agenda. Elections are a primary way to keep members of Congress responsive to, and aware of, the people's needs, interests, and desires. Congressional elections therefore offer insight into how our democracy works.

Political scientists have studied voters, elections, campaigns, political parties, and candidates for elections using various methodologies, but few have analyzed the relationship of candidates, professional campaign consultants, political parties, media, and voters. The intent of this book is to help readers understand the nature of the contemporary campaigns for competitive seats in Congress and the nature of our representative democracy. Each author explores the relationship among candidates, political consultants, campaign organizations, party activists, and interest groups in their drive for campaign cash and ultimately votes. The importance of congressional campaigns for a vital democracy drives this inquiry.

The research reported also comments on the impact of candidates, consultants, and voters on recent trends in campaigns and elections.

The battles to win seats in Congress have gotten nasty, and campaign consultants have been blamed for many electioneering problems associated with this incivility.[1] What does it take to win a competitive seat in Congress? What is the role of campaign consultants in congressional elections? Critics allege that consultants encourage negative campaigning, reduce debates about complex issues to sound bites, escalate campaign spending, suppress voter turnout, corrupt the science of opinion polling through "push polls" (misleading or fake surveys), and marginalize political parties and volunteers in their support of candidates.[2] Given these claims, it is essential to understand the contemporary role of professional campaign consultants and their relationship with the candidates, volunteers, political parties, and voters to explain the way electoral battles for Congress are waged.

Democratic elections are, or should be in an ideal world, competitive events. However, few congressional races can truly be called competitive.[3] Although congressional campaigns are pivotal to our democracy, in 1998 only slightly more than one-third of the electorate voted in the midterm election.[4] Most members of the House of Representatives run in noncompetitive races; they have no opposition in their party's primaries and little in the general election.[5] The competition for a seat in Congress is rarely truly contested.[6] In 1998 forty members of Congress had no major party opposition in the general election, and another fifty-five had minimal opposition. Continuing the trend that began in 1956, 75 percent of 1998 House incumbents received at least 60 percent of the major party vote.[7] Incumbency advantage in name recognition, contacts, and especially fundraising is key to understanding this relationship. As table 1-1 shows, winners in competitive seats usually outspend the losers by a significant amount—our cases are no exception.

Even though most congressional elections are not competitive, American democracy is marked by the presence of what has been called the permanent campaign—the next election campaign begins as soon as the last one has ended.[8] Owing in part to the decline of party in the electorate, these "permanent campaigns" are usually candidate centered with little strategic role for party organizations.[9] Parties have lost control over the recruitment of candidates, and they have relatively little impact on the flow of campaign funds to the candidates.[10] Most candidates self-recruit, receive few funds from the party organization (although that has been

Table 1-1. *Campaign Expenditures for House Candidates, 1998*

Item	*Mean net dollars spent*
All candidates	547,635
Incumbents	652,121
Winners	817,881
Greater than 60 percent of vote	563,298
Less than 60 percent of vote	1,024,336
Losers	1,343,995
Challengers	321,973
Winners	1,148,979
Losers	
Incumbent, greater than 60 percent of vote	133,560
Incumbent, less than 60 percent of vote	618,256
Open seats	769,227
Winners	975,673
Greater than 60 percent of vote	752,460
Less than 60 percent of vote	1,077,520
Losers	543,207
Greater than 40 percent of vote	728,974
Less than 40 percent of vote	69,250

Source: Figures compiled from Norman Ornstein, Thomas Mann, and Michael Malbin, *Vital Statistics on Congress: 1999–2000* (Washington: AEI Press, 2000), tables 3-2, 3-3, 3-4.

changing in recent years), and mount campaigns designed by themselves, their consultants, and volunteers—not the party.[11] Professional campaign consultants from outside the party organization are hired to help the candidates raise funds and get elected.[12] Political parties have thus lost power, while campaign consultants and interest groups have gained influence in elections.[13]

Interest groups are often more important than party organization. They offer candidates campaign expertise, volunteers, soft money, and issue advocacy advertising to help elect candidates for Congress. Although party organizations have lost power, interest groups have gained influence in elections through campaign funds and campaign management expertise.[14] They offer soft money, issue advertising, and volunteers for get-out-the-vote efforts to help elect candidates.

The chapters in this volume also indicate that negative advertising in competitive races is frequent, personal attacks in congressional campaigns and hard-hitting issue advocacy ads from outside groups are frequent, and public trust continues to decline. Consistent with the criticism that uninformative campaign imagery dominates elections, detailed information about candidates in the media was sparse.[15] We found campaigns were more concerned with creating the "correct" image for the candidate than disseminating the candidate's issue positions. The House elections we studied can therefore be called "low information" elections, meaning that very few voters could recall the name of the incumbent, and even fewer could remember anything the representative had done for the district. In most cases, few voters could remember how the incumbent voted on a particular bill. As evidenced by the challengers own baseline surveys, most challengers were even less well known to the public than their competitors. These difficulties were exacerbated by the fact the media rarely covered the congressional races we studied in great detail and public debates were almost nonexistent.

Beyond providing telling information about the media and political parties, the six cases detailed in this volume show that campaign consultants have replaced the party leaders who supervised older party-based campaigns. We found that those who win congressional campaigns, by choice or necessity, have highly professional organizations, retaining general strategists, pollsters, media consultants, field (or get-out-the-vote) organizers, opposition research experts, and fund-raisers.

The six congressional campaigns that are studied here were awash with special interest money. This observation supports the hypothesis that challengers and open seat candidates can not run a competitive race without a stocked campaign coffer and that these resources are usually not provided by the political parties in abundance.

Even though open seats and competitive races are rare in Congress, we selected these races because they illuminate much about the relationship between candidates and consultants. Competitive races effectively "up the ante" by providing a real possibility that Congress, as an institution, may experience some change. Our six cases focus on these rare, but important, races. The primary focus of these case studies is the relationships between the candidates, political consultants, campaign staff, party leaders, and other key participants in the drive for campaign money and ultimately votes. We found that sometimes these relationships are highly competitive among the professionals, the volunteers, and the candidate and, at other times, the campaign organization ran smoothly. The internal battle over the strategy, theme, and message of the campaigns varied significantly in the six cases, but the winners usually had a well-established professional organization that dominated these decisions.

Table 1-2. *Congressional General Election Results, 1998*

	Actual vote	*Percentage*	*Total receipts (dollars)*
California 22d			
Lois Capps (D)	109,517	55.0	1,037,670
Tom Bordonaro (R)	85,927	43.1	372,436
Robert Bakhus (L)	2,597	1.3	less than 1,000
Connecticut 6th			
Nancy Johnson (R)	101,630	58.1	1,791,391
Charlotte Koskoff (D)	69,201	39.6	552,312
Timothy Knibbs (CC)	3,217	1.8	less than 1,000
Georgia 2d			
Sanford Bishop (D)	77,953	56.8	716,604
Joe McCormick (R)	59,305	43.2	457,098
Kansas 3d			
Dennis Moore (D)	103,376	52.4	1,010,145
Vince Snowbarger (R)	93,938	47.6	1,008,912
Washington 3d			
Brian Baird (D)	120,364	54.7	1,671,658
Don Benton (R)	99,855	45.3	875,220
Wisconsin 2d			
Tammy Baldwin (D)	116,377	52.5	1,529,431
Josephine Musser (R)	103,528	46.7	807,504

Source: www.fec.gov/finance/state97.htm, and *The Alamanac of American Politics 2000.*

This book presents a systematic analysis of the nature of competitive congressional election battles by studying six campaigns in 1998 (table 1-2): chapter 2, Capps versus Bordonaro in California's Twenty-Second Congressional District; chapter 3, Johnson versus Koskoff in Connecticut's Sixth Congressional District; chapter 4, Bishop versus McCormack in Georgia's Second Congressional District; chapter 5, Moore versus Snowbarger in Kansas's Third Congressional District; chapter 6, Baird versus Benton in Washington's Third Congressional District (open seat); and chapter 7, Baldwin versus Musser in Wisconsin's Second Congressional District (open seat).

We selected these races because they were all competitive and thus were most likely to illustrate some of the most talked about trends in campaigns and elections—particularly the role of consultants, media, and candidate "packaging." We also made sure that the candidates we examined in detail were from both of the major parties in a variety of electoral conditions. Two cases feature campaigns for competitive open seats:

Washington's Third and Wisconsin's Second. Two races had strong Democrat challengers: Connecticut's Sixth and Kansas's Third, and two had strong Republican challengers: California's Twenty-Third and Georgia's Second. The districts were diverse in several key demographic and geographic characteristics, such as the percentage of rural and urban characteristics, strength of party organization, media coverage, and racial make-up. All the races involved large amounts of campaign spending and, in several cases, soft money and issue advocacy campaigns from the parties and interest groups were prevalent. In all but one case the winner spent more money than the loser, mirroring the general trend in competitive House races (table 1-1).

All of the cases used a commonly agreed on methodology and analytic framework for collecting information and writing about the campaigns. (See the Appendix, "Case Study Framework and Methodology.") The authors of the case studies are scholars who knew the districts intimately, in most cases lived in the district, and often came to know the candidates and campaign staffs well. Although dispersed throughout the United States, the research team met several times before, during, and after the election. Our common framework for data collection and analysis allowed for common generalizations about the competitive congressional campaigns. Collectively, dozens of interviews were completed with candidates, campaign consultants, campaign staff, party activists, interest group representatives, media, and other insiders over the course of the election cycle. These diverse perspectives yielded important insights into the constant campaign for money and votes that candidates face. We used participant observation and often had access to staff meetings, inside memoranda, and information about the campaign budgets, tracking polls, campaign funding, issue advertising, soft money, and coordination with national parties to tell the story of each campaign. Collectively the case studies in this book present original data and insights that describe the world of campaigning, candidates, campaign consultants, and campaign staff.[16]

Most electoral battles for a congressional seat focus on two campaigns, one for money and one for votes. We found that most candidates hate to ask for campaign money, but at the same time it is absolutely necessary to win. They need money to hire professional campaign consultants to engage in their air wars (television, radio) and ground wars (grassroots organization). They even need it for their get-out-the-vote efforts, a service provided by political parties in years past. Significant campaign money and a professionally run campaign are common characteristics of winners in the six case studies shared.

Elections have a strong impact on members' behavior, thus understanding the nature and form of elective campaigns is imperative. In each of the six cases candidates ran highly personalized campaigns in districts with weak political parties. This combination produced varying perspectives, ideologies, political experience, and policy interests among the six winners. Even when the winners were of the same party persuasion, they rarely had a common philosophy pushed on them by the national party organizations. Candidates often ran away from, or against, their party positions, and the five Democrats ignored or ran against their recently impeached president.

Governing is more difficult when the differences among members of Congress outweigh their commonalties.[17] Adding to this problem is that many candidates are, and will remain, primarily beholden to themselves, their contributors, and their local constituents for election and reelection. They are not responsible to their parties, the president, or some larger national public interest. The result of these battles for congressional seats is a body of people who now are expected to work together for the public good. The tone of the six campaigns did not lend itself to this end. The support offered by parties does not lend itself to this end, and the presence of influential consultants, and volunteers from outside the party also does not lend itself to this end.

Our six case studies also show that campaign conduct does have an impact on representative government. They illuminate reasons why consensus is so difficult to achieve in governing. They show how elections tie citizens to government. Tough election battles guide members' behavior in Congress. Candidate-oriented campaigns, combined with weak party organizations and the growing importance of campaign consultants and funds from specialized interests, result in the election of members to Congress with varying perspectives, political leanings, ideologies, and policy interests. With the help of campaign consultants, candidates learn what is necessary to get elected during the campaign season—not what will facilitate effective governance. Large chunks of special interest money, not forging deliberative relationships with fellow members of Congress, helps candidates get elected. Our case studies show that individualism is a necessity for getting elected and that this learned behavior creates a real impediment to forging commonalties among legislators once elected.

Notes

1. Mark Petraca, "Politcal Consultants and Democratic Governance," *PS: Political Science & Politics,* vol. 22 (March 1989), pp. 11–14.

2. Larry Sabato, *The Rise of Political Consultants: New Ways of Winning Elections* (Basic Books, 1981); Petraca, "Political Consultants"; Susan Glasser, "Hired Guns Fuel Fundraising Race," *Washington Post,* April 30, 2000, p. A-1; and Steven Ansolabehere and Shanto Iyengar, *Going Negative: How Attack Ads Shrink and Polarize the Electorate* (Free Press, 1995).

3. Paul Herrnson, *Congressional Elections: Campaigning at Home and in Washington* (Washington: CQ Press, 2000).

4. Norman J. Ornstein, Thomas E. Mann, and Michael J. Malbin, *Vital Statistics on Congress* (Washington: AEI Press, 2000).

5. Herrnson, *Congressional Elections;* and Gary Jacobson, *The Politics of Congressional Elections* (Longman, 2001).

6. Jacobson, *The Politics of Congressional Elections*; and Charles Cook, "House Race Ratings," *Cook Political Report* (Washington, 2000).

7. Ornstein, Mann, and Malbin, *Vital Statistics on Congress.*

8. Sidney Blumenthal, *The Permanent Campaign* (Simon and Schuster, 1992); and Norman Ornstein and Thomas Mann, *The Permanent Campaign and Its Future* (Washington: AEI Press, 2000).

9. Dandy Maisel, *Parties and Elections in America: The Electoral Process* (Rowman and Littlefield); and Paul Herrnson, *Party Campaigning in the 1980s* (Harvard University Press, 1988).

10. Herrnson, *Party Campaigning.*

11. Paul Allen Beck, *Party Politics in America* (Longman, 1997).

12. Herrnson, *Congressional Elections.*

13. Samuel Eldersveld and HanesWalton, *Political Parties in American Society* (Bedford/St. Martin's, 2000).

14. Paul Herrnson, Ronald Shaiko, and Clyde Wilcox, *Interest Group Collection: Electioneering, Lobbying, and Policymaking in Washington* (Chatham House Publishers, 1998).

15. Dean Alger, *The Media and Politics* (Wadsworth Publishing Company).

16. The Capps and Moore cases have been produced as one-hour BBC documentaries and are available free from the Center for Congressional and Presidential Studies at American University.

17. Burdett Loomis, ed., *Esteemed Colleagues* (Brookings, 2000).

CHAPTER TWO

One Year and Four Elections: The 1998 Capps Campaign for California's Twenty-Second District

JEFF GILL

CAMPAIGNS ARE DYNAMIC and fluid endeavors. The choices that campaign managers and candidates make during this process are in general not well understood by academics, journalists, and the public at large. A poor research design for studying the strategy and tactics taken in the midst of a campaign would be to look at final, aggregate statistics such as polls, final vote counts, and Federal Election Commission (FEC) filings without examining the intermediate qualitative factors that drive these numbers. This book takes a different approach to increasing our knowledge about campaign conduct: a chronological case study that describes the *process* of campaigning and the decisions made during the campaign.

Unlike any other congressional district in 1998, there were four elections in California's Twenty-Second Congressional District in which the same two Republican and Democratic candidates appeared on every ballot: two special elections, California's first (and perhaps last) open primary, and the general election. This unusual situation makes the case particularly interesting in several ways. One effect was that campaign

Thanks to Cathy Duvall, Lois Capps, and the entire campaign staff for access, comments, and an inordinate amount of time during a busy election. All errors, of course, remain mine. The author gratefully acknowledges support from the Pew Charitable Trusts through the "Improving Campaign Conduct" grant to American University.

decisions had ramifications not only for the present competition but also for imminent future elections. This feature also meant that available resources had competing short-term and long-term uses. Furthermore, it is difficult to solicit contributions from an individual or a political action committee (PAC) several times in an eleven-month period.

This chapter highlights the historical and short-term factors that influenced campaigning and campaign decisions in California's Twenty-Second district. In many ways the district is atypical in its geographic configuration, ideological and partisan distribution, and ordering of issue salience. The Lois Capps campaign successfully interpreted the relative importance of these attributes and, with some serendipity, received the highest vote total in four immediately consecutive elections. This case study focuses on the factors and decisions that produced these outcomes.

District Description

The Twenty-Second Congressional District consists of all of San Luis Obispo County and nearly all of Santa Barbara County. The Carpinteria area in a far southern section of Santa Barbara County was districted into the Twenty-Third Congressional District to balance out population requirements. Two California State Assembly districts, 33 and 35, have the same coverage as the Twenty-Second Congressional District (except that district 35 also covers a part of Ventura County Twenty-Third Congressional District). The district is heterogeneous in population density with mostly rural areas (farming, ranching, vineyards), two main population centers (Santa Barbara and San Luis Obispo cities), and a few smaller towns and cities (Santa Maria, Morro Bay, Atascadero, Paso Robles, and so on). The population distribution resembles a "bow tie" in that the high-density areas are at opposite ends of the district, and the middle area is sparsely inhabited. There is one large military base, Vandenberg, with a focus on space-flight operations. The area is known in California for its spectacular unspoiled coastline, wines, state parks, and low-key life-style. Each of these attributes is predominantly a function of the distance from Los Angeles and the San Francisco Bay Area, as well as the relative population difference.

Recent History

The Twenty-Second district has been represented by Republicans since World War II. However, the district has historically favored *moderate*

Republicans. Robert Lagomarsino held the seat from 1974 to 1992, when Michael Huffington (previously a Texas businessman and husband of political commentator Ariana Huffington) spent a surprisingly large amount of personal money, for this district, to win the Republican primary. Huffington then vacated the seat after one term to challenge Dianne Feinstein in an infamously negative and expensive race for the Senate. In 1994 Andrea Seastrand, the widow of Eric Seastrand, a long-time popular Republican state assemblyman, won the Republican nomination in a year characterized nationally by an emergent conservative slate of candidates for congressional office. She differed little from those peers, favoring tax cuts, the lifting of restrictions on gun ownership, a complete ban on all abortion, and reduction in the scope of federal government. The Democratic challenger was an uncharacteristic, unpolished politician: a University of California Santa Barbara religious studies professor named Walter Capps. Capps's positions fell somewhat to the left of the district median voter, whereas Seastrand's fell considerably to the right.

The 1994 campaign highlighted an important regional characteristic. Santa Barbara County has more liberals of both parties than San Luis Obispo County. Although the city of San Luis Obispo shares this trait, most of San Luis Obispo County is rural or semirural and overwhelmingly more conservative than the rest of the congressional district. One important exception to this observation is the city of Santa Maria, which is barely within Santa Barbara County on the northern end and more closely resembles neighboring rural San Luis Obispo County. The regional dynamic combined with the candidates' domiciles led naturally to a strong geographic basis for this and future elections. Seastrand won by a mere 1,563 votes because she captured a sufficient number of moderate Santa Barbara Republicans, while Capps could not connect appreciably in any part of San Luis Obispo County. In fact he failed to gain much support even in semiurban areas in the middle and northern part of the district such as Santa Maria, the Five Cities Area, and Morro Bay, much less in the extreme northern part of San Luis Obispo County, which holds the conservative base.

Seastrand went to the House in 1995 as part of the seventy-three freshman Republicans now famous for strongly ideological policy positions. Her conservative floor votes on education funding, immigration, labor, abortion, and the environment pushed her far from the moderate leanings of the district and set the stage for a rematch with Capps in the 1996 election. Because of the closeness of the 1994 race and the dramatic contrast between the policy positions of the two candidates, the 1996 election attracted a large number of outside interest groups.[1] Labor groups, including the AFL-CIO, spent just under a million dollars on advertisements attacking Seastrand's positions. Other groups that spent considerable money on issue advertisements included the National Rifle Association, the Sierra Club, and abortion groups from both sides.

The tone of the election grew noticeably more negative as the closeness of the second competition became apparent. Both sides benefited from significant fund-raising support ($1,266,561 for Seastrand, $962,629 for Capps) and spent nearly all of it ($1,244,151 for Seastrand, $904,831 for Capps).[2]

Both sides went negative, and Seastrand in particular ran a series of negative ads attacking Capps for his refusal to support Proposition 187 (an initiative to strip state-supported benefits for illegal aliens and their families) and highlighting Capps's antideath penalty stance by associating him with Richard Allen Davis, a convicted child murderer. Voter reaction to this campaign tactic and renewed attention to the northern part of the district by Capps helped him win by a respectable margin of 10,312 votes. He won even though he could not campaign all summer because he was injured in a May car crash caused by a drunken driver.

Capps worked during his ten months in the House on bills to streamline Medicare payments for people suffering from Lou Gehrig's disease and to obtain funds for dredging Morro Bay. He also took a very public stand against the Clinton administration's refusal to sign the global treaty to ban land mines. On October 28, 1997, Capps suffered a fatal heart attack at the age of sixty-three in Dulles Airport, when he was returning from his district to vote on a defense authorization bill.

The First Special Election

The January 13 special election to replace Walter Capps provided Republicans with a valuable opportunity to regain a seat held for fifty years before 1996. The immediate choice of the party was Brooks Firestone, heir to a tire and winery fortune. Firestone was a moderate business leader and was then a state assemblyman. He was just beginning a run for the lieutenant governorship when Newt Gingrich called to persuade him to change ambitions. He was also a family friend of Gerald Ford and well known to national Republican leaders. Firestone was considered a perfect candidate for the district by the state and national Republican leaders, as he was pro-choice, favored increased environmental protection, and yet was friendly to business interests. However, conservatives in the district found Firestone far too liberal, characterizing him as a "Christine Todd Whitman Republican." From this group emerged Tom Bordonaro, a San Luis Obispo County state assemblyman and unambiguous conservative. Differences between the two candidates starkly divided district Republicans and reinforced the regional dichotomy.

Bordonaro came from a wealthy family in Paso Robles, located at the northern end of San Luis Obispo. This area is an agricultural valley distinct from the rest of county and bounded by mountains from the sea. It is often referred to by county residents as "over the grade" because of the steep incline on Highway 101 that separates the valley from central San Luis Obispo County. This area is unquestionably the conservative heart of the congressional district and votes overwhelmingly Republican. At the age of eighteen Bordonaro was in a serious car accident that left him paralyzed and with limited use of his arms. The subsequent six months in hospitals helped foster a strong distaste for bureaucracy and the medical establishment in general. Until giving up his seat to compete for the Twenty-Second district House seat, Bordonaro was a state assemblyman and remains managing general partner of the family ranch.

One obvious choice of state and national Democratic Party leaders to run in the January special election was popular state senator Jack O'Connell, who was approached while Lois Capps remained undecided. O'Connell declined the opportunity to be considered, and Capps subsequently decided to run. She had little formal experience in politics but was involved in Walter Capps's life as a member of Congress to a much greater extent than is typical for a spouse. She shuttled with Walter back and forth between the district and Washington and was generally considered an adviser on political issues. Lois Capps worked for twenty years in the Santa Barbara school system as a school nurse and nursing administrator. She also taught early child care development classes at Santa Barbara City College for ten years. These concerns led naturally to her policy interests in health care and education. She also contributed to many local charities and organizations: the American Red Cross, the Family Service Agency, the American Heart Association, the Santa Barbara Women's Political Committee, and her church (Grace Lutheran). While Walter was unable to campaign during the summer of 1996, Lois Capps appeared periodically on his behalf. The challenge for the campaign was to broaden these qualifications to the greatest extent possible over a short period.

By far Capps's greatest asset was her ability to connect with people one-on-one. She conveyed sincerity and concern in a way that is atypical of politicians. To a great extent this is a characteristic shared with Walter Capps. For instance, in the debate sponsored by the American Association of Retired Persons (AARP), she shook hands and talked with all thirty-six people in the room, including the Veteran's Hall janitor as he unlocked doors and set up chairs. This personal quality fostered great loyalty with staff, volunteers, and donors.

Under California law for special elections, all candidates compete in an open contest where the top vote getter from each party competes in a second run-off election provided that no one candidate reaches a majority in the first contest. The governor sets the election dates, and Pete Wilson picked virtually the last possible day allowed by law to give Republicans as much time as possible to organize. The dynamic of the first special election was essentially an ideological battle internal to the Republican Party, as neither of these candidates wanted to directly attack the fifty-nine-year old recent widow.

In many ways the dissension within the district Republicans was symptomatic of national trends. Brooks Firestone was the anointed centrist candidate preferred by state and national party elites, whereas Tom Bordonaro was a prototypical conservative activist. Where this cleavage was most evident was in the paid media run by Bordonaro and outside groups in January. In one example, a television spot highlighted Firestone's opposition to a ban on partial birth abortion by graphically describing the procedure. This commercial was part of a $200,000 campaign ($100,000 per special election) by Gary Bauer and his antiabortion group, Campaign for Working Families.[3] After considerable damage had been done among moderate and conservative Republicans, Firestone finally ran a response ad stating his support for a modified ban. The ad appeared to have little mitigating effect and seemed to solidify Firestone's defensive position.

Firestone, however, had several advantages. He received strong support from the national party and picked up notable endorsements from Gingrich, Gerald Ford, and Steve Forbes. Firestone also had a substantial financial advantage: not only did he receive support from the party, he also put $400,000 of his own fortune into the campaign. Conversely, Bordonaro ran a shoestring campaign. He picked up $1,000 each from fourteen conservative House members but only raised a total of $131,700.[4] This resource gap was somewhat counterbalanced by the outside groups that attacked Firestone. The California Republican assembly spent

$16,100 on a mailing that criticized Firestone's refusal to rule out a tax increase to support Social Security if necessary. Two religious groups, the Christian Coalition and the Catholic Alliance, distributed well over 100,000 voter guides and flyers at churches highlighting the candidates' differences on abortion, gay and lesbian rights, and the death penalty. While the guides did not specifically recommend a vote for Bordonaro over Firestone or Capps, the message was unmistakable.

Outside group support was not restricted to supporting Bordonaro. Planned Parenthood Action Fund, a supporter of abortion rights for women, spent more than $40,000 phonebanking (hiring staff to make unsolicited calls) and mailing against Bordonaro for his "clearly extremist views" on abortion. Americans for Limited Terms and U.S. Term Limits together spent nearly $100,000 airing a radio and television ad against Bordonaro for refusing to sign a pledge limiting himself to three congressional terms as Firestone and Capps had done.

The effect of these outside interest group ads was generally to alienate and annoy district residents because abortion, term limits, and gun control were simply not important to many voters in the district.[5] The single issue ads generally ignored more salient topics such as education, the environment, and economic development. This development created an impression that the special election had become a referendum between two national parties and a dozen Washington-based groups, rather than a local determination of congressional succession.

Lois Capps received the most votes (45 percent) but failed to achieve a simple majority, thus requiring a March runoff election. To nearly everyone's surprise, Bordonaro defeated Firestone for the right to face Capps in the runoff (table 2-1). Firestone's defeat was significant for the Republican Party because the hand-picked successor lost to the self-nominated standard bearer for the right-most faction of the party. Considerable personal animosity developed during the campaign. Because of Gingrich's support for Firestone, Bordonaro stated publicly that Gingrich was interfering in local political processes in the central coast and that if elected he would vote against Gingrich for speaker.

Part of the reason for the January outcome was that the voters who turned out resembled those expected in a primary: generally more ideologically extreme. This result exacerbated the bimodal effect in the district and gave Bordonaro and Capps natural advantages over Firestone. And like a primary, turnout was relatively low compared with that for general elections. The overall effect was to suppress the effect of the

Table 2-1. *California's Twenty-Second District Primary, January 13, 1998*

Item	*Precinct votes*	*Absentee votes*	*Total*	*Percent*
San Luis Obispo County, 124,994 registered voters				
Lois Capps (Democrat)	16,313	12,917	29,230	43.90
Tom Bordonaro (Republican)	16,399	10,890	27,229	40.90
Brooks Firestone (Republican)	4,837	4,392	9,229	13.86
Robert Bakhaus (Libertarian)	282	156	438	0.66
Tod Rosenberger (Libertarian)	184	144	328	0.49
Robert Lovgren (Republican)	53	72	125	0.19
Santa Barbara County, 202,952 registered voters				
Lois Capps (Democrat)	25,254	15,121	40,375	45.71
Tom Bordonaro (Republican)	12,314	4,574	16,888	19.12
Brooks Firestone (Republican)	17,613	12,514	30,127	34.11
Robert Bakhaus (Libertarian)	329	122	451	0.57
Tod Rosenberger (Libertarian)	253	84	337	0.38
Robert Lovgren (Republican)	103	54	157	0.18
District Total, 327,946 registered voters				
Lois Capps (Democrat)	41,567	28,038	69,605	44.93
Tom Bordonaro (Republican)	28,653	15,464	44,117	28.48
Brooks Firestone (Republican)	22,450	16,906	39,356	25.41
Robert Bakhaus (Libertarian)	611	278	889	0.57
Tod Rosenberger (Libertarian)	437	228	665	0.43
Robert Lovgren (Republican)	156	126	282	0.18

Source: California Secretary of State, Sacramento.

district's moderate leanings and hurt Firestone in particular. One effect of Firestone's loss was to magnify existing divisions in the Republican Party. After the January election Ford described Bordonaro as "one of those extreme right wing candidates" in a *New York Times* interview that would resurface later as an October campaign issue.[6] There is also evidence that some moderate Republicans did not substantively participate in the March runoff election because of disenchantment with the Republican candidate.

The first special election was a difficult test for the Capps campaign. Lois Capps kept nearly the entire campaign team from Walter Capps's 1996 election, including the deputy campaign manager and field director Cathy Duvall, who became Lois Capps's campaign manager (Walter

Capps's brother Doug managed his 1996 campaign). This had two important effects. First, it immediately gave her a professional organization that had won a competitive race one year earlier. Second, it provided her with a team that understood her values and priorities. It also meant that the campaign for Walter's successor was run by people who had been profoundly affected by his recent and sudden death. This factor cannot be overstated given the unique personal qualities he possessed and the loyalty that this "nonpolitician" engendered.[7]

The first goal of the Capps team was to define who Lois was going to be to the electorate: what issues she stood for. Three clearly defined themes emerged. Because of her background as a nurse and administrator in the Santa Barbara school system, the campaign decided to emphasize health care and education. These two themes were strongly resonant in a district with a high percentage of seniors and in a state with deteriorating public schools. The campaign message highlighted Capps's background on these issues with the slogan: "the experience of a lifetime." The third theme emerged as an emotional pitch about her desire to "carry on Walter's legacy." Duvall also wanted to avoid going negative in the first campaign, and these positive themes fit perfectly with that decision.

Duvall and Capps had an important strategic decision to make about the procedural ramifications of the special election. Given a limited amount of campaign funds on hand (and of course limited time to raise more), should the campaign spend all its available resources to attempt to win outright in January, or was it better to let the Republicans beat up on one another and then let Capps face the potentially damaged survivor? One factor made this an easy decision. Given a choice, Capps and Duvall would rather have faced Bordonaro than Firestone. There were two reasons for this preference: Firestone was obviously more moderate and cut deeper into the Capps's base of support, and Firestone was likely to be much better financed in a future contest. Duvall asserted that the harder Capps ran in the first election, the more it hurt Firestone rather than Bordonaro. The rationale was that Bordonaro's primary support base was unlikely to respond positively to messages from Capps, but independents, decline-to-states, and third party supporters were far more swayable. Thus running hard in the first special election increased the probability that the second election would be against Bordonaro.

Firestone's loss illustrates the distribution of ideology and partisanship in the district. Rather than a classic unimodal, Downsian (centered around moderates) distribution of ideology, the Twenty-Second district

Figure 2-1. *Alternate Distributions of Ideology*

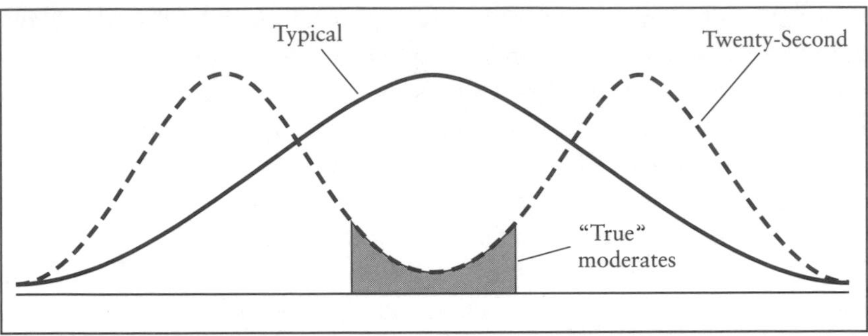

is bimodal (figure 2-1). Candidates can usually count on a large proportion of voters concentrated around the median position. However, in this district voters were concentrated equally around two polarized positions. This means that a liberal-leaning Democrat could count on approximately 40 percent of the voters at the start of the campaign, and a conservative-leaning Republican could count on an equal number of voters at the start of the campaign. Voter registration supported this claim, with 42 percent registered as Republicans and 42 percent registered as Democrats. There is also evidence that registered independents in the district were moderate Republican leaners, as shown by national voting patterns and long-term moderate Republican control of the House seat.

Firestone's loss was caused by Bordonaro's picking up a large proportion of the right-most voters when he entered the contest. This meant that his base of support was now restricted to the center of the distribution where fewer voters existed in this district (the identified "true" moderates in figure 2-1). As one pundit noted about the district, "Moderate Republicans may not be great in number. But they are a swing vote. Especially in affluent suburbs, where voters tend to be economically conservative and socially liberal."[8] Or as Cathy Duvall put it, "The district is just not all that swing," meaning that the proportion of voters around the median position is not sufficiently large enough to drive election results (figure 2-1). In regional terms, Bordonaro acquired the San Luis Obispo County Republicans who tended to be far less moderate than those in Santa Barbara County, with the exception of socially moderate or liberal Republicans clustered in small beach towns. When Bordonaro (and the outside interest groups) aired ads on abortion and other wedge issues, this was a reminder to the social conservatives that Firestone was not really their type of Republican. This distribution of voters played a pivotal role in subsequent contests between Bordonaro and Capps.

The Runoff Special Election

The campaign for the runoff election began literally before the votes from the January special elections were fully tabulated. Every internal field poll conducted by the Capps campaign before the March election showed Capps failing to get 50 percent. They also showed Bordonaro failing to get 50 percent. So the greatest emphasis of the Capps campaign was on turnout and persuading self-identified nonpartisans. However, there was a perception, which the campaign allowed to continue, that its plan was to pursue moderate Republicans who voted for Firestone (25 percent). But Duvall noted that Capps's strengths did not necessarily play into this constituency, with the exception of the abortion issue. So a new message was developed: local economic development. The campaign crafted a new issue focused on attracting and supporting the burgeoning high-technology industry in the district and the creation of public-private partnerships. These issues were purposely directed at moderate *Santa Barbara* Republicans who might be swayed away from a party-consistent vote. This strategy was somewhat half-hearted, as polling data showed little flexibility among core Republican voters. The efforts that developed reflect that these voters were still too tempting and numerous to completely ignore.

The key to the Capps strategy was turnout. Fully one-third of the budget was spent on fieldwork, according to Duvall. The emphasis was on "get-out-the-vote" (GOTV) efforts in order to counter a traditional Republican strength in this area. Besides targeting registered Democrats, the Capps campaign pursued nonpartisans (independent, decline-to-state, third party supporters), and it would have been an additional benefit if these appeals had worked with south San Luis Obispo County Republicans. Although the moderate Republican effort was not completely successful, it seems to have picked up some of these voters. The "Republicans for Capps" message was played throughout this campaign but would be dropped from the plan later in the year.

Even more prominently than in the January election, the runoff campaign was dominated by outside interest groups. The most visible, and negative, was the Campaign for Working Families' (Gary Bauer's group) antiabortion ads. These ads were essentially the same ones that had been directed at Firestone, but now attacked Capps by name: "Tom Bordonaro and the American Medical Association support banning this terrible procedure. But unfortunately Lois Capps does not." The Capps campaign had anticipated these attacks and had already shot a response. It begins with, "First he unfairly attacked Brooks Firestone, now he's unfairly attacking Lois Capps." The subtlety in the ad is an implied alliance with Firestone against unfair negative tactics by Bordonaro: part of the strategy to attract moderates of all types. The Capps ad affirms her "strongly pro-choice" position, making an exception only for late-term abortions. The intent was to take the focus away from a rarely performed procedure, partial-birth abortions, and recenter it on mainstream abortion questions. Soon thereafter, the National Abortion and Reproductive Rights Action League (NARAL) declared its intention to match Gary Bauer's group in spending and began airing ads calling Bauer "extreme" and "dangerous." Eventually, though, the league would only spend about a third as much as the Campaign for Working Families.

Other interest groups spending considerable resources airing single issue ads and sending mail included the National Rifle Association, U.S. Term Limits, Americans for Limited Terms (budgeting $185,000), Americans for Job Security (spending $40,000), and labor groups such as the AFL-CIO. Given that there was only one race taking place at this time (March 1998) in the entire country and given that it was in a competitive district, it became very attractive for these interest groups to participate. However, as the Republican strategist Ed Gillespie noted, "Their strategy is not always to win on Election Day so much as it is to influence public opinion."[9] In total, more than $1 million was spent by outside groups on television advertisements alone during the two special elections.[10]

The net effect of this barrage of outside issue ads was to drown out policy interests natural to the district such as education, federal disaster support (El Niño damage), the environment, and fiscal responsibility. Both candidates made public statements expressing frustration at an outsider-imposed agenda. Capps asked the Democratic National Party not to spend soft money on her behalf or to send big name speakers.

Against this backdrop the campaigns went negative in their advertising. The Capps campaign produced only one such ad, which described Bordonaro as "too extreme for the central coast." Bordonaro ran a series

Table 2-2. *California's Twenty-Second District Special Election Runoff, March 10, 1998*

Item	*Precinct votes*	*Absentee votes*	*Total*	*Percent*
San Luis Obispo County, 126,959 registered voters				
Lois Capps (Democrat)	18,195	17,797	36,174	48.04
Tom Bordonaro (Republican)	20,616	17,223	37,839	50.26
Robert Bakhaus (Libertarian)	864	415	1,279	1.70
Santa Barbara County, 207,747 registered voters				
Lois Capps (Democrat)	32,482	24,736	57,218	57.56
Tom Bordonaro (Republican)	25,249	15,136	40,385	40.63
Robert Bakhaus (Libertarian)	1,191	609	1,800	1.81
District total, 334,706 registered voters				
Lois Capps (Democrat)	50,677	42,715	93,392	53.46
Tom Bordonaro (Republican)	45,865	32,359	78,224	44.78
Robert Bakhaus (Libertarian)	2,055	1,024	3,079	1.76

Source: California Secretary of State.

of negative ads attacking Capps as a liberal. This move was followed up by a substantial mailing campaign funded by the NRCC and the California Republican Party with very negative messages and an eleventh-hour phonebank campaign with unsubstantiated charges about Capps. One Bordonaro statement even (incorrectly) asserted that Jack O'Connell, the Democratic state senator, supported Bordonaro in the contest rather than fellow Democrat Capps.

Bordonaro's status as unwelcome to the national party hurt his fundraising efforts, and his failure to convince moderate voters on social issues damaged efforts to move beyond his base, geographically and ideologically. Capps won the March 10 special election with just under 54 percent of the voters to Bordonaro's 45 percent (table 2-2).

It was clear from the moment this special election ended that a long year of campaigning was inevitable. As Bordonaro tactlessly said, "Now the real race starts. Now we are running against the incumbent Lois Capps, not the widow Lois Capps." Interestingly, each of the next two elections (primary and general) pitted two current officeholders against each other. In such a race each candidate can point to his own and his opponent's legislative record. Although this step implies an issue-dominated race, the opposite was observed. Subsequent campaigning continued to be focused on personalities at the expense of substantive policy debates.

The Primary

Close on the heels of the second special election was the upcoming June primary. Until this point the national parties were not major participants. Bordonaro practically ran *against* the national Republican Party. Once the March special election ended, Capps was a congressperson and therefore of greater interest to the Democratic Congressional Campaign Committee. The Republican Party acknowledged Bordonaro as their candidate for the 1998 general election and began helping him set up a new campaign office.

While Bordonaro's campaign was going through the traditional growing pains associated with enlarging the office and hiring additional staff with newfound national support, the Capps campaign had a strategic decision to make. Duvall explains that it was important to defend the 54 percent as much as possible in the June primary in order to adversely affect Bordonaro's fund-raising capabilities. The more competitive he appeared, the more money he would be able to raise. She also anticipated that Bordonaro would pick up a 5 percent bump in support in the fall election given that other Republican candidates would be on the ballot (although the campaign, as a fund-raising strategy, maintained publicly that this pickup would be 10 percent).

So a decision was made to actively campaign for the June primary even though there was no Democratic challenger. This decision was also driven by the first implementation of California's open primary law, which mandated that all candidates for office, regardless of party, appear on the same ballot (this blanket approach was later struck down by the U.S. Supreme Court on June 26, 2000, although the California secretary of state, Bill Jones, vows to implement some new variant). A strong Bordonaro showing was possible and would be particularly damaging given that Capps's name was on the same ballot. The campaign plan for the primary was not all that different from the previous plan except that seniors were targeted in greater measure, and San Luis Obispo County was given more attention (this decision was notable since Walter Capps never took the county and neither did Lois Capps in either special election). One contributing reason for the attention on seniors was a pullout of health main-

Table 2-3. *California's Twenty-Second District Primary, June 2, 1998*

Item	*Precinct vote*	*Absentee votes*	*Total*	*Percent*
San Luis Obispo County, 129,805 registered voters				
Lois Capps (Democrat)	17,195	15,297	32,492	100.00
Tom Bordonaro (Republican)	16,948	14,527	31,475	92.80
James Harrison (Republican)	1,332	1,127	2,459	7.20
Robert Bakhaus (Libertarian)	538	296	834	100.00
Richard Porter (Reform)	191	165	356	100.00
Santa Barbara County, 210,211 registered voters				
Lois Capps (Democrat)	30,119	17,176	47,295	100.00
Tom Bordonaro (Republican)	21,297	10,778	32,075	85.50
James Harrison (Republican)	3,995	2,057	5,442	14.50
Robert Bakhaus (Libertarian)	908	388	1,296	100.00
Richard Porter (Reform)	302	121	423	100.00
District total, 340,016 registered voters				
Lois Capps (Democrat)	47,314	32,473	79,787	100.00
Tom Bordonaro (Republican)	38,245	25,305	63,550	89.00
James Harrison (Republican)	5,327	3,184	7,901	11.00
Robert Bakhaus (Libertarian)	1,446	684	2,130	100.00
Richard Porter (Reform)	493	286	779	100.00

Source: California Secretary of State.

tenance organizations (HMOs) in San Luis Obispo County. Several HMO programs were doing poorly financially and shut down their programs, affecting seniors in particular. Since both candidates now represented the affected constituents, this event became a natural political issue during the June primary and the subsequent general election.

The June primary brought no new surprises (table 2-3). Capps won San Luis Obispo County by 1,000 votes, which implied a reward for spending more time out of her home area. The total margin over Bordonaro was 16,000 votes, which was largely a function of Santa Barbara County voters.

This description sets the stage for the general election campaign. The summer months remained relatively quiet, as one candidate was a state assemblyman and the other now a freshman member of Congress. Most of the activity involved fund-raising, refining campaign plans, and emphasizing constituent service. The fall campaign essentially did not start until after Labor Day. The summer was not totally uneventful, as Duvall noted that there was concern about the fallout from President Bill Clinton's scandal and the effect it might have on Democratic House candidates. In addition, the lull in activities allowed Duvall to devise a detailed campaign plan, including finer geographic units.

Campaign Structure and Key Issues

The Capps campaign leadership was nonhierarchical and decentralized around five key players. Cathy Duvall was the campaign manager and also a resident of Santa Barbara. She was the primary tactician but developed strategy in a loose, informal committee fashion with Bill Carrick (the media consultant based in Los Angeles), Mark Guma (the direct mail consultant based in New York), Fred Yang (the pollster based in Washington), and of course the candidate. Also included in a number of discussions was Capps's chief of staff, Jeremy Rabinovitz. This was the group that decided all featured issues, themes, and messages. Duvall describes how consensus was built over iterative phone conversations and occasionally conference calls. She asserts that all important decisions were reached by "bouncing out" ideas and reaching a consensus over phone conversations rather than actual face-to-face meetings.

In contrast, Duvall ran the district campaign in a hierarchical, managerial fashion. All *implementation* decisions were made by her except for very low-level issues. Four managers reported directly to Duvall: Ben Romo, deputy campaign manager, Jessica Frahs, finance director, Kevin Easton, field director, and Mollie Culver, San Luis Obispo County coordinator. Jessica Frahs was responsible for coordinating fund-raising efforts and had two subordinates in Santa Barbara County and one in San Luis Obispo County. Kevin Easton had four field coordinators reporting to him: one in Santa Barbara, one dedicated to the University of California, Santa Barbara, and the Isla Vista area around the campus, and two in the San Luis Obispo field office. All financial decisions were approved by Duvall.

Duvall explains that most of the implementation decisions were logistical in nature and "no different than any other managerial enterprise." She felt that at least 90 percent of the work was basic management of events, vendors, volunteers and employees, and finances, little different than private enterprise. However, the real difference in the required style of management was that a campaign is more fluid and unpredictable than other managerial settings. It requires greater flexibility and adaptability in implementation. However, the logistics can be consuming at the expense of strategic planning if the campaign manager is not careful. According to Duvall, "you have a million things that you could do as a campaign, the trick is to figure out which 250,000 are the most important."

Strategy, Theme, and Message

An important new strategy that emerged from a summer of reviewing voter records and updating the detailed campaign plans was the idea that the campaign should focus more in Bordonaro's strong area in northern Santa Barbara County and parts of San Luis Obispo, specifically Santa Maria where Republican wedge issues play well. This strategy was an expression of how comfortable Duvall and the management team felt about southern Santa Barbara County but also underscored the notion that there were some obtainable votes in that area. At the very least, Duvall noted, this strategy would force Bordonaro to spend time and resources defending the area, thus consuming resources that would otherwise be spent elsewhere. She also pointed out that if the polling numbers in other areas changed dramatically, this strategy would be the first part of the campaign plan to be abandoned.

An important aspect of the strategy was the decision not to target Republican voters with any direct approaches. Although some of the later ads can be interpreted as appealing to weak Republicans, Duvall asserted that there was no intention to go after and sway registered Republicans specifically. However, there was a concerted effort to go after moderate voters of *all* kinds. Support was found by campaign staff who conducted a quick poll. Roughly 400 registered Republican women in Santa Barbara City were asked about support for the two candidates. The numbers starkly showed that this group, presumably one of the more persuadable Republican subgroups, was solidly supportive of Bordonaro. However, there was a perception in the media and presumably within the Bordonaro campaign, that Capps was targeting these voters. Duvall explained that it made sense to let this "myth" perpetuate itself for tactical reasons: to make Bordonaro think that he had to defend a Republican segment. Not only was it incorrect that the Capps campaign was targeting moderate Republicans except as part of a strategy to attract moderates in general, Duvall says, there was an incorrect perception that a reasonable proportion of moderate Republicans was already supporting Capps. This second part of the "myth" found its way anecdotally into the print media. Again, Duvall saw no reason to correct this second misperception.

Despite Duvall's claim that the campaign strategy did not include pursuing the Firestone voters, the campaign's ads aimed at conservative Democrats and independents also had an appeal to moderate Republicans. Capps's success with this group in March is hard to ignore. Representative Martin Frost, chairman of the Democratic Congressional Campaign Committee (DCCC), noted that "picking up one-third of Firestone's voters put her up to 53 percent."[11] Several print and television ads used the phrases "an independent voice for the central coast" and "your mainstream choice." This wording could be effective in two ways. First, it fostered a centrist image to appeal to various types of nonpartisans, while simultaneously selling to Firestone Republicans without the potential for turning out Bordonaro supporters, as phonebanking and GOTV efforts might do. Second, it disassociated Capps from the word "Democratic" and therefore created distance from Clinton.

Evidence that the campaign should be seeking support from some more conservative voters can be found in polling and election data. It is clear from the March 10 special election results that Capps picked up some of Firestone's supporters (table 2-2). If one can assume Firestone's January 30,000 Santa Barbara County voters participated again in March, then there was a close split, with 17,000 going to Capps and 13,000 going to Bordonaro. Obviously, this view is a great simplification, but when one notes that 88,000 voted in January and 98,000 voted in March in the county, then 30,000 Firestone voters were simply too important to ignore. However, in March a reasonable proportion of Firestone's voters stayed home rather than cross party lines or vote for what some might have considered an unacceptable Republican candidate. Furthermore, there is polling evidence to suggest that some of the 30,000 Firestone voters were in fact *Democrats* (seniors in particular). In contrast, San Luis Obispo turnout across the first two elections was raised by 6,000 for Capps and 10,000 for Bordonaro. The Capps field polls also demonstrated that there was greater support for Capps among registered Republicans than there was support for Bordonaro among registered Democrats.

The Capps campaign leadership initially decided not to go negative. Although Duvall had developed negative ads for the 1996 contest between Walter Capps and Andrea Seastrand, the perception was that there was much to be gained in the target universe by staying positive, focusing on policy issues, and letting Bordonaro appear to be the more polarizing candidate.

The Capps campaign's central strategy for positioning Bordonaro in voters' minds was to cement his "rightist" credentials. Ad copy featuring the phrase "too extreme for the central coast" played into the moderate leanings of the district. Bordonaro's newfound relationship with Gingrich was highlighted. After Gingrich encouraged Firestone to run and Bordonaro said he would not vote for Gingrich as Speaker, there was little support from the national Republican Party for Bordonaro's race in the second special election. However, limited support emerged after Bordonaro obtained the party nomination in June. One expression of this assistance was contributions from the leadership ($14,495 from the Majority Leaders Fund and $949 from GOPAC). When Gingrich publicly endorsed Bordonaro and agreed to a campaign stop in the late summer, Duvall had the newspaper article photocopied and distributed: "Gingrich Suddenly in Bordonaro's Camp." The point was obviously to tie Bordonaro and Gingrich together in the minds of *Democratic* voters, as this was likely to be a positive reinforcement with a reasonable proportion of Republican votes.

In a sense the strategy of painting Bordonaro as an extremist, negative candidate was one of opportunism. Bordonaro often appeared an extremist, negative candidate when he was articulating policies. In smaller, interpersonal, settings he was quite the opposite: casual, humorous, and generally positive. Duvall claims that not only did Gingrich's endorsement help motivate Democrats to vote, the central campaign strategy, but that Bordonaro's own commercials helped her efforts as well. Bordonaro obviously did not see a potential negative effect to associating his name with Gingrich's. At one debate he even stated, "I've got the ear of Gingrich." In virtually every debate, Bordonaro waved a sheet of paper around proclaiming it to be a letter from Gingrich promising to put him on the Commerce Committee in January 1999. Ironically, neither of them would be a member of the 106th Congress.

Targeting

Duvall asserts that Republican voters were never targeted for phonebanking efforts and GOTV programs despite the perception in the media that Capps was pursuing moderate Firestone Republicans. Therefore her universe of voters was restricted to registered Democrats, decline-to-states, independents, and those voting for minor parties. In rough numbers,

Duvall took approximately 350,000 registered voters with around 43 percent registered Democrats and calculated 150,000 likely and potential supporters. Since 104,262 Democrats voted for Walter Capps in 1996, this meant that there were about 45,000 self-described Democrats that would not vote unless "harassed." Since Capps won in March by about 15,000 votes, this 45,000-strong group was critical to winning the fall election.

A core strategy of the campaign was to get registered Democrats and other non-Republicans out to vote. The Santa Barbara County Clerk predicted an "average" turnout in that county of somewhere between 40 percent and 50 percent.[12] Duvall argued publicly that of 42 percent registered Republicans, most were unobtainable, and therefore winning depended on two factors: getting supporters out to vote and painting Bordonaro as extremist to nonpartisans. Since the district was roughly split in partisan registration, the better-organized campaign would win the first factor. The second factor was part of Capps's central strategy. Those voters registered as independents, with "minor liberal parties," and who declined to state an affiliation were more likely to vote for the incumbent, the less negative candidate, and the more centrist candidate. Since Bordonaro's campaign focused on negative attacks, in ads and in public appearances, the second attribute favored Capps. Duvall was also careful to paint her candidate in moderate, centrist terms as an incumbent without an identifiable left-leaning voting record.

The voter universe was broken down by the campaign into four types of voters, reflecting their likelihood of turning out on November 3: A through D. Those in the D ("deadweight" or "dropped") category were nonvoters still on the books for a variety of reasons. These "voters" were considered a waste of time as nearly all had moved, lived without a phone, or were unavailable for some other reason. The other classes are summarized in table 2-4. The same typology was used in the March special election except that the definitions were necessarily different: A voters participated 3 out of the last 3 elections, B voters participated in 2 of the last 3 elections, and C voters participated in 1 of the last 3 elections.

According to the campaign plan *all* C voters in the district received a GOTV call. No A or D voters were called, and B voters were added to call lists in a very selective fashion determined by area. Some C voters were called more than once if they fit one of four special targeted profiles. These were the "presidential voter" who voted in November 1996 but not since, the "brand new" voter who registered after October 1996 but

Table 2-4. *Counting the Democratic Universe of Potential Voters*

Item	*Party*	*November 1998*	*November 1996*
A voters (likely)			
Voted in 5 of the last 5	Democrat	35,640	29,077
or 3 of the last 3 of 1998	DTS or MLP	6,787	6,196
B voters (probable)			
Voted in at least 2 of the 3	Democrat	24,384	19,352
in 1998	DTS or MLP	7,966	7,222
C voters (occasional)			
Voted November 1996 or 1 out of last 3 plus registered after October 1996	Democrat	21,795	19,669

Note: DTS, Decline-to-state; MLP, Minor Liberal Party.

did not vote in any 1998 election, the "party message voter" who voted in June 1998 but not in any of the specials, and finally someone who voted in one of the specials but not in June 1998. Duvall believed that these voters were particularly susceptible to being "harassed" into the polls. This GOTV effort represented a major emphasis of the campaign plan, including a commitment of significant financial resources, since the outside vendors charged the campaign between $0.38 and $0.50 per call, depending on the size of the order.

The other component of the turnout strategy was to get reluctant voters (C voters predominantly) to vote absentee. Tactics included mailing and handing out absentee ballot applications early in the campaign, phoning those with absentee ballots that had not been mailed, and after the deadline for mailing (Saturday, October 31), calling potential voters to remind them that voting at the polls was now necessary. One problem with this strategy was the necessary delays between voter mailings, county record-keeping, and subsequent availability to the campaign.

A fundamental trade-off existed between narrow targeting and general GOTV programs. Precinct walking was divided between hitting specific households on target lists and uniformly covering a neighborhood. The campaign mostly focused on hitting the target households but made some exceptions. In some neighborhoods, such as Isla Vista, both were done. Particularly late in the campaign, doorhangers (signs draped from doorknobs) were used in conjunction with other Democratic candidates. This helped cut down on the cost ($12,000 minus some costs borne by the

Figure 2-2. *Capps Campaign Doorhangers*

other candidates listed besides Capps), as well as widened the scope of volunteer efforts. These doorhangers were geographically targeted according to the appropriate candidate based. Figure 2-2 shows several examples.

Finances, Fundraising, and Budgeting

Capps received $125,000 from member contributions for each special election. This unprecedented level of support for a nonincumbent was partly a reflection of the depth of feelings that some colleagues felt for Walter and partly because this was the only election taking place in the country at each time (January and March). Furthermore, Capps received $75,000 from leadership and member PACs during the two special elections. This obviously strong expression of early support for the Capps campaign provided a firm fund-raising foundation for the subsequent elections.

The campaign started the general election phase with roughly $170,000 left from fund-raising in the special elections. This advantage was important since Duvall states that she never had to make a decision

Table 2-5. *Approximate Spending Breakdown, General Election*
Thousands of dollars

Line item	*Personnel*	*Nonpersonnel*	*Total*	*Percent*
Fund-raising	43.0	43.0	86.0	11.13
Administration	32.0	61.0	93.0	12.04
Polling	...	25.5	25.5	3.30
Field	43.0	136.0	179.0	23.17
Mail	...	95.0	95.0	12.30
Media	...	280.0	280.0	36.25
Print	...	<1	<1	0.13
Contributions	...	13.0	13.0	1.68
Total	119.0	654.5	772.5	100.00

Source: Lois Capps Campaign for Congress.

to delay or change some campaign expenditure because of concerns about cash flow. Over the course of the general election the campaign raised about $618,000 to net $787,698 ($544,705 from individuals, $239,500 from PACs, plus $3,493 from unitemized contributions).[13] PAC contributions came from labor, progressive political organizations, leadership, and miscellaneous single businesses. The FEC records show 88 percent of the contributions came from within California, and Duvall claims that 58 percent came from within the district. The California Democratic Party also gave $20,000 in 441 Authority (hard dollars) directly to Capps's polling firm, Garin, Hart and Yang, for work on behalf of the campaign. These figures clearly show an organized effort by state and national party officials to assist Capps. This is consistent with the recent strategy of the parties to identify the district where their money can make a bigger difference because of the competitiveness of a given race.

A spending breakdown done immediately after the election shows an estimated total expenditure of $772,500. This sum is organized by the categories listed in table 2-5. It's easy to see that media purchases constituted a large part of the budget: more than 36 percent. The next largest expenditure also reflects the priorities of the campaign plan: field. The cash flow and fund-raising efforts worked sufficiently well that Capps and Duvall decided on the Saturday before the election to give $13,000 in contributions to other races in which there was a cash-strapped Democratic incumbent and to give $10,000 in staff bonuses.

Polling and Opposition Research

Duvall consistently downplayed the roll of polling in her decisionmaking. She asserted that there were three "true" polls in the past eleven months in the form of actual elections and that the electorate was not likely to change dramatically before the general election. The polling did reveal some tactical issues. For example, each of the last three polls showed that Bordonaro had an advantage in San Luis Obispo County excluding the city of San Luis Obispo, but that Capps had a large advantage in the city. This finding fit neatly into the field strategy of precinct walking in the city of San Luis Obispo.

The polls showed another feature with tactical implications. Capps's support with registered Republicans was equal to or higher than Bordonaro's support with registered Democrats across the time periods. In addition, a higher proportion of registered Republicans than registered Democrats declared support for a third candidate or were listed as undecided. Although this situation implied that pursuing moderate to liberal Republicans was a good strategy, Duvall remained fixed on the Democratic turnout focus and pursuing moderate voters of all kinds. The campaign strategy sought to persuade these voters with media and appearances rather than with phonebanking and GOTV efforts, which had the potential to motivate participation from Republicans *not* likely to vote for Capps. The messages aimed at independents, conservative Democrats, and decline-to-states could also be crafted to possibly pick up moderate Republicans as an ancillary benefit. In one expression of this strategy, the Capps campaign developed a pro-business push in Santa Maria, which featured local business leaders supporting Capps.

The Capps campaign also ran focus groups among registered Democrats in Santa Maria. One finding that was consistent with other sources was that these voters tended to describe Bordonaro as "mean" and "negative" regardless of policy preferences or expected vote. This was a feature that the campaign exploited in ad copy, which described Bordonaro in terms that resonated with this perceived image in the electorate and used the word "negative" as often as possible in describing Bordonaro.

Opposition research was practically absent. While this omission seemed ill-advised, it occurred primarily because the opposing candidate was known through the experience of three previous elections in the same year. Duvall hired Ace Smith, a San Francisco-based political consultant, to do some opposition research. Smith was known primarily for suing his alma mater (UC Berkeley) for charging mandatory student fees to sponsor political speeches on campus. She provides little information about the nature of the work done, however. Further basic opposition research was done by browsing web pages.

Earned and Paid Media

The Twenty-Second District is a very inexpensive and efficient television market. There are three network affiliates in the district: KSBY (NBC) in San Luis Obispo, KCOY (CBS) in Santa Maria, and KEYT (ABC) in Santa Barbara. Owing to cable access, these stations have nearly districtwide coverage.

Capps's focus on education and health care was amplified by free media. She made a number of local appearances at schools and hospitals, emphasizing her commitment to these policy areas, and many of these events were covered by print and television journalists. This coverage was more prevalent during the special elections than the primary or general ones. During the general election more earned media coverage was generated because of her incumbent status.

The Capps campaign ran only one ad that was seen as negative. Bordonaro was in the process of running a series of negative ads the week before the primary attacking the "liberal Lois Capps." In response the Capps campaign produced a spot that Duvall describes as "hard hitting but not negative." While these distinctions are often unclear, Duvall claims that the ad was not negative since it was responding to the negative Bordonaro ad and does not represent any campaign strategy to "go negative." This logic implies that voters (viewers really) know the sequence of events, whereas more often they simply see roughly simultaneous runs of negative imagery and words.

The response ad features grainy black and white pictures of Bordonaro with odd facial gesticulations and the following voice-over:

> Tom Bordonaro is at it again. More negative ads. More distortions.
>
> Bordonaro falsely attacked Brooks Firestone. Now Bordonaro falsely attacks Lois Capps.
>
> Why? To hide his record. Tom Bordonaro opposes a women's right to choose; even in cases of rape, incest, and the mother's life. . . .
>
> *KVEC-Radio Debate 2/25/98*

And he would dismantle the Department of Education.

KPRL-Radio Debate, 10/22/98

Former Republican President Ford said Tom Bordonaro is "one of those extreme right wing candidates."

New York Times, 1/20/98

Tom Bordonaro—still too extreme for the Central Coast.

This ad began airing on the Thursday before the election (October 29). On Friday morning Capps was taking questions on a local radio show when Bordonaro called in to complain that the ad was negative and "a lie" since Gerald Ford had endorsed him. Duvall, listening to the show, immediately called in and read the citation and relevant paragraph from the *New York Times* on the air. Bordonaro, furious, called Ford's office. He wanted Ford to recant the statement, declare the ad as inaccurate, or at the very least reiterate the endorsement. John Davies, a Firestone political consultant was also called because Bordonaro wanted Firestone to simultaneously pressure Ford. When Davies called Duvall to check the accuracy of his information, Duvall had the ad transcribed and sent a staffer to hand-carry the ad copy, and the *New York Times* article, over to Davies. Davies replied "it's verbatim" and didn't feel that Bordonaro had much of a case based on the text. Eventually Bordonaro arranged for Ford to call into a Bordonaro press conference and repeat the October 26 endorsement. Meanwhile Duvall was able to sufficiently interest one of the local television stations in airing a press conference in which the Ford article was blown up into poster size and placed prominently as she described the chronology. Interestingly, Bordonaro would later say during a televised debate that Ford had been angered at the Capps response ad and had called *him* as a result.

Late in the campaign when Duvall found that fund-raising was outstripping spending by a reasonable margin, she discovered that it was impossible to spend much more money on television and radio spots. Because of advance scheduling and the small number of local television stations (three), Duvall could not spend more as election day approached. Getting more slots during prime viewing hours (news-time in particular) was simply impossible.

As incumbents, earned media were relatively easy to get for both candidates. Capps in particular had the advantage as the federal-level incumbent. Bordonaro got coverage for each of the Republican national leaders who came to the district, as well as for several press conferences related to legislative activity in Sacramento. Capps got similar coverage for votes in the House on taxes, impeachment, and the omnibus reconciliation bill. The only well-known political figure who stumped for Capps was Dianne Feinstein.

Fieldwork and GOTV Efforts

Turnout was critical to the campaign plan. Since the plan explicitly stated that the campaign would not pursue registered Republicans, 42 percent of the district, winning was dependent on the level of turnout among Democrats (41 percent) and persuaded nonpartisans (less than 17 percent). Duvall distinguished between the persuasion universe, which consists of potential votes among groups that needed to be convinced, notably moderates and conservative-leaning voters independent of party affiliation, and the turnout universe that consisted purely of registered Democrats who would vote for Capps but needed to get to the polls. Duvall liked to summarize turnout as "motivation" and "harassment." Because of the turnout focus, fieldwork played a critical role in the harassment strategy and constituted an unusually large proportion of the budget (table 2-5). In the last week of the election, turnout became more of the focus than persuasion. The campaign did more "harassment" than motivation.

One field project that got special attention was the Isla Vista/University of California, Santa Barbara GOTV effort. Isla Vista is a student-dominated area outside of Santa Barbara that encloses the UCSB campus. Rumored to be the densest square mile of population in the western states, it is composed of apartment buildings and houses that have been divided up into small units and packed with student renters. Substantially higher Democratic registrants combined with the geographic concentration made it a prime target for precinct walking. Duvall would later say that she picked up 2,000 votes "cheap."

Bordonaro was very effective in one aspect of field work: getting his message on the abortion issue out in churches. This venue was a natural advantage for Bordonaro, particularly in areas such as Santa Maria and Paso Robles. One advantage to this approach was that it provided a low-profile way to get the pro-life message out, presumably alienating fewer moderates.

Field efforts and GOTV programs were aided substantially by the unusually large number of volunteers for the campaign. Many of these were repeat volunteers from Walter Capps's two campaigns, but others were clearly drawn by both the stark policy differences between the two candidates and Lois Capps's strong interpersonal skills. This last point cannot be overemphasized: Capps has an unusual ability to connect with voters, volunteers, and donors in a genuine and caring manner. People who meet her in campaign forums or outside of politics get a sense of honesty and concern that is very unlike the glad-handing platitudes that one often gets from politicians.

Outside Forces

Unlike the special elections, outside groups did not dominate the public agenda at the expense of the campaigns. Gary Bauer's group did a small amount of mailing during the summer but otherwise stayed completely out of the race. Having spent considerable money in the spring and losing, he apparently looked elsewhere. More important, Duvall thinks that the intrusive role of the Campaign for Working Families actually helped Capps. In fact, several local observers conjectured that Bordonaro's campaign requested that Bauer's group not run ads in the general election. The Christian Coalition handed out leaflets on the Sunday before election day at churches, but the program was decidedly low key. The League of Conservation Voters committed some of their $2 million national budget to attacking Bordonaro's voting record in the assembly, but little actual work was done in the district.

The two candidates took different approaches on appearances by national party luminaries. Capps specifically asked that no one come to the district to campaign on her part, but she did accept Dianne Feinstein's offer to stump for Capps on October 27, in part because she represents California and in part because of the mentoring relationship that Feinstein had taken on with Capps in Washington. Bordonaro took the opposite tack, with Gingrich, Steve Forbes, Jack Kemp, and Dan Quayle making appearances at fund-raisers and public events. Other than fund-raising, it was not clear whether this helped or hurt Bordonaro. Notable in his absence, for obvious reasons, was Clinton, who had campaigned visibly for Walter Capps in 1996.

Chronology

When asked in late August, Duvall stated that she could not tell what Bordonaro had been doing in terms of strategy or fieldwork. It appears, she said, that his efforts had been concentrated on fund-raising, an area in which the Capps campaign enjoyed a huge advantage. Bordonaro started the summer with a huge 13.9 to 1 disadvantage as of June 30 ($267,845 to $19,270).[14] Bordonaro spent most of the summer growing into an enlarged campaign office in Paso Robles and raising funds, particularly with Republican Party luminaries.

Overhanging the beginning of the fall campaign season was uncertainty about the electoral ramifications of Ken Starr's impending report and Clinton's August admission of impropriety. The campaign was in the field for the September 8–9 poll when the Starr report was turned over to the House. When the data were analyzed, it clearly frightened the campaign. The assumption for most of the summer was that some ground from the last two elections would be lost and that it would be a competitive race, but Capps had too many natural advantages to lose. This comfort level for Duvall was shattered in a Sacramento hotel room at 6:00 A.M., when she got the news that the field poll showed Capps and Bordonaro tied at 46 percent (plus or minus 5 percent, 95 percent statistical confidence interval). A particularly disconcerting aspect of this result was that Bordonaro had done virtually no substantive campaigning to date in this fourth contest. Duvall says that this poll caused the campaign team to ring alarm bells in the district and in Washington. Bordonaro had made up some obvious ground, and the fall contest was starting to look quite different from the previous three. Although it does not look plausible retrospectively, at the time it was hard not to connect the Clinton scandal with this increased Republican competitiveness.

The "46/46 poll" cemented the campaign strategy to not directly pursue registered Republicans with direct mail and phonebanking. Within the campaign team Duvall and Carrick were the least likely to trust polling numbers. Duvall stated that her feel for the status of the race was culled from elites in the district, field feedback, media, calls to the campaign office, volunteers, district and national opinion leaders, as well as polls. However, the 46/46 field poll cast a new light on the campaign. One response was to seek outside financial help more actively: from Emily's list, the DCCC, Democratic National Committee, PACs, and members of Congress. This process was easier now that there was some justification for additional support. The strong Bordonaro showing in the wake of Clinton's admission also renewed the emphasis on turnout among Democrats. A common concern across many Democratic congressional campaigns was that disenchanted Democratic voters would be disinclined to turn out.

The next field poll conducted in the middle of October showed Capps up by three points but with a margin of error of five points (95 percent confidence interval): another tie. For most of the early campaign, both sides had empirical evidence that the race was very close. A Moore Information Poll in late September (n, 400) resembled the Capps field poll with a 45 percent to 42 percent advantage but within the margin of error (4 percent). However, this poll had a subtext of good news for the Capps campaign: 13 percent was self-identified as undecided, and Capps had a favorability rating of 52 percent compared with Bordonaro's 45 percent. These two findings interpreted together (along with the implied confidence interval) indicated that the upside potential for Capps was much better than that for Bordonaro. About the same time (September 18), the Cook Political Report reported that "Capps is in good shape for election to a full-term in November."

While this period of the campaign was the most uncertain (Duvall would later say that receiving the 46/46 poll was the only time she seriously considered losing), Capps started the race with several clear advantages. She began with a large fund-raising advantage, she was an incumbent who voted very circumspectly with regard to the upcoming fall race, her campaign team remained fixed (Bordonaro switched managers), and she had an opponent who quite literally went negative on himself. Polling data and focus groups run by the Capps campaign showed that according to registered Democrats, undecideds, independents, and decline-to-states (that is, the ascribed universe), Bordonaro was frequently associated with the word "mean." Furthermore, there was evidence that the more often this target group saw Bordonaro, the more they were reminded of his perceived meanness. This was a gift to the Capps campaign as it indicated that Bordonaro's ads would have a positive effect for the Capps campaign with regard to their targeted groups. In addition, the more negative the Bordonaro ads got, the greater the magnitude of this effect.

Meanwhile Capps was weighing key votes in the House. She voted for the Republican tax cut measure, which was a safe move to the middle since it was not expected by many to survive the Senate. She anguished, then voted, for the Democratic impeachment inquiry bill rather than vote against impeachment proceedings or for the open-ended Republican bill that passed. She also cosponsored the Patients Bill of Rights, the Small Business Paperwork Reduction Act, the Internal Revenue Service overhaul, and worked to extend the federal moratorium on off-shore oil drilling. All of these legislative achievements focused on centrist-moderate positions in the district and were certainly not done in isolation from campaign strategy.

Capps was also careful to walk a middle ground with respect to the developing scandal in the White House. In an issued statement she described Clinton's behavior as "reprehensible" and stated that "I am appalled by his behavior and outraged that he lied to the American people." But she also urged House Judiciary Committee members "to be thorough, fair, and nonpartisan." The cost of not publicly expressing outrage early in the scandal for California politicians was evident in divergent popularity figures for Senators Barbara Boxer and Feinstein. Dianne Feinstein made explicitly critical public statements early and remained untouched by public opinion on the matter, whereas Boxer hesitated for weeks and appeared to have lowered her polling numbers as a result.

The two campaigns scheduled seven debates starting late (October 21) in the contest. Duvall downplayed the importance of the debates since the campaign plan supposedly focused on turning out supporters rather than converting Republicans. Most of the debates were low-attendance affairs, such as the AARP-sponsored event in which 36 people occupied a cavernous 300-seat hall. Only two such events had any perceivable visibility: the televised debate on Santa Barbara's KEYT and the election eve debate on San Luis Obispo's KSBY. This latter debate with call-in questions showed both of the candidates focusing on favored issues but also showed Bordonaro making repeated negative attacks against a nervous and uncomfortable Capps.

Early in the campaign (October 5) Capps picked up the endorsement of the *San Luis Obispo Telegram-Tribune*. This was a surprise to some observers, as the paper had endorsed Bordonaro over Capps in the special election, and Seastrand over Walter Capps twice. Locals attributed the switch to a new editor and ownership by Knight Ridder versus Scripps-Howard, which owned the paper during the 1994 and 1996 elections. However, Capps had assiduously courted the *Telegram-Tribune* editors, stopping by the editorial office on numerous visits to San Luis Obispo City. She worked especially hard to devote time to issues of local relevance such as the widening of a dangerous rural highway and the flight of HMOs. Accordingly, she was credited by the paper with a commitment to issues specific to San Luis Obispo County. Later on, Capps picked up the endorsement of the *Santa Barbara News Press* and the

UCSB Daily Nexus (which had endorsed Firestone in January and refused to make an endorsement in March). These endorsements, however, were expected.

By late October the fluidity and uncertainty of the polling numbers started to converge. The October 25 field poll showed Capps leading Bordonaro by 52 to 38 (plus or minus 5 points, 95 percent confidence interval). Duvall claims not to have been overly encouraged by this showing and notes that the electorate hadn't changed much since the 46/46 field poll taken on September 8 and 9. This October poll, however, showed Bordonaro ahead 53 to 39 in San Luis Obispo County (minus San Luis Obispo City).

Duvall kept the last field poll numbers within the top campaign team (herself, Carrick, Yang, Guma, and the candidate), fearing an effect on volunteer and staff commitment, as well as the possibility of a leak to the press. Although national pundits were predicting a Capps victory, Duvall preferred to imply that the race was close as a motivation for C voters in particular. Capps would win with a margin near the predicted 52 to 38 difference and eventually carried San Luis Obispo County. One contributing factor was strong turnout there: 54.62 percent of registered voters (41.27 percent of eligible ones) compared with 42.49 percent of registered voters (30.04 percent of eligible ones) for the whole state. Another important factor was strong support for Capps in San Luis Obispo City (plus the second district), traditionally more moderate than the rest of the county. The final poll was 58 to 35 percent and Capps took the city by 61 to 37 percent. Santa Maria was also a success even though it was barely lost (7,202 votes for Capps and 7,313 for Bordonaro), since it had never been close for Capps before.

As election day neared, there was an increasing sense of comfortableness within the campaign headquarters. Although Duvall was careful not to distribute the latest polling numbers, she could be overheard on the phone saying, "It looks like we're going to win this one unless something really weird happens in the last days." She was even predicting a win in the San Luis Obispo County absentee votes: an expression of confidence in the implementation of the campaign plan and the degree to which the campaign outmaneuvered Bordonaro's in that area.

There was also an increasing sense that Bordonaro was trying to move to the middle as a late campaign strategy. Obviously, his polls and field were indicating a perception that he was too far from the median district voter. These attempts were strategically sound but failed to resonate successfully. He picked issues such as Social Security and the environment, issues on which his Sacramento voting record had yet to show a substantial commitment. Finally, Bordonaro's ads became increasingly negative in the final days, often stressing the "liberal" stance of his opponent. Surprisingly, the Bordonaro campaign did not stress economic policy issues that could possibly have played to a traditional Republican strength. However, there are large parts of the district, predominately the urban and beach communities, where commercial development is now often considered a detriment to environmental concerns and a unique central coast quality of living standards.

Volunteers filled the Santa Barbara office on election day and evening with last-minute phone banking of B and C voters. Lois Capps personally made phonebank GOTV calls from 7:00 to 7:40 P.M. Several times she was overheard saying, "Yes, it really *is* Congresswoman Capps. Have you had a chance to vote yet?" Capps seems nervous and the eleventh-hour phonebanking was likely an attempt to stay busy at an awkward time. At about 10:30 P.M. Capps declared victory to a raucous crowd of volunteers, staffers, supporters, and the local media packing a leased downtown Santa Barbara restaurant. Bordonaro never conceded the race.

When the election returns starting coming in on the evening of November 3 it became apparent that the national trends favored Democrats. Early eastern news of Al D'Amato's loss to Charles Schumer and Lauch Faircloth's loss to John Edwards were strong indications of national inclinations. Locally the picture was less clear but for an unusual reason. A critical computer at the Santa Barbara County Clerk's office had a hard-drive failure, delaying the returns from Santa Barbara precincts for hours. However, the news was quite encouraging for the campaign as the local television stations ran counts that were an aggregate of San Luis Obispo County precincts and absentees, plus Santa Barbara County absentees. Even given this temporary handicap, Capps jumped out to a comfortable lead early in the evening.

The results were stronger than predicted. Capps won the district by 54 percent to 43 percent (table 2-6). Given the bimodal nature of the district and the proportion of voters that partisan candidates get immediately on nomination (slightly more than 40 percent), Bordonaro apparently failed to reach out beyond his bequeathed base. An alternative explanation is the relatively poor Republican turnout in the district. Importantly, Capps carried San Luis Obispo County, receiving considerable help from the San Luis Obispo City Democratic turnout in particular.

Table 2-6. *California's Twenty-Second District General Election, November 5, 1998*

Item	*Precinct votes*	*Absentee votes*	*Total*	*Percent*
San Luis Obispo County, 133,809 registered voters				
Lois Capps (Democrat)	23,857	18,939	42,796	51.54
Tom Bordonaro (Republican)	23,529	16,879	40,408	47.72
Robert Bakhaus (Libertarian)	606	369	975	1.15
Richard Porter (Reform)	319	178	497	0.59
Santa Barbara County, 217,022 registered voters				
Lois Capps (Democrat)	43,820	24,772	68,592	58.37
Tom Bordonaro (Republican)	30,414	16,099	46,513	39.58
Robert Bakhaus (Libertarian)	1,162	481	1,643	1.40
Richard Porter (Reform)	504	262	766	0.65
District total, 350,831 registered voters				
Lois Capps (Democrat)	67,677	43,711	111,388	55.09
Tom Bordonaro (Republican)	53,943	32,978	86,921	42.99
Robert Bakhaus (Libertarian)	1,768	850	2,168	1.29
Richard Porter (Reform)	823	440	1,263	0.62

Source: California Secretary of State.

Conclusion

This case study seeks to make the argument that summary statistics, polling snapshots, and postelection interviews do not accurately capture campaign conduct and decisions that take place within campaign organizations. As the four campaigns developed and in particular as the year came to a culmination with the November general election, the decisionmakers in the Capps campaign were faced with a relatively mild set of ethical or value-laden decisions. This occurred partly because of the preferred nature of campaigning expressed by the candidate and partly because of the aspects of the district that are difficult or impossible to control.

When the election returns from March and November are compared, it is difficult to find any dramatically different voting behavior as seen in the third column of table 2-6. Despite a Washington scandal and an election relatively free of outside groups, the voting pattern in the Twenty-Second district appeared fairly stable. This is evidence that the bimodal nature of the district is relatively insensitive to campaign plans that seek to substantively change ideological or partisan preferences. Instead, turnout played the pivotal role, with a minor influence from moderate voters that would not naturally fall to Capps.

When confronted with a series of negative ads by the opponent, Duvall responded with an ad that was moderately negative as well, which is now conventional strategy among campaign professionals. When the campaign decided not to pursue moderate Republicans with direct appeals, it renewed the already existing emphasis on getting out less reliable or committed Democratic voters. But there is evidence that the campaign picked up some moderate Republicans through the pursuit of nonpartisans and conservative Democrats through paid media. This two-faceted strategy is a function of the bimodal nature of the district and the need to segment campaign strategy to fit distinct ideological profiles.

When the candidate was forced to make difficult vote choices in the House, she tended toward moderate centrist positions. When the polling numbers showed that the race was statistically even, Duvall chose not to panic and maintained the existing campaign plan. None of these decisions had strong ethical consequences, and none of these decisions led to substantial vote losses.

To a great extent the Capps campaign was blessed by having an opponent who truly came from a very conservative position, had voted consistently with that position in the state assembly, and presented himself as an acerbic voice from that position. The effect of this behavior in a swing district was to alienate a segment of voters naturally predisposed toward the Republican candidate, despite the candidate's late attempts to move toward the center by softened statements and a refocus on senior issues. Duvall asserted that the reason that the Capps campaign was so fortunate in the choice of opponent was that the Capps campaign had helped that choice to materialize in the first special election by focusing on hurting Firestone and letting Bordonaro do so from the other end of the ideological spectrum. Whether this statement was true or whether the outcome was just fortunate, it meant that there were few difficult strategic decisions to make during the general election.

Notes

1. "Gingrich Suddenly in Bordonaro's Camp," *San Luis Obispo County Telegram Tribune*, July 17, 1998, p. B1.

2. Federal Election Commission, "U.S. House and U.S. Senate Candidate Information for State of California," *FEC Report, 1995–96*, April 14, 1997.

3. Lou Cannon, "Single-Issue Ads Driving California Race," *Washington Post*, February 21, 1998, p. A04; and Dave Wilcox, "Bordonaro, Capps to Stick to the Issues," *San Luis Obispo County Telegram Tribune*, October 12, 1998, p. A1.

4. Federal Election Commission, *FEC Reports on Congressional Fundraising for 1997–98*, April 28, 1999.

5. Wilcox, "Bordonaro, Capps"; and Cannon, "Single-Issue Ads."

6. Richard L. Berke, "Ford Urges G.O.P. to Drop Abortion Issue and Shift Center," *New York Times*, January 20, 1998.

7. For example, see comments by congressional colleagues entered into the *Congressional Record* (http://www.rain.org/~capps/record.html).

8. William Schneider, "When the GOP's Divided, It Loses," *National Journal*, March 21, 1998, p. 662.

9. Ron Faucheux, "The Indirect Approach," *Campaigns and Elections*, June 1998, pp. 18–25.

10. Alan Greenblatt, "Capps Succeeds Her Husband," *CQ News*, March 14, 1998; and Richard E. Cohen, "A Gloomy Day for the GOP," *National Journal*, March 14, 1998, p. 584.

11. William Schneider, "When the GOP's Divided, It Loses," *National Journal*, March 21, 1998, p. 662.

12. Nora K. Wallace, "Officials Fear Voter Burnout by November 3," *Santa Barbara News-Press*, September 24, 1998, p. A1.

13. Federal Election Commission, *FEC Reports on Congressional Fundraising.*

14. Ibid.

CHAPTER THREE

Johnson versus Koskoff: The 1998 Campaign for Connecticut's Sixth District

DIANA EVANS

THIS CHAPTER TELLS the story of the 1998 reelection campaign of an eight-term moderate Republican incumbent, Nancy Johnson, of Connecticut's Sixth Congressional District. Before the preceding election, Johnson had appeared invulnerable, but a shockingly narrow victory in 1996 suggested that she was less secure than she and her supporters believed. Her near-defeat in 1996 and reaction to it in the 1998 campaign provide insight into the role of campaign consultants in determining the conduct of modern campaigns. Johnson's case is particularly interesting because of her long-standing reputation as a popular, secure incumbent, naturally inclined toward genteel, positive campaigns. Although she used consultants in earlier races, she imposed on them the positive style with which she was comfortable. However, her close call in 1996 and the specter of the same challenger in 1998 yanked Johnson into the rough-and-tumble world of modern elections, one in which consultants were allowed to play a larger role in guiding the tone of the campaign. This study examines the role and impact of a candidate who disliked hard-hitting campaigning and a campaign staff and consultants who considered such a style essential to victory in 1998.

Thanks to Richard F. Fenno for his many helpful suggestions and incomparable insights during the course of this study.

Overview of the Election: The District

The Sixth District of Connecticut is, for a small state, far-flung and diverse. It consists of forty-four towns, which in New England are not necessarily municipalities but rather resemble miniature counties. The district's rural and suburban towns tend to vote Republican, but the district also contains five or six small cities, including Nancy Johnson's hometown of New Britain (the largest city), which gives the district its overall Democratic tendency.

The Sixth District has a share of the fast-shrinking New England manufacturing base. It is host to traditional manufacturers such as the Stanley Works toolmakers in New Britain, numerous small machine tool factories; jewelry plating companies and brass platers that have polluted the Naugatuck River with their effluent for decades, as well as a number of modern, high-technology defense contractors. In addition, there are insurance and various health care businesses, among many others. Moreover, the district is ethnically diverse, with a heavy representation of Italian Americans in its northeastern corner and Polish Americans in New Britain. As of the 1990 census, 95 percent of the population was white, only 2 percent black, and 4 percent Hispanic.

The rolling hills of the bucolic northwestern corner of the state are very different in character from the working and middle-class communities that dominate the rest of the district and frequently vote Democratic. The northwestern corner contains a number of communities that consist of refugees from New York, some of them wealthy weekenders, as well as traditional conservative New England Yankee Republicans. Finally, the district contains several affluent suburbs of Hartford, which elect a mix of Democrats and Republicans to other offices.

The district lacks its own major media outlet. Hartford television stations serve almost the entire district. In fact, Hartford, which is in the First District, serves nearly the entire state, with the exception of southwestern Connecticut, which is dominated by New York, and part of the coast. Thus television is very expensive. By contrast, the radio market is more fragmented, consisting of a number of small stations that provide virtually the only radio coverage available to parts of the northwestern corner.

Although the district voted Republican for president in the 1980s, it gave Bill Clinton a plurality in 1992 and a bare majority in 1996's three-way race. Even before Johnson's close call in 1996, the Sixth was not a district that the Republicans could take for granted in House races. Before her first victory in an open seat race in 1982, the seat was held for eight years by Toby Moffett, a liberal Democrat. Before his tenure, the district elected a Republican, Tom Meskill, and then a Democrat, Ella Grasso, both of whom went on to be elected governor.

Background: The 1996 Election

The 1998 election campaign in the Sixth District can only be understood in the context of the 1996 election, as Johnson's 1998 campaign for a ninth term in the House of Representatives was in many ways an outgrowth of the unexpected trauma of the preceding election. The key to victory in 1998 would be to repair whatever damage was reflected in the 1996 results and attempt to bring her standing among her constituents back into line with the pre-1996 norm. Before 1996 Johnson was by all accounts a good fit with a district in which she typically won by margins in excess of 60 percent, despite her urban constituents' tendency to vote Democratic. Yet that year, she eked out a margin of fewer than 1,600 votes against Democrat Charlotte Koskoff in her second challenge to Johnson. Indeed, the race was so close that early network television projections initially called Koskoff the winner. It was clear early on that Koskoff, newly energized by her unexpectedly strong showing, would challenge Johnson again in 1998.

Given the benefit of hindsight, one serious mistake is apparent to the observer of the 1996 campaign. Johnson's final poll was taken more than a month before the election; there were no subsequent tracking polls to gauge the impact of a late advertising blitz that might be mounted by her opponent. And Koskoff did mount an advertising blitz. Given her 3 to 1 funding disadvantage (she raised $270,576 to Johnson's $825,021), Koskoff opted to conserve her media dollars until near the end of the campaign. During the final ten days, and particularly the last three days of the race, she flooded the radio airwaves with advertisements criticizing Johnson on various issues, most notably charging her with "bending the law" for House Speaker Newt Gingrich in a House ethics committee inquiry chaired by Johnson. Thus, Koskoff was able almost invisibly to erode what had been a comfortable margin for Johnson in September. Johnson's September poll had her support at 60 percent, a number that had not moved since earlier polls and was consistent with, if a bit lower than, her margin in previous years.

By all accounts, however, the major flaw in Johnson's 1996 campaign was the failure to respond in kind to her challenger's attacks. In the first place, she felt that her position as chair of the House ethics committee enjoined her from responding to criticisms of her handling of the proceedings against Gingrich while they were in process. At the same time, her campaign staff members felt under siege on the issue, yet they were unable to respond to press inquiries and the challenger's charges.

Besides the liabilities inherent in the Gingrich issue, crafting a succinct message was difficult, as Johnson was resistant to simplifying complex policy issues for campaign purposes. Without a strong challenger in previous campaigns, the perils of that inclination had not been so apparent. A final handicap was Johnson's unwillingness to campaign in a hard-hitting way. Her television ads were positive, stressing her own accomplishments; indeed, according to her 1996 campaign manager, her only critical piece was a mailer that contained the following urging: "Don't get caught in Charlotte's web." Her natural inclination to campaign in a genteel, civilized way had always worked before, and she evidently was unable to shift gears in 1996. Indeed, it took her near-defeat that year to shock Johnson into making the changes that might insulate her from similar damage in 1998.

The 1998 Election

Johnson reacted swiftly to the near-disaster. She put into place a reconstituted team with key new members immediately after the election. Early on, they decided to wage a nearly year-long campaign, giving her a head start that would allow her to set the agenda from the beginning, which she had not done in 1996. A major part of her strategy was to stress her moderation on the issues. The first salvo in the campaign was a television ad that began running on December 27, 1997; the ad was an advocacy piece in which Johnson advertised her role in writing successful legislation to fund health care for uninsured children. Several other ads were run in the months before Koskoff's first ad in early October forced the campaign staff to turn its attention to responding to Koskoff's charges.

Johnson's stress on centrist positions did not go unnoticed by conservatives in the district. Incensed by what it called Johnson's "dart to the left," Waterbury's conservative newspaper printed two blistering editorials excoriating her recent record. For example, "She recently boasted about how she has voted with her Republican colleagues only 68 percent of the time this year, down from nearly 100 percent two years ago. . . . Rep. Johnson continues her headlong dash over the ideological hill and takes her cue from the liberal vanguard, but it's not too late for her to return to her Republican roots." Later, the same newspaper charged, "Mrs. Johnson is no conservative and is a Republican in political affiliation only."[2]

Despite the criticism from the right, Johnson received the unanimous endorsement of the Republican Party on July 18 at the party's nominating convention. In the meantime, Charlotte Koskoff had received the Democratic nomination on July 13, after decisively defeating a possible primary challenge by wealthy opponent Jim Griffin.[3]

Griffin's campaign was notable primarily for an odd incident, as a result of which he was accused by his campaign manager of assault. In the campaign manager's account, Griffin had been convinced before the Democratic convention that he would receive the needed 15 percent of the delegates' votes to force a primary. On learning a few days before the convention that his staff had undercounted the necessary number of delegate votes and that he lacked the support to engage in a primary, Griffin reportedly grabbed his campaign manager by the throat and choked him, banged his head repeatedly against the wall, and shouted military commands. Later, following his loss at the Democratic convention, Griffin was said to have asked his campaign staff to stay and help him with a possible independent bid for the Sixth District seat. They all refused; Griffin essentially disappeared from sight after that.[4]

The first scuffle (figuratively speaking, in this case) of the general election campaign occurred in mid-September, when two of Johnson's campaign staffers from her nearby headquarters saw Koskoff with a film crew outside the gates of Stanley Works, the major industry in Johnson's hometown of New Britain. They returned to the site with a video camera and began taping the event. Koskoff aborted her own filming and angrily accused the Johnson campaign of sabotaging her ad.[5] Johnson's campaign manager Cheryl Lounsbury responded, "I wonder why Charlotte's reaction is so strong. Is she embarrassed she got caught in a negative campaign ad?"[6] The location of the filming confirmed Lounsbury's expectation that Koskoff would again raise a charge that she had levied in previous campaigns; that advance notice allowed the Johnson team to begin formulating a response ad in advance of the airing of Koskoff's first attack ad.

At about the same time (and reported in the same newspaper articles), the National Republican Congressional Committee released the results of a poll taken by Johnson's pollster, Linda DiVall, which showed a thirty-five-point lead for Johnson.

On October 8, Koskoff began running the first of three television ads, airing the charge that constituted her entire media campaign. Her approach was the one that had served her so well in 1996: attack Nancy Johnson. This time, Johnson was not only ready but far more willing to respond in kind. She softened some of the response ads, rewrote others with a stress on policy detail, and generally applied some degree of braking on the inclinations of her staff and consultants. Nevertheless, for the first time in her career she ran ads that not only responded to her opponent's attacks but hit back and hit hard. Within twelve hours of the appearance of Koskoff's first ad, Johnson began running an ad that started as follows: "Charlotte Koskoff's negative ads are a lie." Thus began a public relations and advertising war that lasted the rest of the campaign.

A week-long series of debates in mid-October highlighted a variety of issue differences between the candidates, which will be detailed below. Despite the variety of issues addressed in the debates, Koskoff did little to define herself in the campaign. Instead, she confined her ads to attacks on Johnson on the issue of jobs and related conflict-of-interest charges, even though she apparently received little traction with those ads over the course of her media campaign.

Among newspaper endorsements, Johnson received the nod from major newspapers, including the *New York Times* and the *Hartford Courant*, while Koskoff received endorsements from several smaller papers. The *Courant* credited Johnson for her accomplishments on health care, especially for uninsured children, arts funding, environmental protection, and women's issues, among other things. And like the *New York Times*, the *Courant* stressed Johnson's value as a moderate in the majority Republican Party.[7]

On November 4, Johnson won with 58.1 percent of the vote to Charlotte Koskoff's 39.6 percent, with turnout at 44.8 percent of the eligible electorate. Nevertheless, Johnson maintained the level of support indicated by her September poll, unlike 1996 when a comfortable September lead was dramatically eroded by Koskoff's late but intense radio advertising. Last time, Koskoff's charges went unanswered. This time, Johnson not only answered the charges and fired back with her own, she also defined the agenda long before Koskoff could afford to start advertising. Additionally, she used the advantages of incumbency to revive her reputation in the district as an accessible, responsive, moderate Republican. This time she lost only four of her forty-four towns, including her working class home town, compared with thirteen in the previous election. If the spread was not quite as large as it had been before 1996, it was nevertheless a resounding victory.

In what follows, I fill in the broad outlines of this account with details concerning the candidate, the campaign staff and consultants, and their roles in guiding the course of the campaign.

The Key Players, the Candidates, and the Issues

Nancy Johnson has held the Sixth District seat since 1982, following three terms in the state Senate. She has been known at home for her accessibility and constituency service, a home style that not only matches her personal inclinations but also helps her win the loyalty of some constituents who do not agree with her policy stances.[8] In her Washington work, she has been known for fiscal conservatism, marked by her early support of President Ronald Reagan's budgets. "In 1984 House votes, Johnson concurred with the president and with the conservative coalition of Republican and Southern Democrats more than half the time, something (Stewart B.) McKinney (R-CT 4) and most of the other 'Gypsy Moth' Eastern Republicans did not do."[9]

Johnson's fiscal conservatism has been tempered by social liberalism. She is firmly and passionately pro choice, against school vouchers, and generally concerned about the rightward swing of her party on social issues. In 1991 she joined with like-minded Republicans to establish the "Tuesday lunch bunch," a group of moderate Republicans who met weekly to map out strategies to moderate Republican policymaking in the House.

At the same time, she played a role in Newt Gingrich's rise to power, seconding his nomination to the Speaker's post with these words, "[Gingrich is] the most visionary thinker in American politics today." Given Gingrich's phenomenal unpopularity, those words came back to haunt her in 1996. More than her support for Gingrich's election as Speaker, she was dogged by allegations concerning her role as chair of the House ethics committee in its probe of charges against Gingrich in the 104th Congress. The charges, to which Gingrich eventually admitted, were that he brought discredit on the House by giving false information to the ethics committee about the links between a college course he taught and

GOPAC, a partisan political action committee that he headed, and failed to get adequate legal advice about federal tax law prohibiting the use of tax exempt funds for partisan political purposes. Johnson's committee recommended and the House approved a historic reprimand of the Speaker and a $300,000 fine. However, Johnson herself was criticized for not settling the matter until after the 1996 elections, when many Democrats thought that the committee's conclusions might have influenced voters' decisions. Her challenger used the issue to devastating effect in that election.

Once Johnson's term on the ethics committee ended, she focused again on the kinds of legislation popular in her district, including taxes, health care, and education. As the fifth-ranking Republican on the Ways and Means Committee, she was well-positioned to be effective on the tax and health care issues. As chair of the Subcommittee on Oversight, she was able to play a key role in the reform of the Internal Revenue Service. As a member of the health subcommittee, she sponsored successful legislation to help the states provide health insurance for uninsured children. In addition, the evidence indicates that Johnson moderated her voting record. Her ADA voting score (a measure of liberalism) for the 105th Congress rose to 55, compared with a score of 20 for the 104th Congress and 35 for the 103d Congress.

Charlotte Koskoff has challenged Nancy Johnson three times. It could be argued that she is not a high-quality challenger in Gary Jacobson's terms, as she has never held elective office.[10] Instead, her political experience before her three campaigns against Johnson consisted of service on her Democratic town committee and the state central committee. She is a lawyer and retired professor of education at Central Connecticut State University in New Britain. Her lack of a record of elective office entailed the usual positives and negatives for her strategy—on the one hand, she had no record to criticize, which forced Johnson's opposition strategy to rely on newspaper quotes as a substitute; moreover, it allowed her to present herself as "the gutsy outsider" who could bring a fresh viewpoint to Congress. On the other hand, in a year in which constituents were relatively happy with their lot as Connecticut emerged from a long recession, her inexperience allowed Johnson to stress the value of her own record, seniority, and power in Congress.

Until Koskoff began attacking her, Johnson's message focused entirely on her legislative initiatives and accomplishments. However, as the campaign heated up, the relative issue positions of the candidates became clear. In many areas, the differences between them were matters of degree; in others, their approaches were quite different. The contentiousness of the campaign obscured the fact that the candidates frequently agreed on the problems that needed fixing, if not on the solutions, including patients' rights relative to health maintenance organizations (HMOs), education, Social Security, and Medicare. Over the course of the campaign, some of the issues in contention were the following:

—Taxes. Johnson was a primary sponsor of the 1998 House Republican bill to cut taxes by $80 billion over five years; Koskoff criticized her for not devoting the entire budget surplus to saving Social Security.

—Social Security. Johnson favored allowing people with private pensions to invest in other ways a portion of earnings that now goes to Social Security. Koskoff opposed any reallocation of Social Security contributions.

—HMO reform. Both favored more patients' rights, but Johnson favored mediated settlements of patients' disputes with their HMOs; Koskoff favored the legalization of patient lawsuits.

—Medicare. Johnson favored and Koskoff opposed HMOs for Medicare recipients. Both argued that Medicare should be saved, but specifics during the campaign were few.

—Fast track authority and NAFTA. Johnson supported and Koskoff opposed both.

—Term limits, which Johnson opposed and Koskoff favored, promising to serve only three terms if elected.

—Capital punishment, which Johnson favored for some crimes and Koskoff opposed.

—Last, but certainly not least, Johnson's coauthorship of a 1996 amendment that would have prohibited the U.S. Customs Service from tightening the rules concerning products that could be labeled "made in the U.S.A."

The details of how the dispute over the last issue played out in candidate ads will be elaborated below. But because it was the sole subject of Koskoff's three television ads, it became the main issue in the final weeks of the campaign. The policy differences described above were articulated in the press and candidate debates, but in her ads, Koskoff did nothing to define herself and her views. Meanwhile, Johnson traveled the parallel tracks of responding to Koskoff's attacks and putting forth her own accomplishments.

The Campaign Managers and Consultants

Johnson's campaign team combined players from previous races with new ones who were experienced in the sort of tough campaign that she endured in 1996. Critical continuity and experience were provided by Johnson's campaign manager, Cheryl Lounsbury. Lounsbury was a trusted long-time friend who early in Johnson's tenure in Congress served Johnson as a fund-raiser, then as assistant director and finally director of her district office. Additionally, she managed all of Johnson's campaigns except for her first in 1982 and the near-fatal 1996 campaign, although she served as a consultant for the latter. Lounsbury had long been on Johnson's "kitchen cabinet" and played a key role in the early strategy sessions for the 1998 campaign before becoming campaign manager in June of 1998. Lounsbury had moved to a job in the private sector some years earlier and at the time of the campaign worked for a medical research firm as head of patient recruitment for clinical trials of new drugs. The remarkable degree of Johnson's faith in Lounsbury is indicated by the fact that Johnson hired her to run the campaign even though Lounsbury retained her "day job" and oversaw the campaign by telephone during the day and in person through long hours each night and weekend.

Another long-time member of Johnson's campaign team was Linda DiVall, who has done voter surveys for Johnson since her first race in 1982, when DiVall worked for the National Republican Congressional Committee. She is president of American Viewpoint, which she founded in 1986. One of the top tier of Republican pollsters, she polled for Bob Dole in 1996; in the 1998 midterm elections, she polled for fifteen congressional races. DiVall's long relationship with Johnson offered a substantial advantage, as DiVall has asked some questions every time, allowing accurate assessments of long-term shifts in voter attitudes.

Besides the continuity provided by Lounsbury and DiVall, key changes in Johnson's Washington staff helped to form her 1998 campaign team as well. In a swift reaction to the 1996 election, Johnson hired a new administrative assistant for her Washington office, David Karvelas. Karvelas, a former Associated Press reporter, had worked on Representative Dick Zimmer's unsuccessful 1996 campaign against Robert Torricelli for New Jersey's open Senate seat, a race that was described as "one of the nastiest campaigns in New Jersey history."[11] Karvelas thus brought with him experience with the kind of campaign that Johnson had just barely survived, as well as the skills to operate in that kind of environment. According to Lounsbury, Karvelas "thinks like a reporter" and helped Johnson develop media-savvy explanations for the events of any given day on the Hill. The resulting press releases were intended to begin repairing her image in the months before the start of the campaign.

Karvelas soon hired David White, promoting him to press secretary early in 1998. White had previously worked for Zimmer's district and Washington offices and on House committee staffs before joining Zimmer's 1996 Senate campaign. Following that race, he worked for Jamestown Associates of Princeton, New Jersey, which had supplied Zimmer's media consultants. White took a leave from the Washington office in September and moved to the district to become deputy campaign manager. Given his media experience, White handled most of the press contacts; moreover, during the day he ran the campaign in close consultation with Lounsbury.

In a key shift from the 1996 race, Larry Weitzner, the principal of Jamestown Associates and creator of Zimmer's 1996 ads, was hired to do Nancy Johnson's media for the new election cycle, replacing the firm that previously had served as her media consultants. Weitzner, assisted by Adam Geller (also with Jamestown), also worked on the reelection campaigns of George Pataki and Alfonse D'Amato, as well as a number of House campaigns. In addition, his firm provided consulting for the moderate Republican Leadership Council. Given Weitzner's experience in New York and New Jersey campaigns, which are notably less mannerly than the typical Connecticut race, Johnson acquired a media consultant who was experienced in the trench warfare of modern campaigning.

Thus the leadership of Johnson's 1998 campaign team combined continuity with Johnson and Sixth District politics with a new orientation toward the sort of tough campaign that almost defeated her in 1996.

Laying the Groundwork: Polling and Opposition Research

Immediately following the 1996 election, Johnson commissioned a poll by her long-time pollster, Linda DiVall. That poll, which found Johnson's support to be at just 50 percent, was designed to diagnose the problems that nearly cost her reelection. The results confirmed Johnson's closest supporters' analysis: her close shave was caused by four factors, three of which were particular to her:

—One, as chairwoman of the House ethics committee, she presided over the proceedings on the ethics charges against Speaker Newt Gingrich in the 104th Congress. The media and her challenger branded her as his apologist. Her campaign manager believed that apparent leaks from a Democrat on the committee, coupled with Johnson's unwillingness to counterleak concerning the confidential proceedings, left unanswered the charges of partisan coddling of the Speaker.

—Two, she was perceived as being out of touch with the district. The ethics matter along with the newly increased responsibilities of being both in the majority and a subcommittee chair on the Ways and Means Committee had kept her from coming back to the district as often as usual; her constituents felt that she was not around enough.

—Three, for the first time, she was perceived as being more conservative than most of her constituents. Her strategists attributed that shift in perception to the national media's concentration on conservative Republicans during their first term in the majority. They felt that as a consequence, despite Johnson's leadership role among moderate House Republicans, her opponent was able to paint her as more conservative than she actually was, thus moving the district's perception of her to the right.

—Four, Republican presidential candidate Bob Dole managed to win only 37 percent of the vote in the Sixth District; Johnson's strategists believed that his poor showing had dragged down the Republican underticket. The fact that the Dole campaign by all accounts pulled out of Connecticut at least two weeks before the election meant that considerably less money was spent on Republican races generally than otherwise might have been the case.

Overall, the poll showed that Johnson's negatives were significantly higher than normal.

Besides the postelection poll, in late 1997 pollster DiVall and media consultant Weitzner conducted a series of focus groups in the district to flesh out the findings of the poll and provide the basis for a campaign strategy. Taken together, the poll and the focus groups made it clear, among other things, that voters in the Sixth District, as elsewhere, cared about health care, education, and taxes. Because of her senior rank on Ways and Means, Johnson was in a position to be effective on all of those issues; thus her early ads featured her accomplishments in those areas. The earliest ad, which began running in late December of 1997, concerned health care, an area felt to be one of Johnson's strongest as well as one of the most important to voters.

In April of 1998, four months into the year-long campaign, DiVall did another survey. The results showed that the early ads as well as Johnson's other efforts had moved her numbers in a more positive direction. The campaign team judged that the strategy was on track.

DiVall conducted another survey in September, which gave Johnson a thirty-five-point lead (58 percent supported Johnson, 23 percent favored Koskoff). DiVall described the results as showing that Johnson was strong with her Republican base and seniors, along with a significant number of Democrats. In another encouraging sign for Johnson, the poll showed that 64 perent of voters in union households approved of Johnson, who enjoyed an overall job approval rating of 70 percent. (Importantly, however, Koskoff had the energetic support of the AFL-CIO and several other large unions.) The results were released to the press by the National Republican Congressional Committee, thus giving the report greater public credibility than it would have had if it had been announced by the Johnson campaign, The aim, of course, was to stem any momentum Koskoff might develop and dry up her funding sources. However, Koskoff had not yet run her first ad, and no one had forgotten that she did her worst damage in 1996 in the last ten days of the campaign.

In mid-October, six days after the unveiling of Koskoff's first television ad and Johnson's response ad, DiVall did a tracking poll to determine the effect of the two ads. The results showed that Koskoff's ad was not working for her; in fact, Koskoff's negatives had increased, and her positives had not moved; meanwhile, Johnson's positives had increased, and her negatives had gone down. Lounsbury marveled, "Koskoff must not have polled! She should have seen her ad wasn't working and pulled it." Instead, she continued to run on the same message in subsequent ads.

Nevertheless, the last tracking poll, conducted two weeks before the election, showed that union members were "coming home strongly to the Democrats" in four key towns: New Britain, Bristol, Torrington, and Southington. DiVall therefore advised that the message and targeting be tightened by focusing mailings on federal benefits that Johnson gained for those towns, which they did during the last two weeks of the campaign. At the same time, however, union locals were sending out mailers to their members attacking Johnson and reinforcing Koskoff's charges.

Over the course of the campaign, DiVall participated in assessing strategy, message development, and tactical shifts. She played a broader role as well. DiVall noted in an interview that this campaign was different from Johnson's previous races; in the past, Johnson had always driven things herself. Because of her scare in 1996, she recognized that she had to give up some of that control, but she was unaccustomed to having others tell her what to do. DiVall's role was to help "nudge Nancy toward what her team had come up with," using her own seniority and their long relationship to reinforce the wisdom of the team's recommendations.

Unlike the polling, the opposition research was not done by professionals. Rather, it was done during the summer of 1998 by two college interns (who later became paid employees of the campaign) Jamie Cheshire and Jared Rodrigues. Because Koskoff had never held elected office, it was necessary to draw her issue positions entirely from her public statements. To that end, the interns gathered relevant newspaper clippings from March 24, 1994 (the year of Koskoff's first challenge) until the present. As will be seen, the quotations that they unearthed played an important role in Johnson's first response ad. Following the format recommended by the national party, Jamie Cheshire organized the clips by subject into a "quote book," which was the source used by deputy campaign manager White when he needed a countercharge to something that Koskoff had thrown at Johnson.

In addition, the interns scoured town halls and Superior Courthouses throughout the state for legal documents that might prove useful. As both Koskoff and her husband were attorneys, there was quite a bit to be found. Some of the documents, in the staff's opinion, could potentially have been embarrassing, particularly some relating to real estate investments. However, only one such item was ever used, and that was not particularly negative in itself. To be specific, when Koskoff charged Johnson in her first ad with "slipping" language into an amendment that would, she asserted, have exported district jobs to China, Johnson's response ad used a newspaper quotation from 1994 on Koskoff's support for tax increases in Clinton's 1993 budget. However, when he talked to the press about the jobs issue, deputy campaign manager White noted that Koskoff owned property in Washington, D.C., and suggested that the investment indicated her indifference to the economy of Connecticut. Such documentary evidence of Koskoff's finances was not used in ads, however.

When staffers were asked during the campaign whether they would use any of the rest of the very thick book of opposition research that they had assembled, one intern said "If David [White] had his way, we'd use more of it"; the other asserted that Johnson would not allow it. Those statements neatly summed up a major dynamic of the campaign: Johnson's staff wanted a more hard-hitting approach, while Johnson herself resisted many of their recommendations. Of the opposition research,

White said, "We never used most of it. I didn't bother to even put it to Nancy because I knew she wouldn't use it." White regarded it as a reserve weapon, to be used only if the campaign was in trouble and really needed it. Because Johnson's poll numbers held up throughout the campaign, most of the opposition research remained in reserve.

Fund-raising and Campaign Finance

Not surprisingly, fund-raising began immediately after the 1996 election. Even though Johnson had outspent Koskoff by 3 to 1 in 1996, Koskoff had nearly won; thus there was a sense of urgency about fund-raising in the new election cycle. In a break with her normal practice, Johnson installed her 1996 field director, Christina Stamos, in an office in the basement of her home to begin raising money. Additionally, Todd Meredith of Morgan Meredith and Associates was hired to do political action committee (PAC) fund-raising. The district fund-raising plan was developed by Stamos and Lounsbury; Stamos and Meredith worked together on both district and D.C. events. District events began with a series of small coffees with supporters not only to raise funds but also to find out what had gone wrong in 1996 and mend any fences that needed it. Additionally, there were two major events in 1997: a summer fund-raiser attended by Governor John Rowland and a November breakfast attended by Budget Committee Chairman John Kasich. By the end of 1997, Johnson reported receipts of $624,071, which amounted to three-quarters of her total receipts for the entire 1996 election cycle. By the same time, Koskoff had raised $202,214, also three-quarters of her receipts for the 1996 election cycle. Despite the incumbent's usual fund-raising advantage, Koskoff was clearly being taken seriously as a candidate.

There were three direct mail fund-raising efforts in 1997 and five additional mailings in 1998. The consultant wrote the drafts of the letters, which were then sent to Johnson, who rewrote them, then to Lounsbury who revised them, and to Johnson again for final revisions. The dynamic of the process was similar to that seen on other aspects of the campaign: for most of the race, Johnson wanted a great deal of substance on public policy in these mailers; she resisted abbreviating her views in print and transforming them into bullets, believing that her job was to educate her constituents on the issues and her role on them. However, she eventually adopted the approach of the consultants and staff; as one of her staffers said, "Toward the end, she got into the bullet thing because she said no one reads the details."

In addition to the use of mailers, twenty-four fund-raising events were held outside Washington in 1998, most of them in Connecticut, most of them hosted by a member of Johnson's fund-raising committee. Together, local events and mailers earned nearly a half-million dollars in 1998.

Fourteen PAC events were held in Washington in 1998. They were handled largely by the fund-raising consultant, Todd Meredith, working with Stamos and Johnson's PAC steering committee consisting of PAC representatives from a variety of industries. Most of those events were industry specific, including events for the pharmaceutical and chemical industries, as well as the National Retail Federation, Tenneco, the letter carriers (U.S. postal workers), and pathologists. There was one general, "cattle-call" PAC event, which alone raised $172,000. The PAC events started at $500 per person, but toward the end, the cost was $1,500 a head. For an additional $500 one could return to Johnson's Washington home after the PAC reception for dessert and conversation with senior members of the Ways and Means Committee, of which Johnson is herself a senior member.

It is normal for candidates to spend hundreds of miserable hours on the telephone, "dialing for dollars." When asked how much time Johnson spent in that manner, Lounsbury replied, "None. She hates to fund-raise. She'll fund-raise for other candidates—it continues to be very important to her to build the moderate wing of the Republican Party"—mainly by appearing at fund-raisers for other House candidates in open seat races. Lounsbury made the calls to top corporate executive officers, asking for large donations; "they expect that," largely because she had done it for so long that they were accustomed to receiving calls from her. The larger point here is that Johnson's high rank in the majority party on the powerful Ways and Means Committee eased her fund-raising path considerably.

The following table provides the breakdown of receipts and expenditures for Johnson and Koskoff as well as the Concerned Citizens Party candidate for the 1996 and 1998 election cycles.[13]

As is typical, the lion's share of Johnson's $1.77 million budget was spent on media: approximately 65 percent of the budget was allocated to that effort. Of that amount, about two-thirds was spent on television, while roughly one-third went for mailers. Very little was spent on radio, which Koskoff did very little of herself this time, and newspaper ads, which the staff did not consider particularly useful. An additional 10 percent of the

1997–98 receipts (dollars)		*Received from PACs (dollars)*	*Expenditures (dollars)*
Johnson	1,768,305	1,017,391 (58 percent)	1,721,382
Koskoff	551,102	148,473 (27 percent)	550,463
Knibbs	189	0	126
1995–96			
Johnson	825,021	435,082 (53 percent)	931,406
Koskoff	270,576	108,307 (40 percent)	273,133
Knibbs	0	0	430

budget went for polling expenses. Approximately 10 percent was allocated to the field; the remaining 15 percent was for salaries and overhead. Overall, 90 percent of the budget was spent from September on, when the intensity of media buys and the number of ads increased dramatically.

Campaign Conduct: Strategy, Theme and Message

Immediately following Johnson's narrow victory in 1996, she turned to an analysis of what went wrong. The postelection poll and focus groups indicated the three major weaknesses detailed above: perceptions that Johnson had spent so much time in Washington that she had become a Washington insider, out of touch with her constituents; that she had become too conservative for her district; and that she had unduly protected Newt Gingrich during the ethics committee proceedings. From these findings, the strategy, theme, and message of the campaign emerged.

Clearly, some of the factors that damaged Johnson in 1996 would not be operative in 1998, while others could be fixed. First, the Republican ticket in 1998 would not be topped by a losing presidential candidate, but by an incumbent governor, who, as it turned out, enjoyed a stunning degree of popularity. Second, because Johnson rotated off the ethics committee in 1997, a potent negative would be nearly two years behind her by the 1998 election. Additionally, her traditional image in the district of accessibility and approachability could be revived, as could the perception of her as a moderate Republican in line with her constituents's views.

Thus, pre-campaign strategy involved the following:

—Get back out into the district. For most of the 105th Congress, Johnson spent Friday through Sunday in the district, attending several events each day. During the 104th Congress, the press of business especially in the ethics committee had kept her in Washington often until Friday night, and she typically returned to Washington on Sunday night or Monday morning. Thus, her new district schedule (which returned to her pre-104th Congress pattern) gave her 50 percent more time in the district, allowing her to raise her visibility. Also as an aid to repairing her constituent relations, she installed as her new district director an old friend, Ted Fusaro. Fusaro was well connected with the local Republican town committees, which were key to her field operation once the 1998 campaign began in earnest.

—Stress her moderation on the issues and distance herself from the conservative wing of the Republican Party to appeal to the key swing voters in the district. Her media-savvy new administrative assistant David Karvelas and press secretary David White helped with that early in the new congressional term. White later brought his media skills into the campaign, where he served as deputy campaign manager. White and Karvelas raised Johnson's profile in the press, stressing her moderate positions. Johnson herself believed that part of her job was to educate people about her record and the reasoning underlying her actions; she tended to do so in great, sometimes indigestible, detail. Yet her inclination to elaborate too much played well into the need to stress her moderation, as it demonstrated that her positions were not drawn from hard-line ideology. Her time in the district helped her to develop her message as well. Her "town meetings" provided the setting in which to discover which issues resonated with the voters; meetings with local newspapers' editorial boards served a similar purpose.

—Begin raising money immediately, which she did by keeping on a 1996 campaign staffer, Christina Stamos, who cultivated Johnson's district finance committee and organized early fund-raising mailings and events in the district; Washington fund-raising also proceeded apace.

In January 1998, Johnson's campaign team—Karvelas, Lounsbury, DiVall, and Weitzner—assembled to map out the campaign plan. However, as noted earlier, they had previously begun to define the strategy, theme, and message of the campaign. Before the first of the year they had decided to follow the recommendation of media consultant Weitzner to conduct a nearly year-long campaign, running the first television advertisement on December 27, 1997. In the planning process, continuity and familiarity with Johnson's style and preferences were provided by Lounsbury and DiVall, who had been part of Johnson's team for many years. The core of the strategy was a continuation of Johnson's postelection, precampaign strategy: she must maintain high visibility in the district to counter the perception that she had become a Washington insider who was out of touch with her constituents. Second, she needed to convince her constituents that she was a moderate Republican, not a Gingrich clone.

To help reinforce the message of her moderation and independence on particular issues, decisions were made to seek group endorsements, such as the League of Conservation Voters and the Sierra Club. Additionally, at the national level the Democratic Party, which had not supported Koskoff in either of her two prior races, had ranked the 1998 race as a top target following Koskoff's near victory in 1996. Thus, part of the campaign strategy was to build Johnson's strength early so that the targeting level would be dropped, which indeed it was, to a third-tier race, by October.

Finally, the team felt that it was essential to prevent a repetition of a key advantage enjoyed by Koskoff in 1996; in that race, the challenger had controlled the agenda, keeping Johnson on the defensive. Fundamental to the strategy of the 1998 campaign was to turn the tables, having Johnson seize control of the agenda early on and keep it throughout.

The theme of the campaign focused on the value to the district of Johnson's experience and accomplishments in Congress, especially her role in the passage of legislation that provided significant benefits in such areas as health, Social Security, and education, all which were of interest to her constituents. Implicit in the theme was the suggestion that her constituents benefited from her place not only in the majority but in a leadership position on one of the most powerful committees in the House, which allowed her to play a key role in passing such legislation. The fact that those bills provided general benefits to the nation was not stressed, as the campaign team sought to focus on the district benefits flowing from Johnson's Washington insider status at the same time that they eschewed the damaging label.

The message evolved over time. In midsummer, Johnson and the staff narrowed the field of issues that would be the vehicle for Johnson's message. Because Johnson herself was so issue oriented, the staff faced a twofold problem: persuade her to narrow the number of issues and simplify her discussion of them. Johnson's resistance to talking in sound bites and penchant for discussing the complex ramifications of dozens of policy areas prompted both admiration and frustration in her staff. An early handout detailing her accomplishments encompassed nearly three dozen issues in eight issue areas. For example, early in the campaign, she stressed her contribution to welfare reform and to balancing the budget, but she later omitted those issues and focused more strongly on taxes by means of her proposal to return some of the budget surplus to the voters through her sponsorship of the $80 billion House Republican tax cut bill in September. A major focus of both the staff and consultants was to persuade her to distill her message to a few issues and points that would resonate and stick with the voters.

By September, the message had been distilled to the following points:

—Taxes and jobs. Johnson's efforts to reduce taxes on small businesses would promote jobs; her successful efforts to reform the IRS protects constituents from an aggressive government agency.

—Education. Johnson's "five-point plan" to make college more affordable would provide among other things a $1,500 tax credit for college costs, allow deduction of interest on student loans, help families save for education, and encourage employers to pay tuition for their workers.

—Health care. Johnson wrote the law providing health care to uninsured children, called the HUSKY plan in Connecticut. Additionally, she argued that she "fought successfully to save Medicare from bankruptcy, and added new protective benefits"; further, she fought for a patient's bill of rights relative to HMOs.

—Social Security. Johnson wrote legislation to cut taxes on Social Security benefits.

—Environment. She helped gain for the Connecticut River a coveted federal designation as a National Heritage River.

Part of the campaign strategy was to court group endorsements in areas that would allow Johnson to make inroads into Koskoff's support, a major component of which had been labor unions. According to Lounsbury, they had never aggressively gone after group endorsements before, "mainly because Nancy won't change her legislative positions for endorsements." This time, however, the staff actively communicated with key organizations, sending them her bills, votes, and press releases relevant to their interests. When the time came for the groups to decide on their endorsements, the staff challenged them to say why they would not endorse Johnson. It was a strategy that paid off in several key instances, garnering new endorsements that reinforced her moderate image. Furthermore, the campaign carefully timed the release of announcements of group endorsements to keep up the momentum of the race.

Implementation of the endorsement strategy began in early June when the campaign announced the endorsements of four construction unions. Those endorsements were intended to counteract to some degree Koskoff's support from the AFL-CIO, which provided important campaign assistance, including a series of mailers critical of Johnson.

Additionally, on July 7 Johnson announced the endorsement of the League of Conservation Voters; the representative of that organization was joined at the press conference by officials from several state environmental groups. However, the state chapter of the Sierra Club, internally split between Johnson and Koskoff, delayed its endorsement of Johnson until September, when the national Sierra Club ran radio ads for Johnson. In the process of reporting the LCV endorsement, at least three district newspapers noted that Johnson had not received that group's support in 1996, when the group gave her a rating of 54 on environmental issues, compared with a much-improved rating of 94 in 1997.[14]

Perhaps Johnson's greatest coup in regard to endorsements was winning the backing of the National Education Association in mid-September. Koskoff, a retired college professor, had received that group's endorsement previously, but Johnson's work on legislation to make college more affordable as well as her bill to guarantee health care coverage for children were cited by the president of the national association as influences on their decision.[15] However, the Connecticut Education Association's PAC was reported as having voted earlier in the year to support Koskoff once again; its decision was overruled by the executive committee, a serious blow to Koskoff.[16] The announcement of this endorsement is a prime example of the strategic release of information: the Johnson campaign announced the NEA endorsement immediately after Koskoff's first attack ad. The timing, according to Lounsbury, was intended to "level the playing field with the press," and, it must be assumed, to demoralize Koskoff, who clearly had expected the NEA's support once again.

Paid and Earned Media

The earned and paid media campaigns were carefully coordinated by deputy campaign manager White. With respect to paid media, Johnson had the airwaves to herself from the broadcast of her first ad in late 1997 until the appearance of Koskoff's first ad on October 8, 1998. During that time Johnson ran five different television ads, buying time primarily on the three major network-affiliated stations, two in Hartford and one in New Haven (there is no television station in the Sixth District). At this point, of course, all were advocacy ads highlighting her accomplishments and positions in a number of policy areas.[17] The first concerned her bill to provide federal funds to help states extend health care benefits to uninsured children. Another took credit for creating jobs through her efforts at cutting taxes and simplifying the tax code.

Yet another early ad concerned her five-point plan to make college education more affordable. A fourth ad, run in the summer of 1998, also focused on taxes, listing among Johnson's accomplishments the $500 per child tax credit, a cut in Social Security taxes for seniors, reduction in small business taxes to stimulate job creation, and her leadership in the successful effort to reform the Internal Revenue Service. Another ad proclaimed her a "national leader on health care," noting that she helped write the law to save Medicare and give seniors new preventative benefits, as well as advertising her efforts to pass a patients' bill of rights in the House and the children's health care plan. That ad ended with the following: "Strong, steady leadership, getting results," reflecting the major theme of the campaign: her experience and effectiveness in policy areas that her constituents cared about, making public policy that would improve their lives. In a few cases, sixty-second radio ads expanding on the message were run in some areas in conjunction with the television ads.

Johnson's 1998 legislative initiatives were heralded in a steady stream of press releases that reinforced her message on her accomplishments and generated considerable press coverage. Those issues include the passage of her children's health insurance plan; the introduction in May of her five-point plan to make college more affordable; the signing of the Internal Revenue Service reform bill; and her initiative on a $78 billion tax cut plan in September.

During those nine months, Johnson was able to run an entirely positive campaign to define herself in the voters' minds, "reminding them of who she is," in the words of her strategists. By the time Koskoff went on the air, it was too late to do serious damage to an incumbent who had already made the case for her moderation and legislative effectiveness, and whose connection to Gingrich during the ethics probe was but a faded memory.

Nevertheless, Koskoff certainly tried to damage Johnson, and when she did, Johnson's team was ready with its comeback. During the final weeks of the campaign, White, Lounsbury, and other campaign staffers talked daily with the consultants about tactical matters such as the design of new mail pieces and responses to Koskoff's statements; responses were played out in both the paid and earned media efforts. Especially with respect to Koskoff's charges against Johnson, the underlying strategy was, in White's words, to "refute and countercharge."

The real battle between the candidates began when Johnson's staffers discovered Koskoff filming her first ad on September 17 outside the gates of the toolmaker, Stanley Works. They easily guessed that the ad would be an attack on Johnson's record on jobs in general and probably on what came to be known as the "made in the U.S.A." issue. Their assumption was right: in her first ad, aired on October 8, Koskoff charged Johnson with "slipping" special interest language into a bill to allow an unnamed company, identified in later ads as Stanley Works, to label as "made in the U.S.A." products that were made in Taiwan. That ad also noted that Johnson had received more than $20,000 in campaign contributions from the same company.

The campaign's treatment of Koskoff's charges on this issue was probably the most important area of coordination between the earned and paid media campaigns. The policy issue was a complicated one, and the campaign team decided not to respond substantively in a paid ad but rather to characterize Koskoff's charge as a lie in the response ad and, at the same time, use contacts with reporters to defend Johnson's actions and make countercharges against Koskoff.

The campaign hardly could have responded to Koskoff more quickly. The day that her ad began running, she held a press conference outside Stanley Works's gates to introduce the ad and air her charges against Johnson. However, the ad had already run; thus White, the consultants, and Lounsbury had already had time to devise the specific response, especially given that they already had inferred the probable nature of the charge from Koskoff's attempt to film her first campaign ad outside Stanley Works in September.

Thus the press packet was already prepared, and White and his assistant attended Koskoff's press conference (which could be seen taking place from the windows of Johnson's district office) and began handing out the packet and talking to reporters then and there.[18] In his conversations with the press, White charged Koskoff with being unconcerned with the economy in the district, the evidence for which was the fact that she and her husband owned hundreds of thousands of dollars worth of property in Washington, D.C., which, White argued, "does nothing for jobs or taxes in Connecticut."

Backed by the press packet, White refuted point by point the claims in Koskoff's ad and provided detailed information on the "country of origin" policy that the U.S. Customs Service proposed changing. First, he pointed out that the measure in question was an amendment to a Ways and Means Committee trade bill that was cosponsored by Democratic Representatives Barbara Kennelly of Connecticut and Richard Neal of Massachusetts; he denied that it was secretly "slipped in" as Koskoff charged. Second, he noted that it applied to all companies in the category in question, not just Stanley. Finally, and most important, he argued that the amendment would actually have protected, not endangered, the jobs of Stanley workers.

The real argument occurred over the interpretation of this complex issue. This battle was key, as it constituted Koskoff's entire paid media campaign; if her interpretation had prevailed, Johnson would have successfully been tarred as indifferent to the economic concerns of her working class constituents.

The amendment in question, which ultimately died in the Senate, would have prohibited the Customs Service from reversing a policy that allowed tool companies that use raw metal forgings produced abroad as the basis for tools made in their U.S. factories to label those tools as made in the United States. If the Customs Service had its way, companies would have been required to label such tools according to the country of origin of the forgings, not the finished product.[19] Johnson and her campaign staff defended her proposal as one that would save jobs; without her amendment, people would choose hand tools labeled as produced in the U.S.A. over those that were not so designated, resulting in a decline in Stanley's sales. On the other hand, Koskoff interpreted the amendment as a threat to jobs in the district, as it removed the incentive for companies to make tools from materials produced in the United States.

White further argued that the policy had nothing to do with a "made in the U.S.A." issue; rather it was, he said, a "country of origin" issue. His approach thus constituted an attempt to change the subject from American jobs to something more arcane and less incendiary.

White's effort to defuse the issue was remarkably successful. The subsequent press coverage included much of the information in the press packet, and the campaign's own tracking poll showed that the issue not only did not resonate with the voters, but that Koskoff's negatives increased within a week of the airing of the ad and Johnson's response.

White himself felt that the effort was successful and was pleased with the press coverage; he said, "They knew Nancy wasn't bought off."

With respect to the paid media campaign, once Johnson's team became aware in September of the probable thrust of Koskoff's first ad, they began to craft the elements of their response ad, and in the meantime continually monitored Koskoff's media buys. Thus, they knew when the ad would go up and were ready to finalize and tape the response ad, which they were able to get on the air within twelve hours of the appearance of Koskoff's ad.

Johnson's ad responded in kind to Koskoff's attack. It was to some extent a contrast piece, comparing the two candidates' positions; however, its emphasis also was on the attack. The script was as follows: "Charlotte Koskoff's negative ads are a lie. The truth is Nancy Johnson voted to help factories keep jobs in Connecticut. That's why unemployment is the lowest in a decade. It's Charlotte Koskoff's support of higher taxes that will cost us jobs and hurt working families. She supported the biggest tax increase in history—even raising taxes on Social Security benefits. Charlotte Koskoff has started her campaign by lying to you. So how could you believe anything she says?"

Johnson's charge that Koskoff had "supported the biggest tax increase in history—even raising taxes on Social Security benefits" was based on newspaper clips from 1994. Koskoff angrily pointed out that she could not have done what the ad implied, never having held public office; yet her defense carried the inherent disadvantage of forcing her to admit her lack of experience in a year when voters seemed to value exactly that.

Koskoff's second ad repeated the initial charge, pairing it this time with another conflict-of-interest accusation involving Johnson's ownership of up to $250,000 in Stanley Works stock. Although the amendment in question had been introduced in July 1996, Johnson's connection to it received unfavorable attention in the press in October 1997, when her financial disclosure report listed the stock. According to one press account, "Johnson came under fire last October from Democrats and union leaders for trying to shelter the New Britain-based company."[20] In light of that publicity, Koskoff undoubtedly thought her attack would be more successful than it was. In response to the charge, Johnson's campaign proudly noted that the stock in question was inherited from her father-in-law, who had been a foreman at Stanley Works. That interpretation worked on two levels: as a realization of the American dream for a Stanley worker and as a symbol of Johnson's long and deep ties to and investment in the community.

A "brush fire" poll by DiVall showed that the issue not only had not helped Koskoff but seemed to have hurt her, yet she continued to run ads on that theme to the exclusion of all others. All three of her television ads were attack ads, while Johnson ran a series of ads that consisted mostly of a combination of contrast and advocacy.

Koskoff's first attack ad and Johnson's response caused quite a stir in the press. For Johnson herself, the response ad was a qualitative change in campaign style. She had never before run an ad that anyone could have interpreted as an attack. By all accounts, she found such ads distasteful. Yet her new administrative assistant David Karvelas persuaded her early on that she must never again allow an attack to go unanswered. The strategy for responding to attacks during the campaign, according to deputy campaign manager White, was to briefly address the attack itself, push it aside, and come back with an attack on Koskoff, preferably on a related issue. That pattern is clearly evident in the script reproduced above and in White's handling of the press.

The major question of this study, the role of campaign consultants, appears in a light rather different from the popular image of consultants driving the tone in a highly negative direction. Although Johnson acknowledged the need to respond to attacks, her natural revulsion for negative campaigns tempered the exact form of the responses, as the development of the first response ad illustrates. That ad, written like all the others by Jamestown Associates using the points supplied by the campaign team, showed an unflattering black-and-white still picture of Koskoff. The initial version, however, was even more unflattering, featuring a slow-motion tape of Koskoff talking. In the words of one staffer, "It made her look horrible." Johnson vetoed that in favor of the still photo. She also was uncomfortable with calling Koskoff's charge a lie but in the end was swayed by her staff and her own frustration with what she considered the nasty tone and factual distortion of Koskoff's ad. She was finally persuaded that she had no choice but to respond as she did.

Nevertheless, her first instinct had been to explain her position. Her staff and consultants talked her out of doing so on the grounds that first, it would be impossible to do effectively because the issue was so complicated. Second, it would make her appear defensive; and third, she would forgo the chance to throw back a countercharge. Thus, she approved the media consultant's characterization of Koskoff's attack as a lie and opted for White to explain her position to the press and for Johnson herself to deal with it in debates.

The tracking poll taken six days after Koskoff's ad and Johnson's response showed that Koskoff's numbers were deteriorating, while Johnson's positives had improved. White said that the campaign's earlier polls had already showed that Koskoff's attack, which they anticipated, would not work. He said, "I was amazed that was the best thing she could think of to hit us on!" The polls showed that most people did not believe Koskoff's attack; they in fact did believe that it was a lie, as Johnson charged. Moreover, earlier polls showed that jobs were not a big issue in the district, which was finally enjoying a recovery from Connecticut's long recession.

The process of devising the response to Koskoff's second attack ad was essentially the same, although the media consultant, Larry Weitzner, did not think it necessary to move quite as fast, as the first response covered the second ad as well. Thus, after the first response ad had reached 1,000 gross rating points, he began running the second one.[21] That ad was a contrast piece, noting Johnson's endorsements from the NEA, environmental groups, labor unions, taxpayers' groups, and a "Democrats for Johnson" group. The script was only mildly negative, but the ad was devastating nonetheless: it featured a video clip from the first debate in which Koskoff stammered and stumbled and finally admitted that she could not answer a question on immigration. That was followed up this way: "We can't afford on the job training. Nancy Johnson for Congress." Once again, the consultant said that Johnson was uncomfortable with the approach and insisted that the ad be "tasteful," which in this case meant starting with her own strengths and only then contrasting that with Koskoff's inexperience. As before, Johnson exerted control over the process but allowed a more negative tone than she previously would have permitted.

Thus, the ad that ran was a compromise between the harder line recommended by consultant Weitzner and Johnson's desire to conduct a more genteel campaign. But her conviction that Koskoff had to be answered, constantly reinforced by her staff and consultants, not to mention the election returns of 1996, persuaded her to allow a tougher approach. As Johnson herself said the day before the second response ad ran, "I've never done this before, but it's a different world now." She observed that her more pugnacious new staffers were in fact good for her "given the way things are now."

Koskoff's last ad ran during the final week of the campaign. It made use of an opinion piece written by the managing editor of the *Journal Inquirer* (more on that article and its use shortly). That article expressed the opinion that Johnson had not rebutted Koskoff's charges because they were all true. In a turn-about, the ad featured a clip of Johnson saying "We need new blood," and the announcer said, "Mrs. Johnson, we agree." No response ad was ever run, although one had already been prepared; it was a contrast piece featuring Johnson's and Koskoff's positions on taxes, jobs, Medicare and Social Security, and the death penalty. But Weitzner said that they decided, first, that no further response was needed. Tracking polls continued to show that Koskoff's ads were not working. "She took a bad tack of calling Nancy a crook. She doesn't look like a crook or talk like one. She has a reputation for integrity." In the end, they ran a mostly positive advocacy ad that featured Johnson's accomplishments on children's health care, Medicare, and taxes. Then the ad reminded voters of those ads they did not believe: "No wonder the *Hartford Courant* endorsed Nancy Johnson and rejected Charlotte Koskoff for running negative ads that lacked substance. Vote for experience, integrity, and results."

The earned media effort on Koskoff's final attack on Johnson was more frustrating for the campaign staff than such efforts on previous ads. Following the airing of the third ad, the staff spent several hours assembling another press packet (which they called the "whack pack") to send to the *Journal Inquirer*, the paper that supported Koskoff's charges. With it, Johnson faxed a heated letter to the publisher requesting that she publicly denounce Koskoff's claim on the grounds that it was false and that Johnson had indeed refuted her charges point by point. That letter was faxed on October 28. The publisher not only declined to disassociate her newspaper from the claim in Koskoff's ad, two days later the paper published an editorial that praised Koskoff for raising the conflict-of-interest issue and blasting Johnson for her "it's a lie" response.

On the whole, the campaign's use of the media was far more successful than in the preceding incident. As noted earlier, a key part of the earned media campaign was its use of endorsements to generate favorable media attention and thus make a statement about Johnson's strengths. Endorsements were indeed trumpeted by the campaign. When Johnson received the backing of the four construction unions, it was heralded at a campaign event in working class New Britain, a city she lost last time. The event was duly reported by the local newspaper.[22] Similarly, the League of

Conservation Voters' endorsement of Johnson was announced at a local press conference attended not only by the political director of the LCV, but by representatives of a number of other environmental organizations. That event received coverage in several of the largest newspapers in the district. In an interesting sidelight, one of the articles about the latter event was written by Kelley Beaucar, a reporter for the New Britain *Herald*, who was shortly to become Koskoff's press secretary. Although the article was balanced on the whole in its treatment, its first sentence was the following: "While [Johnson's] opponents are calling her a political chameleon. . . ."[23] In fact, White observed that the *Herald* failed to report on important press releases, including one concerning the support of "Democrats for Johnson," a group that included a former mayor of New Britain. He felt that the *Herald* had adopted something of a hands-off policy, covering neither candidate very well, perhaps because of the role of the paper's former reporter in the campaign. Nevertheless, in general, reporting on press releases on endorsements was widespread.

Summing up Johnson's general approach to media communications, Lounsbury said, "Nancy is an educator. She insists that her ads contain issue information." Johnson was able to follow that inclination to a greater degree in her ten direct mail pieces than in her TV ads. With respect to targeting the direct mail, Lounsbury said, "Nancy has a philosophical belief that election time is to educate all of her constituents. She wants to mail everyone in the district." That, of course, is very expensive and has the added disadvantage of possibly activating her opponents; thus, her campaign team "fought her on it." In the end only one piece was mailed to all households. The rest were targeted, especially to seniors, "who need a lot of attention. . . . they can easily get stirred up on Social Security and Medicare, so you have to mail them constantly." They also did mailings to every voting household in towns she lost last time, in particular, the working class cities of New Britain and Bristol, forcing Koskoff to defend her base during the last days of the campaign.

For the mailers, as for all her ads, Johnson rewrote what the consultants and her staff produced; they rewrote it again, and through a process of debate, a final product was agreed on. As a highly experienced candidate with strong views about how a campaign should come across to the voters, Johnson exerted a great deal of control over the final product of the media campaign. As a nearly defeated incumbent, however, she came to terms with the modern campaign environment, giving her campaign team more freedom to attack her opponent than ever before.

Field Operation and Get Out the Vote

The field operation was an entirely in-district affair. As a long-time incumbent, Johnson had connections that she needed to reinforce, but she and her campaign team saw no role for consultants. The field director was Paul Carver, who planned the strategy with Johnson, Ted Fusaro, director of her district office, and campaign manager Lounsbury. The strategy itself consisted primarily of cultivating the Republican town committees, the key to her base, in the forty-four towns in the Sixth District. Carver had been chair of the New Britain Republican town committee, as had his wife, who was also currently a member of the Republican state central committee. As Carver said, "You have to know the personalities on the town committees. I've known some of them for 20 years."

Carver began implementing the field strategy in February 1998, concentrating at first on the 13 towns that they lost in the 1996 election, talking to the town committee members to find out what they thought the problems were. In April, once the newly elected committees and their chairs were in place, Carver worked with them to select a town coordinator for Johnson's campaign from each town; that person was responsible for coordinating field operations in the town. Their responsibilities included letting Carver know about events in the district, such as small local fairs; staffing a Johnson-for-Congress booth at the fairs; getting people to come to events that Johnson would be attending; introducing her to people at the events; and clipping and faxing articles about the campaign or the candidates that appeared in local newspapers. The town coordinators also notified Carver of locations at which lawn signs could be put up and helped erect them. On election day, they helped turn out the Republican faithful and handed out literature outside the polling places.

During this process, Carver learned what was being talked about locally and took it back to the campaign team. He saw his role there in part as speaking for the conservative Republican base. He argued that "when you're pushing Nancy's moderate, independent voice," don't forget you still need those Republican votes: "You don't rub their noses in her moderation."

Besides the normal town committee efforts to identify Republicans and be sure they voted, the Johnson campaign relied heavily on the efforts of the incumbent Republican governor's campaign in most of the forty-four towns in the district to get out the vote (GOTV). In addition, Johnson employed a professional phone bank for targeted calling to voters in four key towns during the last two weeks; calls were made to Republicans and independents in New Britain, Southington, Bristol, and Torrington, three of which Johnson lost in 1996. People who indicated that they were likely to vote for or were leaning toward Johnson were called back and urged to vote during the weekend before the election. Efficient targeting of the calls was made possible by the state Republican Party organization's huge voter data base, discussed below.

Although she lost two of the targeted towns, her returns were 10 percentage points higher in three of the four than in 1996.

Outside Influences

Beginning in May 1997, the state Republican Party organization began to assemble a massive voter information file for the entire state. Using data banks, census data, outside research agencies, and voter records in town clerks' offices, the organization developed information on individual voters that included such standard data as occupation, income, race, party affiliation, and whether the individual voted in recent elections. The Republicans also collected data on such consumer matters as magazine subscriptions and television viewing. Not surprisingly, the year-long effort cost more than $100,000. These data were made available to all Republican campaigns, including Johnson's, to use in their mail targeting efforts and GOTV activities.

Otherwise, as Johnson's fund-raising success shows and her long experience would indicate, her campaign did not need much outside help. The NRCC sent two people; one came for three to four days in July to help the two interns with opposition research, but their efforts were already well under way; the interns found his help of little use. The other helped where she was needed, from envelope stuffing to phone calls. However, this support obviously was not high-level expertise, and although it was appreciated, it did not seem to be particularly needed. Outside assistance of much greater importance consisted of issue advocacy ads run by three organizations: Americans for Job Security, the Business Roundtable, both of which ran television ads, and the Sierra Club, which ran a radio spot.

Americans for Job Security (AJS) was an organization formed by the American Insurance Association president Robert Vagley along with that group's allies. The AJS ran three television ads costing $85,000 in Nancy

Johnson's district around the April 15 tax filing deadline. The ads, which ran every day for two weeks, featured "everyday Americans" talking about the problems posed by high taxes and concluded with the announcer saying "Join Nancy Johnson in the fight for real tax reform." Dave Karvelas, Johnson's administrative assistant, was quoted as saying that Johnson was at first concerned about uninvited help but was relieved when she saw the ads. "'It certainly is not going to hurt her to have ads on TV that recognize her accomplishments in tax reform,'" he said.[24]

Additionally, during the first week of September the Sierra Club ran a radio ad for Johnson praising her record of support for environmental causes.[25] That ad was part of a $600,000 national Sierra Club issue ad campaign that targeted twenty-seven congressional races, a campaign that included only one other Republican. Those ads from an organization that normally supports Democrats were a major coup for Johnson, as they reinforced the message of her moderate Republicanism.

Finally, in October the Business Roundtable ran an ad praising Johnson's efforts on a laundry list of issues: health care, education, jobs, and "an America opening foreign markets around the globe, spreading peace and prosperity." The camera panned over a number of babies; in an apparent effort to be sure that no remaining bases went uncovered, the group included three white, two black, and two Asian babies. The staff seemed mildly amused and not displeased by the ad, but Johnson herself, like many candidates, argued that outside ads "don't help much; they can dilute your message." She did not think that the "babies" ad had done anything to help her.

Conclusion

By any measure, Johnson's 1998 campaign was a resounding success. Although at roughly 58 percent of the vote she fell short of her usual victories of more than 60 percent, she nonetheless far exceeded her narrow 1996 margin against the same challenger. The table below presents

	1996 returns	*1998 returns*
Johnson	113,020	101,630
Koskoff	111,433	69,201
Knibbs	3,303	3,217
Total votes cast	227,756	174,048

the returns for both 1996 and 1998. The vote total of a fourth minor party candidate in 1998 (733 votes) was excluded from the table for purposes of comparability.

Despite the far lower number of votes cast in the 1998 midterm election than in the 1996 presidential year contest, Johnson expanded her vote margin over Koskoff from 1,587 votes in 1996 to 32,429 votes in 1998. The lower turnout hurt Koskoff far more than Johnson. Although Johnson received 11,390 fewer votes in 1998 than in 1996, Koskoff's drop over the same period was 42,232 votes.

Johnson's spectacular recovery was partly because of the changed political context: her release from the Gingrich ethics probe along with a strong Republican candidate at the top of the ticket rather than one who had given up on Connecticut as Dole had in 1996, taking his money with him. Nevertheless, the strategy of immediately increasing her presence in the district as well as highlighting her moderation laid the groundwork for a year-long campaign that allowed Johnson to set the agenda. Although Koskoff raised more money than she did in 1996, enabling her to run television ads (which she had not done in 1996), she evidently did not have enough money to advertise for more than a month. Even though Johnson had to respond to her charges, she nevertheless had nine months of advocacy ads on a variety of major issues under her belt before she ever had to publicly turn her attention to Koskoff.

Critical to Johnson's political recovery was the team she hired after the 1996 election. Her media-savvy new administrative assistant Dave Karvelas helped her to think strategically about how she presented herself to the district. Additionally, by bringing back Cheryl Lounsbury, her long-time campaign manager, Johnson had another strategic mind in a key position, one who knew her well and could be sure that the plans laid by the campaign were consistent with Johnson's character and inclinations. That said, it is also clear that both Karvelas and Lounsbury worked hard and successfully to pull Johnson into a more aggressive posture. Yet there were limits that Johnson refused to exceed, regardless of any wishes her staff might have had. Her known reluctance to use most of the opposition research is a case in point.

The consultants fit neatly into the new dynamic, working collaboratively with Johnson and her staff. The pollster, Linda DiVall, had a long relationship with Johnson, and was trusted by her. The new kids on the block were the media consultants, Jamestown Associates. Yet they probably were integrated into the campaign more smoothly than they otherwise might have been by the fact that David White, Johnson's new press secretary, had worked for Jamestown before joining Johnson's staff. Jamestown was thus the natural choice for this race, given not only its experience with Karvelas and White but also its work on Zimmer's race, which had been far more rough-and-tumble than the usual Connecticut campaign. In view of what Johnson saw as a highly negative Koskoff campaign in 1996, she felt that she needed consultants and staff who had the skills to function in the modern world of campaigning.

The consultants worked with the campaign staff on strategy and tactics. The media consultants, in particular, worked up scripts and overall designs for ads and mailings. Nevertheless, there was never any question that Johnson was in charge. Her years of experience and strong policy orientation had defined her in a way that would have constrained the maneuverings of any campaign team even if she had been willing to be molded by them, which she was not. Within that context, the campaign staff played a dual role. While they worked to induce Johnson to respond more aggressively to her opponent, they also mediated and moderated the suggestions of the consultants. As Lounsbury said, "the staff knows Nancy . . . the consultants will recommend something and you say 'no, that won't work.'" Nevertheless, the staff also argued with her on many media pieces, urging her to be tougher.

Johnson's ethical standards provided the governing norms. She was willing to attack her opponent on her statements about Johnson but was unwilling to make personal attacks. As Lounsbury said, "There were things we could have gone after [Koskoff] on, but it's not her style." That statement as much as anything summarizes the limits of the consultants' influence on this strong-willed, long-established incumbent.

Notes

1. "Rep. Johnson Darts Left," *Sunday Republican*, April 19, 1998, p. 2A.
2. "The Left Defects," *Republican American*, July 13, 1998, p. 10A.
3. Unlike most states, Connecticut operates under a "challenge primary" system in which a primary can only be waged by candidates who gain at least 15 percent of the delegate vote at a party nominating convention. In the Sixth District race, no challenger to the party-endorsed candidate in either party crossed that threshold.
4. Steve Collins, "Campaign Manager Accuses Griffin of Assault," *Bristol Press*, July 14, 1998, p. A3.

5. Robert C. Pollack, "Johnson-Koskoff Mudslinging Takes to the Streets," *Record-Journal*, September 16, 1998, p. 17.

6. Matthew Hay Brown, "GOP Actions Irk Koskoff Ad Team," *Hartford Courant*, September 16, 1998, p. B5.

7. "Sixth District: Nancy Johnson," *Hartford Courant*. Monday, October 26, 1998, p. A8; and "For Congress in Connecticut," *New York Times*, October 31, 1998, p. A14.

8. Her successful home style has given her the leeway in Washington described so insightfully by Richard F. Fenno Jr. in *Home Style: House Members in Their Districts* (Little, Brown, 1978).

9. Alan Ehrenhalt, ed., *Politics in America* (CQ Press, 1985), p. 276.

10. Gary C. Jacobson, *Money in Congressional Elections* (Yale University Press, 1980), pp. 106–07.

11. Philip D. Duncan and Christine C. Lawrence, *Politics in America, 1998* (CQ Press, 1997), p. 901.

12. David A. Smith, "Foes in 6th Spar over Poll, Filming," *Republican-American*, September 17, 1998, p. 3A

13. Although Knibbs reported spending only $129 for the entire campaign, he received 3,099 votes, an enviable ratio of votes to spending.

14. "Environmental Group Endorses Johnson," *Manchester Journal Inquirer*, July 7, 1998, p. 8; and Kelley Beaucar, "Environmental Groups Back Nancy Johnson for Re-election," *New Britain Herald*, July 8, 1998, p. A3; and Kelley Beaucar, "Johnson Gets Support from Unlikely Places," *Bristol Press*, July 8, 1998, p. A1.

15. David A. Smith, "NEA Flips, Gives Support to Johnson," *Republican-American*, September 18, 1998, p. 4A.

16. Ted Kenyon, "Johnson Gets Teachers' Backing," *Journal Inquirer*, September 19, 1998, p. 18.

17. Definitions of ad types are taken from Kathleen Hall Jamieson, Paul Waldman, and Susan Sherr, "Eliminate the Negative? Defining and Refining Categories of Analysis for Political Advertising," unpublished manuscript, Annenberg School for Communication.

18. Asante Green, "Koskoff Goes on the Offensive," *Herald*, October 9, 1998, p. A1.

19. The Customs Service dropped the proposed change following a letter from the chairmen of the House Ways and Means and Senate Finance Committees asking them to do so.

20. Steve Collins, "Koskoff Ad Attacks Johnson," *Bristol Press*, October 9, 1998, p. A1.

21. Gross rating points constitute an estimate of the number of people exposed to an ad and the number of times they are likely to have been exposed. A run of 1,000 gross rating points means, roughly, that the average voter saw an ad ten times.

22. Elizabeth Ganga, "Four Local Unions Endorse Johnson," *Herald*, June 3, 1998, p. A3.

23. Kelley O. Beaucar, "Johnson Gets Support from Unlikely Places," *Bristol Press,* July 8, 1998, and "Environmental Groups Back Nancy Johnson for Reelection," *Herald,* July 8, 1998, p. A3; and "Environmental Group Endorses Johnson," *Journal Inquirer*, July 7, 1998, p. 8.

24. Jackie Koszczuk, "Method in the Madness," *Campaigns and Elections,* June 1998, p. 25.

25. Johnson was one of only two Republicans included in the Sierra Club's issue ad campaign. The other was Connie Morella of Maryland.

CHAPTER FOUR

High Turnout in a Low-Turnout Year: Georgia's Second District

CHARLES S. BULLOCK III

1998 was not an off-year election. Bill Clinton ran for re-election. Bill Clinton ran a survival campaign. It wasn't Sanford Bishop that drove up the turnout in the district. It was Bill Clinton.

Marvin Robertson, Joe McCormack's agriculture consultant

ECONOMIC PROSPERITY, like the interstate highway, has largely bypassed Georgia's Second Congressional District. The Second is tucked into the state's southwestern corner with Tallahassee and its always competitive Florida State University football team to the south and the statue to the boll weevil to its west in Enterprise, Alabama. Ties to both states are close. Tallahassee and Thomasville, Georgia, share one of the district's major televisions stations. Some students along the district's border cross the Chattahoochee River to attend private school in George Wallace's Barbour County. The district's most famous native son, Jimmy Carter, promised that if elected governor he would invite Wallace to address the Georgia General Assembly.

Agriculture plays a bigger role in the Second than elsewhere in the state, and the member of Congress from this district invariably serves on the House Agriculture Committee. This flat landscape, which looks more like Iowa than north Georgia, leads the nation in the production of

I appreciate the help provided by my research assistant, Bill Gillespie.

peanuts. But not all of the nuts grow underground here. In the heat of the summer, vast groves of pecans, upper branches intertwined to form a green canopy, look inviting to the passing motorist. The district also produces traditional southern crops like corn and in the fall, vistas of Dixie snow (cotton) undulate to the horizon. Monstrous, mobile irrigation systems, looking like brontosaurus skeletons, extend for hundreds of yards more than ten feet above the ground to water row crops. In celebration of that southern breakfast staple that Yankees never learn to appreciate, the town of Warwick held the First Annual Grits Festival in 1998. Nearby Cordele honors a product with a wider acceptability, calling itself the "Watermelon Capital of the World." And Whigham is the home of the annual "Rattlesnake Roundup."

Not all of this rural district is given over to row crops. Pine forests spread further than the eye can see and where these are planted—as opposed to having been distributed by nature's hand—they are arranged with military precision. Planted woodlands are often owned by timber companies, while those that remain wild and tangled with blackberry brambles and honeysuckle interrupted here and there by fields of broom sedge are now used for recreation. Turpmtime Plantation owned by the fictional Atlanta developer Charlie Croker in Tom Wolfe's *A Man in Full* is located in Baker County just south of Albany, the largest city in the Second District. And while Turpmtime is the creation of Wolfe's vivid imagination, there are real life estates from which the author in the white suit could draw inspiration. Baker is the home of the vast Ischaway Plantation of Coca Cola's Woodruff family, a domain that rivals Croker's holding. Plantations in nearby Thomas County have long provided a winter retreat for northerners, including President Dwight D. Eisenhower's Treasury secretary George Humphrey, who often invited the president down to shoot quail.

Background

With thirty-one counties, the Second District contains almost 20 percent of Georgia's 159 counties. Many of the counties are small, rural, and forgotten by all but those who live in them or come from them. Several of those along the Alabama border have been losing population, and the county that experienced the greatest percentage decline during the 1980s is in the Second District. Two counties, Schley and Miller, which between them have fewer than 10,000 people, have a single precinct each.

The district includes one metropolitan area and laps at the edges of two others. Albany saw its population dip in the 1980s, so that in 1990 it had fewer than 80,000 people. This, the county seat of Dougherty County and home of traditionally black Albany State University, dealt Martin Luther King his greatest defeat when its police chief peacefully arrested civil rights marchers and dispersed them among jails throughout southwestern Georgia. The chief saw to it that his officers did not resort to violence, and soon the media moved on to cover more interesting stories, and King shifted his efforts to Selma.[1] Currently, Albany is 55 percent black and its white mayor, Tommy Coleman, used black support to unseat the incumbent.

The district extends north to the edge of Columbus and contains much of Fort Benning, where paratroopers are taught how to jump from planes and survive. With Tallahassee to the south, most of the district, and certainly the bulk of its population, is closer to the capital of Florida than to Atlanta. Through the counties along the eastern edge of the district flows I-75, along which midwesterners speed to Disney World and other Florida sites, stopping in south Georgia only to refuel with cheap gas and perhaps buy jeans at a Levi's outlet store. Truckers stop and mingle with local good ol' boys at the "We Bare All" restaurants along the interstate.

Democratic dominance that once covered the South like kudzu has been most difficult for Republicans to root out in rural areas like the Second. When Jimmy Carter won a state senate seat, the first of four elections that led to the White House, the decision was restricted to the Democratic primary, which he survived only after going to court to overturn actions by a county boss who had stolen the election.[2] Local offices are still decided in Democratic primaries in much of the Second. This area has never had a Republican representative in Congress, and twenty-five of the counties supported Bill Clinton's re-election. Georgia Democrats turned in even stronger performances in 1996. All but one county voted for Max Cleland (D) to succeed Senator Sam Nunn and for Democrats for three statewide posts on the ballot. Before 1996, only one Republican state legislator came from this part of the state. A successful Republican recruitment and campaign effort that year boosted the number to three, but the Second continued to send only Democrats to the state senate.[3] With Democrats so entrenched, why would a Republican choose the Second for a serious effort? Unlike most of the country where 1998 marked the fourth time that the present districts were used, Georgia redrew its congressional districts before the

1996 election. In 1995 the Supreme Court upheld a district court decision that the Eleventh District violated the Fourteenth Amendment's equal protection clause because the legislature relied too heavily on race when drawing it. Subsequently, the district court found a similar infirmity in the Second District. With two of the eleven districts invalidated, much of the state had to be reconfigured. When the legislature failed to pass a plan, the task fell to the three-judge federal panel, and it designed the current map. Had the Second not been transformed in 1996, Joe McCormick (R) would never have challenged incumbent Sanford Bishop (D).

Bishop came to Congress in 1993 after fourteen years in the Georgia House and two more in the state senate. The Mobile native came to Georgia to attend Morehouse, the premier black private school for men. Bishop earned a law degree from Emory, on the opposite side of Atlanta from Morehouse, then settled down to practice law in Columbus. He was not yet thirty when he won a seat in the state House. As a moderate, he got along well with that body's conservative, rural, white leadership.

Two forces united to give Bishop the opportunity to go to Congress—the Department of Justice and the incumbent. Georgia, like most of the South, is subject to section 5 of the 1965 Voting Rights Act and as such must obtain preclearance from federal authorities before implementing changes that affect elections. The state could not finalize the redistricting necessitated by the 1990 census, which gave Georgia an additional House seat, until it obtained the approval of the Justice Department or the District of Columbia district court. In the early 1990s, the Justice Department interpreted section 2 of the Voting Rights Act as requiring that whenever possible, districts had to be drawn so that blacks or Hispanics would constitute a majority of the population. This objective took precedence over values such as compactness and respect for county lines and other political boundaries. The result in southwest Georgia appears in figure 4-1, which shows the ragged eastern edge of the Second District and the narrow, contorted necks reaching into Meriwether and Bibb counties in order to collect pockets of blacks while avoiding nearby whites.

The Second District was the third drawn in Georgia with a majority black population. The state legislature's initial effort produced a district less than 40 percent black, a racial makeup much like that during the 1980s. After the Justice Department rejected that plan, pointing specifically to the failure to draw a majority-black district in southwestern Georgia, a second plan increased the percent black to 49 by including the

Figure 4-1. *Georgia's Second District, 1993–96*

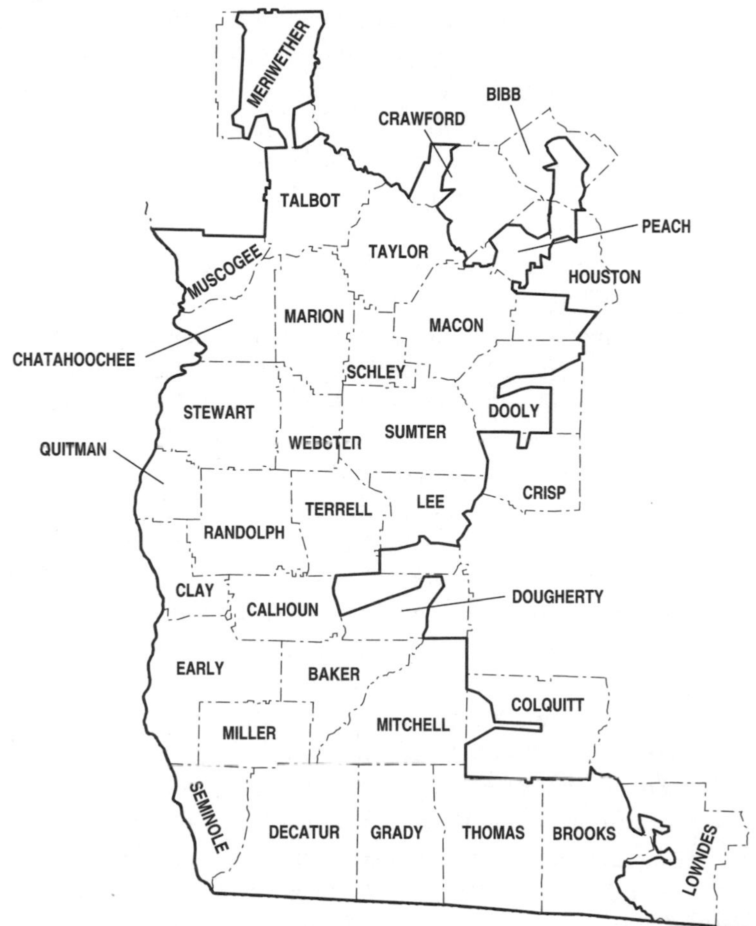

southern half of Columbus (Muscogee County), where the bulk of the city's black population lives. The department rejected this plan, asking why the black population in Savannah had not been incorporated into a majority black district. To satisfy the Department of Justice, the legislature extended the Eleventh District in a ribbon along the Savannah River to Georgia's port city. With 50,000 African Americans from Savannah added to the Eleventh District, Macon's black population could be shifted from the Eleventh to the Second and thereby boost the latter's population to

57 percent black. To create a majority black district in the southwestern corner, technicians in the Legislative Reapportionment Office went block-by-block, putting majority-black census blocks in the Second, while majority white blocks went to the neighboring Third or Eighth districts. All along the eastern boundary, counties were divided with surgical exactness. Black neighborhoods in Albany, Valdosta, Cordele, Moultrie, Perry, Vienna, and Warner Robbins went into the Second.

Creating a majority black district ensured the election of a Democrat and probably meant that once the white incumbent left, an African American would be elected.[4] Unlike in South Carolina's Sixth District, twelve-year incumbent Charles Hatcher (D) did not step aside for a black. Although popular with the district's farmers, Hatcher had a problem. He had more overdrafts (819) at the House bank than all but one other member. His perceived vulnerabiliy and the availability of a majority-black district drew three serious African American challengers, one from each of the urban areas touched by the district. Bishop, who had represented the Columbus area in the legislature, finished second in the primary with 21 percent of the vote, thereby edging out a state representative from Albany by 2,300 votes. While Hatcher led the field with 40 percent of the vote, the black candidates polled a combined 54 percent in the primary. In the runoff, as reported in table 4-1, Bishop's vote total almost doubled while Hatcher saw 4,000 votes slip away, allowing Bishop to snare the nomination with a 53 percent majority.

Although the district had more white than black registered voters, Bishop had no trouble besting a Republican doctor and took 64 percent of the vote, running four points ahead of Bill Clinton in the district. Despite having spent his life in urban areas, Bishop immediately got a seat on the House Agriculture Committee. His assignment to Veterans' Affairs also provided opportunities to secure benefits for constituents since a number of military personnel once stationed at Fort Benning retire to the Columbus area.

Bishop recognized the conservativism that characterized the district's white population and charted a course away from the bulk of the congressional black caucus members. It may well be that in this rural district black voters were less liberal than African Americans in major urban areas. Even if the ideology of African American voters in southwestern Georgia was not significantly different from that of blacks in Atlanta or Detroit or Los Angeles, this district's electorate was less heavily black than many others since black turnout lagged behind the white rate.

Table 4-1. *Electoral History of Georgia's Second District, 1992–98*

Year	*Election*	*Candidate*	*Number of votes*	*Percent of vote*
1992	Democratic primary	Charles Hatcher	40,833	40
		Sanford Bishop	21,692	21
		Mary Young Cummings	19,363	19
		Lonzy Edwards	11,819	12
		Phil Whigham	4,762	5
		Stephanie Kaigler	4,253	4
1992	Democratic runoff	Sanford Bishop	41,953	53
		Charles Hatcher	36,778	47
1992	General	Sanford Bishop	95,789	64
		Jim Dudley	54,593	36
1994	Democratic primary	Sanford Bishop	33,862	67
		James Bush	16,757	33
1994	General	Sanford Bishop	65,383	66
		John Clayton	33,429	34
1996	Democratic primary	Sanford Bishop	56,660	59
		W. T. Gamble	31,615	33
		Walter Lewis	7,116	7
1996	Republican primary	Darrel Ealum	11,665	62
		Chris Hatcher	7,195	38
1996	General	Sanford Bishop	88,256	54
		Darrel Ealum	75,282	46
1998	Republican primary	Joe McCormick	9,820	53
		Dylan Glenn	8,828	47
1998	General	Sanford Bishop	77,953	57
		Joe McCormick	59,306	43

Bishop might have survived had he staked out more liberal positions like those of John Lewis and Cynthia McKinney, two other black Georgia Democrats, but doing so would inspire more spirited opposition. Taking moderate positions and concentrating on the problems of farmers allowed Bishop to expand his re-election constituency.[5]

By 1994 Bishop had distinguished himself as the least liberal member of the black caucus and the only black member of the blue dog caucus, a gathering of conservative Democrats. Bishop shifted rightward between 1993 and 1994, and in the latter year his scores on the indexes compiled by COPE and the Chamber of Commerce were in line with what Hatcher had done. Bishop's voting record protected him, so that the losses suffered by Democrats elsewhere in Georgia and across the nation in 1994 did not affect the Second District, where the incumbent had a modest, two-point sophomore surge. Bishop faced only token opposition as the GOP nominee spent less than $10,000, while the incumbent poured almost half a million dollars into the campaign. Bishop rolled up an equally impressive margin in the primary, where he disposed of James Bush, a senior Hatcher staffer who sought to rally the former incumbent's followers and others who considered Bishop too liberal.

Had Bishop's initial district remained unchanged, he would have been unbeatable in general elections. His serenity was shattered when the district drawn by the court in 1995 reinstituted the practice of using counties as the building blocks and excised the black concentrations in Columbus and Macon that had boosted the black percentage. The new district, shown in figure 4-2, had a 39 percent black population. If the electorate divided along racial lines, Bishop would soon be a private citizen.

Sensing the incumbent's possible vulnerability, four white challengers came forward in 1996. Two primary opponents filed, with the more serious being a former Bishop staffer, W. T. Gamble, son of a rural county commissioner with strong ties to peanut producers. Bishop managed almost 60 percent of the primary vote but faced his stiffest general election competition.

The survivor of the GOP primary, Darrel Ealum, secured 46 percent of the vote, making this the third most competitive district in Georgia. Ealum came close despite being outspent by almost $450,000 and not having the wholehearted support of his primary opponent.

In his first three general elections, Bishop got essentially all of the black vote, a pattern replicated by Democratic nominees in Georgia congressional elections regardless of their race.[6] Table 4-2 shows that Bishop improved his share of the white vote between 1992 and 1994 but suffered a slight erosion against the better-funded Ealum. Had Ealum managed 73 percent of the white vote, as Jim Dudley did four years earlier, and had the distribution of the black vote remained as it actually was in 1996, Bishop would have lost. The incumbent's voting record enabled him to secure enough white votes to survive both primary and general election challenges (since receiving his new district, Bishop has tended to stand with Georgia's white Republicans more consistently than with the two other black Democrats when congressional roll calls have mobilized the conservative coalition of Republicans and southern Democrats.

Figure 4-2. *Georgia's Second District after 1997*

Table 4-2. *White Support for Candidates in General Elections in Georgia's Second District*

Percent

Year	*Democrat*	*Share of white vote*	*Republican*	*Share of white vote*
1992	Bishop	33	Dudley	67
1994	Bishop	43	Clayton	57
1996	Bishop	38	Ealum	62

Source: Estimates made from Gary King's ecological inference technique, appearing in Charles Bullock III and Richard E. Dunn, "The Demise of Racial Districting and the Future of Black Representation," *Emory Law Review,* vol. 48 (Fall 1999), pp. 1209–53.

Bishop's 1996 performance with the white electorate must be put in perspective. Yes, he failed to get a majority of the white vote, but that year no Georgia Democrat in a contested congressional seat secured a majority among whites.[7] Bishop's 37 percent was the second-best performance for a Democrat and was just 3 percentage points less than millionaire Michael Coles, who received an infusion of AFL-CIO contributions, managed against Newt Gingrich.[8] Bishop ran several percentage points ahead of Bill Clinton among white voters and was just three points behind Max Cleland, who managed a plurality victory in the U.S. Senate contest. The voting patterns in high-profile contests in Georgia suggest that the race of candidates is not a factor. In 1996 Democrats managed between 30 and 40 percent of the white vote regardless of their race, whether they confronted an incumbent, or the office was at stake.

The voting behavior of whites in the Second District in statewide contests shows that Bishop ran ahead of President Clinton, who managed about a third of the white vote. Bishop, however, ran behind Max Cleland and the Democratic candidates for secretary of state and two seats on the Public Service Commission. Cleland ran almost ten points ahead of Bishop, while the Democratic candidate for the PSC performed about five points better than Bishop. These results suggest that although race of the candidate might be a bigger factor in southwest Georgia than statewide, it is no longer determinative of outcomes.

The 1998 Republican Challengers

With only three Georgia seats held by Democrats and in light of Bishop's narrow escape in 1996, he became the GOP's top Georgia congressional target in 1998. Though the 57 percent black Second District was virtually impossible for a Republican, at 39 percent black, the district offered a chance—if everything went right. Georgia Republicans were not alone in seeing an opportunity in the Second. During the campaign cycle, this district regularly appeared on lists of districts thought to be competitive. In mid-September, Stuart Rothenberg rated the Second as a district in which the Democrat was favored but added an enticing, "Looking for a long-shot to bet?"[9]

The McCormick campaign compiled figures to show how congressional candidates ran in the counties now part of the Second District in 1992 and 1994. Before the 1996 redistricting, a number of counties were divided between the Second and Eighth districts, and some counties now in the Second were wholly in the Eighth. In 1992 a Democrat won the Eighth; in 1994 it elected Republican Saxby Chambliss to an open seat. Combining the votes for congressional candidates in the thirty-one counties now in the Second shows that in 1992, Democrats accumulated 52 percent of the total; two years later, the combined GOP vote exceeded the Democratic vote by 4,000. Republican candidates got a 52 percent share in 1994 even though they narrowly lost Dougherty County. A Republican who achieved the vote percentage that Republicans running for Congress in these counties attained in the last off-year election could win!

Two prospects emerged. Both were young; neither had officeholding experience, although both had worked in others' campaigns. Neither had deep roots in the district. Strikingly for the GOP, only one (Joe McCormick) is white; his opponent, Dylan Glenn, is black.

Joe McCormick

In October 1997, when the loser from 1996 showed no interest in an encore, Joe McCormick, chair of the Dougherty Republican Party, stepped forward. The owner of an equipment rental business, McCormick ran on the theme, "A Businessman for Congress."

McCormick grew up in New York, but his wife Celeste comes from a prominent Albany family. McCormick, who settled in Albany in 1994, had managed the campaign of the first Republican elected to the state House from the area and helped Ealum and Bob Dole in 1996. Before coming to Albany, McCormick served on the staff of the director of political operations in the Bush-Quayle re-election campaign.

When McCormick entered the contest, he imported much of his staff from the Ealum effort. General consultant Lou Kitchin had managed Ealum's 1996 general election effort, his most recent responsibility in a career that began thirty years earlier when he guided Fletcher Thompson (R) to victory in Georgia's Fifth Congressional District. During the next three decades Kitchin managed the campaign of South Carolina's first Republican governor and Joe Skeen (R-N.M.), who came to Congress by way of a write-in victory. Kitchin, the scion of a North Carolina family that has sent four members to Congress, worked for Ronald Reagan for more than a decade, beginning with his 1976 effort to deny Gerald Ford a full term.

Other key campaign personnel lacked Kitchin's vast experience but had deep roots in the district. Campaign manager Kent Sole, the son of a political science professor, grew up in Americus and represented Sen. Paul Coverdell (R) in south Georgia for much of his first term. Bryce Johnson, the chair of the Worth County Republican Party, had the title of field representative but functioned as a human computer programmed to spit out analyses of voting patterns in the district, with estimates of vote shares by county needed to secure victory under various scenarios. Johnson's estimates showed that to defeat the incumbent, McCormick would have to cultivate the farming community and reap a record harvest of white votes. Essential to this effort was agriculture consultant Marvin Robertson, who held a doctorate, taught at the high school and college levels, and had recently retired from a journalism career when McCormick embarked on his candidacy. For six years Robertson had prepared *Farm and Plantation*, a publication that at times was a standalone weekly and at other times an insert in the *Albany Herald*, the district's largest daily newspaper. Each issue of *Farm and Plantation* featured a farm family, and as Robertson traveled the district for McCormick, he encountered these individuals whom he once interviewed. The press officer had worked as Ealum's campaign manager.

McCormick and Glenn ran very different campaigns, with the businessman working as an insider using the local GOP organization while Glenn traded on contacts he had developed while in Washington, D.C. McCormick built outward from his Albany base where he had the support of the four Republicans officeholders. Johnson reports that McCormick had most of the district's bigger contributors in his corner.

The edge in local fund-raising was helpful to a point, but McCormick lacked a network of affluent Republicans around the country. Consequently, he was impoverished compared with this opponent. Ultimately, McCormick raised $170,000 for the primary, largely from within the district, and in the July 1, 1998, filing he reported only four non-Georgia contributions, which totaled $1,700. McCormick tried to turn necessity into a virtue and made no attempt to raise money outside the district. He felt that to do so would undercut his contention that the people of the Second District—and not outsiders—should determine the representative. He highlighted the local funding of the primary on the bottom of his May newsletter: "Fundraising . . . It is your campaign." McCormick has raised 98 percent of the funds in the district!

Although he was in a relatively inexpensive media market, McCormick ignored television until the last three weeks of the primary, when he bought time on the 6 and 11 o'clock news on the Albany and Thomasville-Tallahassee stations. Furthermore, he increased the advertising for his rental business, believing that since he was running as a "conservative Albany businessman," the ads would promote his business, increase his name recognition, and underscore the image that he was stressing while helping distinguish him from his primary opponent. These ads ran on cable stations in Americus, Albany, and Cordele.

Since he relied less heavily on television to reach voters, McCormick had to take another tack. His campaign manager said in a June interview, "We are running a typical 1960s campaign without television."[10] That meant that McCormick turned to traditional techniques for contacting voters, such as spending two hours daily during primary season to go door to-door tracking down voters who had participated in past GOP primaries. When no one was home, he left campaign literature on the door. Campaign manager Sole attributes these personal contacts with providing the margin of victory in the primary, since the opponent avoided going door-to-door in the oppressive heat and humidity.

McCormick also made extensive use of signs with a hundred four-by-four signs and a thousand standard-sized yard signs. Some of Glenn's supporters charged that McCormick made a subtle racial appeal by including his picture on many of the signs. The logic behind this argument is that because of Glenn's extensive television advertising, most voters knew Glenn was black, and McCormick showed himself to be white by putting his picture on his signs.[11] David Pace, a Washington-based Associated Press reporter who visited the district during the primary, observed, "Everywhere Dylan went, people recognized him from his TV commercials so his name ID is up."[12] Of course, if McCormick had matched Glenn ad for television ad, information about the racial difference would have been disseminated that way. Although most Georgia candidates do not include a picture on their yard signs, the practice is not unheard of, and a minor Republican gubernatorial candidate in 1998 often had a picture on her signs.[13] With black Republican candidates being so uncommon in Georgia, most voters would have assumed that McCormick was white.

Both candidates advertised on radio. McCormick concentrated on the Albany, Thomasville, and Valdosta stations that had a religious emphasis in their programming and on a Thomasville station that had an easy-listening format along with farm news. Glenn, who boasted that his candidacy would bring new and younger voters to the GOP, bought time on stations that appealed to those listeners.

Owing to funding constraints, McCormick's campaign made less use of outside consultants and professional help than did his opponent. A woman who worked for a local television station developed McCormick's television commercial. McCormick did no polling until late in the primary when he used a Tallahassee firm for an inexpensive look at voter inclinations.

Dylan Glenn

In mid-1997 an articulate twenty-eight-year-old political consultant returned to his boyhood home on the northern edge of the district and began laying the foundation for a challenge. Dylan Glenn had been away for years, going to high school in the District of Columbia and then attending Davidson College. After graduation, he worked as a policy adviser in the Bush administration and with the Republican National Committee.

Glenn's candidacy delighted national and state Republican leaders, who sought to attract black voters and believed that having African American candidates would help convince black voters that their concerns would receive a serious hearing in the GOP. Glenn was the star of a set of twenty-one black candidates who filed for the Georgia Republican primary in 1998.[14] This more than doubled the number of blacks running as Republicans in 1996 and was reported to be the largest number of African American Republican candidates in any state.[15] In Glenn, Republican leaders saw a younger J. C. Watts (R-Okla.), someone who could be an articulate spokesperson for the party and especially effective among African Americans.

Commitment to Glenn was so strong that party leaders sought to dissuade others from entering the hunt. As an indication of the support from GOP leaders, Glenn received campaign contributions from Haley Barbour, Donald Rumsfeld, Senator Lauch Faircloth (R-N.C.), and Representative Henry Bonilla (R-Tex.).

His work as a political consultant brought Glenn into contact with Ron Jensen, and the two joined forces in a Washington-based political consulting firm. Jensen, who served as Glenn's chief consultant, is older than Glenn and has worked in scores of contests across the country, although in 1998 his other major client was a candidate for mayor of

Louisville, Kentucky. Not only was Glenn's chief consultant from outside the district, so was the campaign manager. Jim Dykes, the campaign manager, came from Arkansas and had met Glenn when working on the Jack Kemp presidential campaign.

Glenn's Washington experiences and the uniqueness of being a viable black Republican enabled him to gather fruit from a national money tree. He ultimately raised more than $400,000 and listed among his contributors General Colin Powell and David Rockefeller. The Second is one of the nation's poorest congressional districts, so having access to pocketbooks from around the country proved very helpful. Glenn's friends held fund-raisers for him in New York and Washington, D.C. Of the $452,000 he raised, 83 percent came from outside the state, with almost as many contributors from New York (107) as from Georgia (120), and the New Yorkers gave $18,000 more than the home state crowd. There were another nine states and the District of Columbia from which seventeen or more individuals gave totals of more than $10,000. The McCormick camp saw Glenn as the party's chosen one and believed that the national party put him into contact with prospective givers. "How many 28-year-olds do you know who know that many people who will contribute big bucks to a campaign?" asked McCormick's campaign manager.[16]

Having full coffers allowed Glenn to take to the airwaves early and to remain a presence until the primary. He bought time on WALB in Albany, the only market having a signal largely confined to the district and covering about 60 percent of the district, beginning in early March. Glenn's campaign also bought time on WCTV, which serves Thomasville, Georgia, and Tallahassee, and WSST, the cable outlet in Cordele. Glenn had sufficient funding that he could run ads on popular shows such as the *Oprah Winfrey* show.

Glenn had Steven Reed Curcio produce a campaign video that he distributed widely. When I visited his headquarters in June, Steve Meir, a student intern was on his way out with an armload of the videos. Three pieces of direct mail had been sent by mid-June. These and three more pieces went to a list of 15,000 individuals who had previously participated in GOP primaries. Lance Tarrance polled for the Glenn campaign.

The 1998 GOP Primary

Big name contacts provided Glenn with more than money, and some of them came into the district to appear at events with him. Senator Thad

Cochran (R-Miss.), for whom Glenn had worked, visited the Second early in the campaign and spoke forcefully on Glenn's behalf in the campaign video. Shortly before the primary, former presidential candidate Jack Kemp dropped into the northern end of the district and announced his support for Glenn. In an unmistakable sign that McCormick was regarded as the party's red-headed stepchild by many of the movers and shakers, Speaker Newt Gingrich hosted a fund-raiser for Glenn at a private club in Atlanta. Typically, party leaders avoid openly taking sides before the primary unless one of the candidates is mired in scandal or, like former Klan leader David Duke, is an embarrassment.[17]

The overt involvement of GOP leaders on behalf of Glenn had a mixed impact on the race. Certainly, Glenn benefited from the money that the outsiders helped raise, and the publicity generated by their support boosted his name recognition. On the one hand, some voters may have been impressed by the circles in which the young candidate moved so easily. On the other, some resented the efforts of outsiders to influence the district's choice of a nominee.[18] In this district in which Atlanta seems far away, some local GOP leaders viewed the involvement of major players from the national scene as interference rather than assistance. McCormick fanned this criticism: "The people here would like to be able to choose their own nominee. His campaign is funded by donors from New York and Los Angeles and Utah. And there's already a backlash against that."[19] Let the national party stay on the sidelines until the local electorate determines the standard bearer—as would be the practice in any other district—and then, the McCormick camp suggested, help from Atlanta, Washington, and any other quarter would be welcomed.

Not only did McCormick decry outsiders' support for Glenn, McCormick consultant Lou Kitchin painted Glenn as an interloper from Washington.[20] In a Thomasville debate McCormick emphasized, "We need someone who has been participating, not someone sent down from Washington to run for office."[21] This attack seemed designed to attract conservatives who have long railed against the national government for interfering with decisions best made locally. Linking Glenn with Washington tied into the charge in McCormick's first mail-out to likely GOP voters that "*It's time we put an end to bureaucratic and wasteful 'Washington-Knows-Best' approaches.*" The carpetbagger assault put Glenn on the defensive in the closing days of the campaign as he tried to explain that he is a fifth-generation Georgian, while McCormick has been in Georgia less than five years. Glenn's reliance on outsiders for money and high-profile endorsements, ironically, helped drive home McCormick's charges that Glenn was not of the district and therefore would not be responsive to district needs should a conflict arise between the preferences of the district and Glenn's well-heeled supporters.

In distinguishing himself from Glenn, McCormick chose dimensions that would also differentiate himself from Sanford Bishop should the two square off in the general election. During the primary and the general elections, McCormick touted his link to business. His campaign manager said during the primary, "Dylan has no experience. Joe has a business." Later he made the same point vis-à-vis Bishop. "Joe is the only candidate who has run a business and knows what it's like to deal with OSHA. Sanford is a lawyer from Columbus. Sitting in a [congressional district] office in Albany with a secretary is not running a business."

Another distinction emphasized by McCormick was that among the three candidates only he had a family. "If you're gonna be pro-family, it helps to have a family. People are entrenched here. They are entrenched in their families and they are entrenched in their communities," explained Sole. Helping drive home the family point was McCormick's attractive wife—a former beauty queen—who was heavily involved in the campaign. An ad that the campaign judged particularly effective, based on the number of favorable comments it generated, showed the couple fifty feet up in the air atop one of the forklifts McCormick's business rented.

Despite the emphasis on differences, the opponents shared many policy preferences. According to McCormick, "I talk about how I differ from Dylan. We differ in our interests and our life experiences. We would not differ much in voting records." Later he told a reporter, "Ideologically, we're very much in-line."[22] Sole reports that Glenn said during the primary that "if the two of them [Glenn and McCormick] represented adjoining districts, they would probably vote the same in Congress."

The two did differ, however, on the issues they chose to emphasize. In the primary and general election campaigns, McCormick went with the traditional, dominant economic interests of the district—agriculture and the military, while Glenn gave top billing to economic development. McCormick sought to get leaders in the farm community involved in his campaign, using the successful effort of Saxby Chambliss (R) in the adjoining district as a model. Glenn hoped that his theme, "A New Voice for a New Century," would appeal to voters regardless of race and age and bring young, black voters to the GOP.

The military plays a major role in the economy of the Second District with a contribution that McCormick puts at $1 billion a year. Stressing his commitment to maintaining the Defense Department presence in the district gave McCormick another chance to distinguish himself from the other two candidates. “I’m the only veteran that is running. That makes a big difference when you go to Valdosta where Moody Air Force Base might be threatened with closure,” McCormick explains.

McCormick’s staff perceived a difference in styles between the two candidates. During the summer Sole said, “We are taking on a constituency advocacy position. We act as if we are already the member of Congress. We seek to find out what we can do for voters.” In contrast, he said of Glenn, “If it’s a military problem, Dylan says, ‘I know Colin Powell.’ Or if it’s a problem with development, Dylan says, ‘I know Jack Kemp.’ ”

McCormick won the nomination with 52.7 percent of the vote. Despite losing the popular vote, Glenn carried sixteen of the thirty-one counties, and the two candidates tied in another county. The voting pattern revealed the friends and neighbors tradition that V. O. Key noted in southern Democratic primaries a half century ago.[23] The fourteen counties that McCormick carried included his home and the six counties that surround it. His advantage in these seven counties came to 1,098 votes, more than his 992-vote victory margin districtwide. More than half the margin came in his home county of Dougherty.

Glenn also carried his home county and its neighbors; however, Chattahoochee County had a tiny turnout, so even though he rolled up a margin of almost six to one there, it amounted to just fifty-three votes. In carrying six of the seven other counties in the northern end of the district, Glenn’s margin came to a scant 106 votes. To compensate for his disadvantage in vote-rich Albany, Glenn focused on the counties along the Florida border. Glenn’s biggest margins came in Lowndes (222 votes) and Decatur (105) counties, as he lost only one of the six southernmost counties.

Some outside the district interpreted the result as a racist rejection of an African American candidate. Here, they said, was yet another instance in which a qualified black suffered at the hands of intolerant white voters. A Democratic office holder in the district observed, “People in southwest Georgia don’t join the Republican Party so that they can vote for a black candidate.” And there were doubtless some whites who did respond solely on the basis of race. In fairness, however, it must be acknowledged that in defeat Glenn showed notable strength in the white community. This becomes evident when one sees how little support Glenn generated in black precincts despite his efforts to win over black clergy and his addressing black congregations. Although he hoped to attract a thousand black voters to the GOP primary, it does not appear that he even came close to that number. In seven overwhelmingly black precincts in Albany (that is, more than 90 percent black in registration), Glenn and McCormick divided a total of ten votes. In two of the precincts, not a single voter participated in this contest. With McCormick living in Dougherty, Glenn might have been expected to do less well there than elsewhere in the district. While no primary precincts outside of Albany matched the black concentrations found there, an examination of heavily African American precincts in other counties fails to uncover evidence of widespread black support. A review of nine heavily black precincts in eight counties shows that they cast fewer than 200 votes, with Glenn taking 58 percent. It is likely that even though at least 80 percent of the registered voters in these precincts were black, the bulk of the ballots actually came from whites.[24] Since Georgia has an open primary system in which voters do not register by party but instead decide which party's primary they want to vote in when they arrive at the polls, nothing prevented African Americans who wanted to support Glenn from doing so. Thus all but a handful of Glenn's votes came from whites, and the white Republican electorate divided almost evenly between the two candidates. It seems likely that Glenn's percentage of the white vote cast in the primary exceeded the share of the white electorate who had voted for Bishop in the past (table 4-2).

A curious duality surrounded press views of the primary contest. The national press gave this contest inordinate attention with articles in the *New Republic, Time,* and *Roll Call* and briefer notices in the *New York Times, Richmond Times-Dispatch*. and the *National Review*. The Home Box Office channel sent a film crew in to look at Glenn's campaign. McCormick typically did not rate even a mention in these pieces.

The national press followed the lead of the party and treated Glenn as the de facto nominee, but the closer one got to the district, the less plausible a Glenn victory seemed. David Pace, the Washington Associated Press reporter assigned to cover Georgia, visited the district in June, and his story provided a more balanced coverage of both candidates' efforts and prospects. While seeing positive attributes in both candidates, Pace thought that Glenn would be handicapped by his youth and his weak ties to the district. "There is the age factor; Dylan looks young! And there is also maybe a problem with his having come back to the district recently."[25]

A potential danger in a closely contested primary, like the one McCormick won, is that during the general election campaign the party will continue to be riven along the fault lines exposed during the nomination stage. According to several observers, that problem haunted Ealum in 1996. If, however, the party can reunite after a primary, the competition may prove beneficial. James Barnes and Gregory S. Thielemann have argued that contested primaries strengthen the GOP in the South.[26] The competition may draw new voters to the GOP primary, and participating in the primary can lead voters across a psychological divide so that they become more likely to think of themselves as Republicans. News coverage given to candidates in a spirited primary also promotes name recognition in ways that would not happen if the nomination had gone by default because no one else entered the lists.[27] Kitchin and agriculture adviser Robertson agree that the primary was critical for strengthening McCormick. By forcing McCormick to work harder and polish his skills, "Dylan Glenn made Joe McCormick into a candidate," according to Kitchin.

General Election

For the first time, Bishop escaped primary opposition in 1998, which enabled him to husband resources. As of July 1, 1998, he had raised $378,000, with 62 percent of the money coming from political action committees (PACs). He had almost $225,000 on hand, substantially more than McCormick had managed in his entire campaign up to that point.

A poll conducted for Bishop in April 1998 showed him having a broad base of support with a favorable to unfavorable advantage of 72 percent to 15 percent among whites. Blacks provided near unanimous support. The ratio of favorable to unfavorable evaluations was high among all income and education groups. The Lester and Associates' survey found that only a fifth of the respondents wanted someone new to represent the district. In match-ups with the two GOP candidates, even among Republican identifiers, Bishop trailed by only a few percentage points. Among independents and Democrats, Bishop enjoyed a commanding lead.

Bishop's popularity stemmed from his attentiveness to the district's agrarian interests. From his perch on the Agriculture Committee he had worked to shore up the district's peanut farmers. Besides helping farmers, he voted with the National Rife Association and compiled the most conservative record of any member of the congressional black caucus. Nonetheless, Bishop was more liberal than any of the Republicans in Georgia's delegation and according to the *National Journal* ratings, sided with liberals about two-thirds of the time.

Given Bishop's popularity, defeating him would require lots of hard work, money and luck. Challenger McCormick did not shy away from the two elements he could influence.

Fund-Raising

Since national Republicans and even some leaders in the state hierarchy had turned to Dylan Glenn as the putative standard bearer, the McCormick staff relished its acceptance by the party establishment in the general election. The lean diet during the primary made the helping hand extended to McCormick particularly valuable since it contained money. "We're a nationally funded race," Sole said proudly. The significance of this status was that "this will not be a contest where we just have a few thousand dollars to put into television advertising."

Several members of Georgia's congressional delegation hosted fund raisers for McCormick, some of which were held in Washington, D.C., providing the opportunity to tap PAC resources. After McCormick's nomination, Speaker Gingrich moved quickly to placate the candidate he had spurned during the summer and signed fund raising letters and gave the maximum allowable from his PAC. McCormick was one of twenty challengers to receive attention from the New Conservative Leadership Fund (NCLF), a fund-raising effort sponsored by conservative Republicans from the class of 1994. Founded by National Football League star receiver Steve Largent (Okla.), the NCLF collected \$5,000 from each member of Congress who joined and solicited funds from PACs and individuals. Five of the NCLF-supported candidates came from the South, and McCormick joined Bill Randall from Florida's Third District in challenging black Democrats in districts redrawn following constitutional challenges. Ultimately the NCLF gave McCormick about \$15,000.

As efforts to raise money for the general election heated up, McCormick ran afoul of Federal Election Commission (FEC) rules when he sent a solicitation to names gleaned from Glenn's contributor list. Glenn backers received a letter signed by Newt Gingrich and addressed to "Dear

Friend of Dylan Glenn."[28] Lifelong Democrats who received this solicitation complained to Glenn, who reported, "They are upset and I am upset. I feel somewhat violated."[29] The Glenn camp found McCormick's behavior particularly galling since in the primary McCormick had criticized his opponent for fund-raising outside the district, but now the victor was approaching those same outsiders. This caused hard feelings with Glenn whom McCormick was trying to incorporate into his general election effort. McCormick could not afford to lose the support of those who had voted for Glenn in the primary. McCormick blamed staffers, saying they were unaware of the FEC ban on using contributor lists from other candidates when they sought the money.

Despite the mis-step with Glenn's backers, McCormick proved to be an effective fund raiser. Through mid-October, he raised $431,973 of which more than a quarter of a million came from individuals.[30] Indeed he got at least $30,000 more from individuals than did Bishop who reported $225,000 from individuals in his postelection FEC filing. The two campaigns raised most of their money in-state and McCormick had 181 Georgia contributors who gave larger average contributions than the approximately 300 Georgians who backed Bishop with money. Bishop, as is typical for incumbents, had more luck trolling among PACs where, according to his November 22 report, he snared $479,000 compared with $63,000 for the challenger. Despite Bishop's greater success with PACs, McCormick demonstrated sufficient viability that some of the district's bigger givers, such as Gold Kist poultry and the Synovus financial empire, hedged their bets by contributing to the challenger. McCormick's final funding total came to about $500,000, an amount that exceeded Bishop's spending in 1992 or 1994 but was well short of the $708,000 raised by the incumbent in 1998. After the campaign, Bishop still had $100,000 on hand while McCormick was saddled with a $30,000 personal debt.

Polling and Opposition Research

Many believe that to defeat an incumbent the challenger must make the incumbent and his or her record the issue of the campaign. Often this tactic involves criticism of the incumbent's past roll call behavior. It may involve what the incumbent considers distortions, or it may attack the incumbent for activities related to his or her vocation.

McCormick chose a temperate approach when criticizing Bishop. In his initial mail-out, McCormick asserted, "Sanford is not a bad guy, he is just the wrong guy!" This tack recognized public attitudes toward Bishop, attitudes which Bishop's poll had captured. As McCormick campaign manager Sole acknowledged, "Sanford Bishop is not disliked in the district." The task for the McCormick campaign was to alter Bishop's image from nice guy to misguided Democrat.

Despite the conservative tendency of the district, McCormick did not attack Bishop when he voted against the Republican proposal for impeachment hearings on President Bill Clinton. Although the McCormick office received numerous calls critical of Bishop's decision, the campaign concluded that the costs associated with negative campaigning more than offset any advantage that using this vote to pin the liberal label on Bishop might provide.[31] A poll completed for McCormick in mid-October indicated that President Clinton's negatives outnumbered his positives by a margin of 55 to 37 percent, so criticism of the Bishop vote might have been an option.

The decision not to go after Bishop's impeachment vote may have been prompted by concern about a backlash. In mid-October Kitchin expressed satisfaction that the campaign had not gone negative. With white women potentially the critical swing group, attacks on Bishop might be counterproductive. According to the consultant, "Women don't like attack ads. Men can handle it; men may even enjoy it. But you lose support among women when you go on the attack." McCormick believed Ealum's weak appeal among women had been his Achilles' heel. "Darrel Ealum lost, in part, because he didn't get the women's vote. He had too hard an edge."[32]

Moreover, McCormick's October poll, conducted by Cherry Communications in Tallahassee, showed Bishop's positive evaluations falling and his negatives rising. Since a late August poll done by John McLaughlin, Bishop's favorables had sagged from 64 to 52 percent while his negatives had risen eleven points to 27 percent. A larger share of the electorate viewed Bishop unfavorably in October than at any point in three polls conducted for Ealum in 1996.[33] Since August, McCormick's positives had grown from 30 to 36 percent, but his negatives had almost tripled from 8 to 21 percent. In August the challenger trailed the incumbent by more than two to one, but by October McCormick had narrowed Bishop's advantage from forty-seven to thirty-eight.[34] The campaign was making headway without going on the attack, and in light of the sparks being struck in the contests for governor and lieutenant governor, a less hostile approach might be the better way. McCormick acknowledged after the election, "I wanted to come out swinging on TV, but once we sat down and analyzed the poll results, we concluded it wouldn't make sense to go negative."

Despite a desire to go after Bishop, McCormick indicated an overriding concern that his campaign be fair to his opposition. "I wanted to contrast myself with Bishop but wanted to do so in a way that was credible and dignified, if that term is appropriate. I wanted it to be something that I could defend. I did not want to go after him with a hatchet. That's not my style." Both McCormick and Kitchen mentioned the devastating ad that Bishop had run in 1996 after being harshly attacked. The ad began with "Hello, I'm the Truth," to which a character representing Ealum responded, "I don't think I know you." The 1998 challenger wanted to avoid a similar putdown.

Advertising

With more money available, McCormick turned to television earlier in the general election than in the primary and began airing two ads in Albany on October 5. One showed the candidate in several contexts—with children at a school, with his agriculture adviser in a field, and in a well-known Thomasville drug store where retirees gather to discuss politics. The other featured McCormick's attractive wife speaking about her husband's honesty, integrity, and service as a U.S. Army ranger. This "Celeste" ad elicited widespread approval, and the gains registered in the October poll were interpreted as evidence that the ad was working. Plans to prepare additional television advertising were shelved in light of the positive response to the ads being run coupled with the progress registered as Bishop's lead had been cut from twenty-eight points in August to less than ten in mid-October.

While the television ads had positive messages, some of the radio spots criticized Bishop's roll call votes. One ad condemned the incumbent for supporting President Clinton's needle exchange program directed at drug addicts. A second ad recalled Bishop's vote for the General Agreement on Tariffs and Trade, which, McCormick charged, hurt Georgia peanut producers. The third one targeted Bishop's amendment that would have eliminated the word "God" from the Religious Freedom Act. McCormick's push polling had revealed that respondents became less likely to support the incumbent when confronted with this information. Providing respondents with this information transformed McCormick from trailing by ten points to a four-point lead.

Initially, $200,000 had been budgeted for television, a figure later increased by 10 percent. Mike Gannon, out of Atlanta, who also worked for Georgia's GOP attorney general nominee, filmed McCormick's commercials. The campaign budget set aside $35,000 for radio. Ultimately, $40,000 was spent on radio ads which McCormick estimates gave him four times the presence Bishop had on radio.

Earned Media

As the only GOP congressional objective in Georgia and one of the few dozen seats in play nationwide, the Second District received extensive attention from the state's Republican members of Congress and visits from several national figures. The appearance of Georgia Republican leaders Senator Paul Coverdell, Newt Gingrich, and National Republican Congressional Committee (NRCC) chair John Linder at endorsement rallies and the visits of Marilyn Quayle, Bob Dole, and Representative Steve Largent (R-Okla.) each provided opportunities for raising money, inspiring volunteers, and attracting media coverage.

The extent of media coverage of these events pleased McCormick. "In this district, the media coverage was more than fair. I would say it was very fair," said the candidate as he looked back ten days after the election. He continued, "I can't imagine getting more media coverage. We got tremendous amounts of earned media." To the extent that he had complaints, they emphasized some headlines and not the accuracy or amount of the reporting. For example, the lead to the story written when Largent came to Valdosta focused on what the former NFL star said about Kosovo rather than his endorsement of McCormick's candidacy.

Evaluations of the coverage of candidate debates and forums was less positive. Television did not cover the debate in Valdosta—where McCormick needed to win over Glenn supporters—nor the two forums attended by the candidates. The debate in Americus, where McCormick felt that he did especially well by launching criticisms of the incumbent's voting record that the latter could not defend, aired only on the local cable outlet. A debate in Albany where McCormick was present while Bishop participated by way of a telephone hook-up appeared on local-access television but not on either commercial affiliate.

Get Out the Vote and Field Operations

McCormick expected about 115,000 voters to go to the polls based on turnout in 1994 in the counties that currently comprise the Second District and that he would poll a narrow majority.[35] The GOP get-out-the-vote effort consisted of two parts. The state party bore the responsibility for mobilizing Republicans who were defined as those who regularly voted in GOP primaries. These households received calls from the state party. To McCormick fell the task of getting the swing vote to the polls. Some sixty McCormick volunteers called 40,000 households during the final two weeks of the campaign and urged a vote for their candidate.

Another state party initiative mailed out absentee ballot requests to more than 650,000 likely GOP supporters.[36] This marked the first time that Georgia voters were encouraged to ask for absentee ballots—Georgia law does not provide for early voting as Texas and some other states do. Anecdotal evidence suggests that the GOP effort increased absentee voting. For example, Dougherty County received 2,000 absentee ballots in 1998 compared with 800 in 1994. While McCormick ran 22 percentage points higher among absentee voters than he did with those who voted at the polls, he was disappointed with the 60 percent of the absentee votes that he received.

The challenger ran a vigorous campaign. Although he did not return to the door-to-door efforts of the primary, he traveled the district constantly and spent much of the fall touring the district by bus. He would be in one community for breakfast and another for lunch and claims to have visited almost all of the district's civic clubs. He tried to shake at least 150 hands a day in the far-flung district where concentrations of voters are often hard to find.

Outside Influences

While Bishop used the magnetic power of incumbency to raise more money than McCormick, the challenger believes that as a result of Republican Party advertising more was spent on his effort than on the

Democrat. Johnson estimates that the National Republican Congressional Committee spent upward of $80,000, while the Republican National Committee (RNC) spent between $250,000 and $300,000 promoting a favorable image for McCormick. With regard to the RNC effort, Johnson recalled, "They bought television time for four weeks on all the media markets that touched the district. At the 6 o'clock news there would be two spots from the RNC, one from our campaign and one or two from Sanford."

Most of the advertising paid for with soft money emphasized GOP positions in favor of sending money to local school districts, saving Social Security, protecting Medicare, and cutting taxes. These ads appeared on television stations in Albany, Tallahassee, Columbus, Macon and Dothan, Alabama. They contained the tag line, "Call Joe McCormick and tell him you appreciate his stand on these issues."

In the closing days of the campaign, the tenor of the ads sponsored by outsiders changed as the NRCC picked this district for its hardest-hitting attack on Clinton. A voice asked, "Should we reward Democratic plans for more big government? More big spending? Should we reward their opposition to more welfare reform? And should we reward not telling the truth? That is the question of this election. Reward Bill Clinton? Or vote Republican?" Only three southern Democratic incumbents were targeted for this ad.[37] One assumes that selection of these districts rested on a belief that the president's phenomenally high job approval ratings did not apply here. Evidence from McCormick's mid-October poll, which showed Clinton's unfavorables outnumbering his favorables by a fifty-five to thirty-seven margin, suggested that the president may have lost it with Monica Lewinsky.

Although not a random sample, calls to the *Albany Herald* following President Clinton's August 17 admission of an affair with Lewinsky revealed widespread anger at the president's prevarications. Among the more than 500 responses registered in twenty-four hours are the following:

> I was very interested in what he had to say. I was listening for the words "I'm sorry" or "sin" or "adultery." Now, of course, we heard none of them. But when you consider that he has Jesse Jackson as a spiritual adviser, which you might liken to having Rodney King as a legal adviser, I don't suppose that you could expect anything less.

> The whole thing has left a bad taste in my mouth. I do not think the president should escape the consequences of his poor judgment. He's still being evasive and deceptive. He should be held accountable if it is proven that he broke the law.
>
> I think that the man should resign 'cause he has absolutely no morals. He'll lie in a heartbeat—you can tell when he's lying because his lips are moving.

In retrospect, despite the criticisms registered immediately after the president's admission, the NRCC attacks may have backfired. Surveying the wreckage a few days after the election, GOP House Conference Chair John Boehner told Wolf Blitzer on CNN's *Late Edition* that these ads had been "a big mistake," an assessment echoed by at least some in the state GOP headquarters. Nor did McCormick consider the ads helpful. He did not criticize the president while on the campaign trail and when questioned about the ads, responded that he wanted to keep attention focused on the issues and not on the affair.[38] Immediately after the vote, Kitchin had seen Bishop's opposition to the GOP impeachment proposal as potentially helping the challenger, but he too expressed reluctance at making this an issue. A spokesperson for Bishop claimed that few callers criticized the incumbent when he rejected the GOP approach.

Besides the backlash triggered by the anti-Clinton ad, Bishop benefited from the Democrat's united campaign. He joined the statewide Democratic bus ride as it wound through the district.[39] On board rode the Democratic team that included nominees for governor, lieutenant governor, attorney general, state school superintendent, secretary of state, and the U.S. Senate. In addition, out-going Governor Zell Miller who boasted 85 percent job approval and the ever-popular, all-time home run recordholder Hank Aaron gave their blessings to Democratic candidates. Bishop was one of three Democratic candidates—the other two sought statewide offices—for whom Miller cut a supportive ad.

U.S. Agriculture Secretary Dan Glickman also visited the district, as he had done two years earlier, to urge farmers to stand by Bishop. In 1998 the agriculture secretary held out the lure of federal disaster assistance for drought-devastated farmers. He warned one hundred tillers of the soil who had gathered in an air-conditioned, converted barn, "I can tell you one person who will be at my side when I design that package. His name is Sanford Bishop. That other fellow isn't going to be at the table."[40]

"That other fellow" and Speaker Newt Gingrich immediately castigated Glickman for politicizing relief to struggling farmers and called for a House investigation. "I think the nation's farmers expect the secretary to do the right thing based on who needs emergency help without regard to party," said the Speaker.[41]

Two years earlier Glickman had joined Bishop to back up the candidate's claims that he had saved the peanut program from elimination. A McCormick staff member groused that in 1996 it had seemed that Glickman lived in Georgia's Second District.

Perhaps national Democrats did not believe that Bishop was threatened. That would explain why he did not attract help from visible non-Georgians other than Glickman. Nor did he benefit from party television advertising although the coordinated get-out-the-vote effort did promote Bishop's chances.

Issues

Given the rural nature of the Second District and its dependence on the output of the soil, it is not surprising that agriculture became McCormick's major issue. In 1996 the incumbent had stressed his role in protecting the peanut program and had been rewarded by the votes of farmers. To get to Congress, McCormick would have to cut into Bishop's support at the grass roots in the farming community.

Agriculture

Immediately upon entering Congress Bishop set out to expand his reelection constituency by serving on the House Agriculture Committee where he worked to protect peanuts, the district's most valuable crop.[42] McCormick attacked Bishop's claim that he made a unique contribution to the two-vote margin to sustain the peanut program by attracting support from congressional black caucus members. "We went and did some research and we found that the peanut program got more votes from the black caucus when Charles Hatcher represented the district," the challenger reported.

Besides challenging Bishop's claim to be the patron saint of peanuts, McCormick sought to develop a grassroots organization among farmers. Agriculture consultant Marvin Robertson created McCormick's Agriculture Task Force in mid-1997, building on a similar organization that

Chambliss had established in the eastern counties of the Second when they belonged to the Eighth before the 1996 redistricting. According to Robertson, "Saxby gave us a strong agricultural organization along I-75." McCormick began campaigning among farmers with an appearance at the Sun Belt Exposition in 1997. This event staged in Moultrie is the largest farm show with field demonstrations in the nation. Thereafter, Robertson had the candidate at every meeting of farmers in the district and even took him to a meeting of young farmers in Savannah, well to the east of the district.

McCormick hoped that several components of his background would help win over farmers. For example, he had personal contact with a number of farmers since about 30 percent of his rentals go to them. McCormick also expected to benefit from having a peanut grower for a brother-in-law and a former National Peanut Queen for a wife.

A mail-out to 4,000 farmers designed by McCormick's agriculture consultant questioned whether Bishop was the key protector of the peanut by emphasizing the importance of being with the majority party. Part of the missive outlined the challenger's stand on farm issues. Another portion, after evoking the names of Georgia congressional legends Sam Nunn, Richard Russell, Carl Vinson, Walter George, and Herman Talmadge, all of whom flourished as members of the majority party, then pointed out, "On the Agriculture Committee, the leaders in the House in January will include Larry Combest (R-Tex.) as chairman. He is a friend of peanut and cotton farmers and from a district where these crops are a major part of the economy." The letter, signed by Saxby Chambliss of Georgia's Eighth District and Terry Everett of Alabama's Second District—which neighbor Georgia's Second to the east and west—noted that

> Agriculture interests in South Georgia also recognize the power of the majority. With the Republican majority on the House Agriculture Committee including the 2nd District of Alabama and the 8th of Georgia, only the 2nd District of Georgia is missing to give majority party representation across the Southeastern peanut belt. We need Joe McCormick in the U.S. House sitting with the majority party on the House Agriculture Committee to help shape farm policy. . . . As a member of the majority, Joe will have access to the Speaker and the House Leadership that sets the agenda and determines what bills reach the House floor.

Challenging Bishop's image as savior of the peanut program was part of a broader attack on his effectiveness. Campaign manager Sole charged, "Bishop hasn't had a major agricultural bill in six years. Bishop has just supported Saxby on agricultural issues. Sanford has missed the boat on agriculture."

A month before the election, McCormick thought that his message that the district would be better served by having a member of the majority party and criticism of the incumbent had taken the peanut issue away from Bishop. Kitchin concurred, "Bishop is having to rebuild his base with farmers and is finding that a number of people who have supported him in the past are now supporting us." Even earlier in the fall, Sole had reported, "We are getting support in the agri-businesses such as peanut shellers and cotton gins." Interviews conducted by *New York Times* correspondent Kevin Sack indicate that despite McCormick's efforts, many conservative farmers continued to credit Bishop for his work on their behalf.[43]

Other Issues

The district's second most significant economic sphere is the military. McCormick recruited two retired generals, Ed Cassidy who commanded the U.S. Marine base in the district and Troy Tolbert, former commander of Moody Air Force Base in Valdosta, to serve as advisers. In the primary, McCormick claimed to be the only veteran running in the Second District. The challenger emphasized his attendance at VMI and his service as a U.S. Army Ranger in his literature and in the television ad done by his wife. McCormick contended that his military background prepared him to defend the district's installations should they be threatened by a future base closing commission. McCormick charged that Bishop ignores the district's military installations so that when constituents have concerns in this area, they turn to Chambliss or Coverdell. The challenger also criticized the incumbent for having forsaken the House Veterans' Affairs Committee for the House Select Committee on Intelligence. McCormick believed that the swap would hurt the incumbent with the district's 60,000 veterans.

Bishop countered that none of the district's bases had closed on his watch.[44] He also challenged McCormick's claim to be the only veteran and joined the Caucus for Vietnam-Era Veterans. In the 1998 edition of the *Almanac of American Politics*, the incumbent indicates service in the

U.S. Army in 1970–71. In previous editions of the *Almanac,* military service was missing from his career entries, and *Politics in America, 1998,* still had no entry for Bishop under military service. McCormick released documentation of his service with the U.S. Army Rangers and called on Bishop to do the same.

The candidates offered different takes on the state of the district's economy. Assuming that contented voters are more likely to stick with the status quo, Bishop boasted that the economy was strong, and the that district had 40,000 additional jobs.[45] McCormick's rejoinder was that the district remains among the nation's least affluent and "We're in an economic recession in southwest Georgia."[46] McCormick offered that his experience as a small entrepreneur would help him attract industry to southwest Georgia.

McCormick sought to make family values an issue by noting that unlike his opponent, he was married.[47] Celeste McCormick underscored this point through her active participation, which Kitchin saw as especially skillful. "Of all of the candidates I have worked with, there has only been one candidate's wife who is better than Celeste and that is Barbara Bush. Celeste is really good in doing woman-to-woman. You often have wives who you worry about what they will say when they represent their husbands, but you don't have to worry about that with Celeste." Her presence as a spokesperson is in keeping with the pattern observed by media monitor Professor Kathleen Hall Jamieson who characterized 1998 as "the year of the woman in campaign advertising."[48]

Besides making a television ad, Celeste McCormick participated in a number of "women only" events hosted in homes. A PBS radio correspondent who attended one was impressed by Celeste's interaction with guests who came heavily from farm families. By meeting farm wives, Celeste helped Joe pursue two objectives. First, it dovetailed with efforts to negate Bishop's past success with farmers; second, it might narrow the gender gap that often plagues Republicans.[49]

In recent years, the "L" word has often proved fatal to Democrats. and knowing that, Republicans try to pin the liberal label on their opponents. [50] McCormick's emphasis on the military, his business experiences and family all sought to differentiate him from his opponent along an ideological spectrum. Bishop's moderate voting record and his work on behalf of farmers, who in Georgia are not likely to consort with the American Civil Liberties Union, frustrated the challenger. McCormick and his staff frequently criticized Bishop for voting conservative only a third of the time but being able to convince voters that this one-third was the dominant feature of the incumbent's record.

Election Results

The elections of 1998 were among the most incumbent friendly ever with more than 98 percent of the House officeholders returning to the 106th Congress. No incumbent in the South stumbled, so McCormick suffered the fate of all other challengers in the region.

The McCormick camp had expected to improve on Ealum's showing. Partly because of the greater visibility accorded the McCormick-Glenn face-off compared with that given the Ealum primary, McCormick began the general election effort better known than Ealum. McCormick's August poll showed his name recognition at 38 percent; two years earlier, Ealum had 13 percent name recognition ten weeks before election day.

The 1998 challenger built on this early advantage. "We will raise more than two times as much as Ealum. We will get more PAC money," Kitchin predicted a month before the election. And, as of the mid-October FEC filing, McCormick had obtained more than $430,000, already eclipsing Ealum's final figure by $100,000. Moreover, Kitchin, who served as consultant to the Ealum general election effort, considered McCormick a better candidate and thought that the improved quality of the product that he was working with in 1998 would be worth at least 4 percentage points—which would put the race into a dead heat.

When the votes were counted, however, McCormick managed 43 percent of the vote, compared with 46 percent for Ealum, and carried only four counties. Ealum won seven counties and only in Lee and Thomas counties did McCormick outpace his predecessor. In two small counties, the GOP vote share fell by more than 10 percentage points from 1996. In Dougherty, where Kitchin thought it imperative that his candidate break even, McCormick replicated Ealum's performance, taking just under 38 percent of the vote.

In losing, McCormick drew 59,306 votes, just 700 votes fewer than the analysis based on 1994 voting patterns that suggested a Republican would receive, and more than enough to win. In seventeen counties McCormick actually exceeded the projections based on the previous midterm election. He lost, however, because Bishop ran 22,000 votes above the 1994 figure and in two counties actually got more votes than in 1996 when district turnout ran about 20 percent above the 1998 effort.

Kitchin thought that his candidate would win until he drove past some of Albany's black precincts on election day and saw turnout more like a presidential than an off-year. "I knew they weren't turning out for us," Kitchin said. "The thing that worries a consultant is when you see a large turnout and you know you're not the cause of it."

The unexpected turnout in 1998 stemmed from several elements largely beyond McCormick's control. Georgia's Second District must be one of few in the nation affected by a contest for lieutenant governor. Mark Taylor, Democratic nominee for the state's second highest office, comes from a prominent Albany family and represented the area in the state senate beginning in 1987. In the past, south Georgia frequently provided leadership to the state and counted among its contributions governors Eugene Talmadge (1933–36, 1941–42) and his son Herman (1949–54), E. D. Rivers (1937–40), Marvin Griffin (1955–58), Jimmy Carter (1971–74), and George Busbee (1975–82). In recent years not only has the lower half of the state failed to send one of its own to the governor's mansion, not since 1988 had a south Georgian been elected to any statewide office. Local pride showed through in the runoff for lieutenant governor as Taylor regularly won south Georgia counties by margins of seven or eight to one and took more than 90 percent of the vote in a few counties. With Taylor on the ballot, a strong temptation to vote Democratic might siphon off potential GOP votes, and Taylor led the ticket in the Second District with more than 96,000 votes, 9,000 more than the Democratic gubernatorial nominee.

Before the election Kitchin said hopefully, "We share a lot of Mark Taylor supporters. A number of people who support Mark Taylor have also contributed to our campaign." Maybe so, but the enthusiasm registered among friends and neighbors for Taylor created an undertow that sucked McCormick down. The challenger carried only four counties with his most impressive success coming in Lee, Albany's white flight county, which gave McCormick a 63 percent victory. He lost narrowly in Lowndes (48.2 percent), where the Republican candidate for lieutenant governor managed barely a third of the vote. In Dougherty, home county for both McCormick and Taylor, the congressional challenger's 38 percent of the vote far outpaced Taylor's GOP opponent, who registered an anemic 15 percent.

Although McCormick did not campaign against the president, Democrats used the threat of impeachment to mobilize black voters, and McCormick suffered along with other Republicans. Albany mayor Tommy Coleman, who headed Bishop's 1992 campaign, noted, "Bishop does not have a great grass-roots effort to get out the vote. He tends to leave that up to others." Johnson from the McCormick campaign agreed, "I don't attribute the Democratic turnout to Sanford. It was more the result of Roy Barnes [gubernatorial nominee], Mark Taylor and the whole Democratic Party." Since Georgia voter lists identify the race of registrants, messages could be targeted to black households. The state Democratic Party claimed that it contacted the household of each black voter five times during the closing week of the campaign. One contact was a recorded message from President Clinton, and some voters who found it on their answering machine thought that the president had indeed called. A second recorded message featured Fourth District Congresswoman Cynthia McKinney.

Actions by Republican candidates also contributed to black turnout. Republican candidates for governor and lieutenant governor ran what many blacks saw as race-baiting ads. In the final week of the campaign as he saw white male support fading, GOP gubernatorial nominee Guy Millner charged that his opponent supported racial quotas. Blacks found even more offensive a commercial in which Mitch Skandalakis, the GOP lieutenant governor nominee, called Atlanta's black mayor Bill Campbell an "incompetent boob" and threatened to "kick Atlanta's (bleeped out)." A Democratic mail-out to black households played off the Skandalakis ad. It showed Skandalakis and Millner with bold lettering warning, "We're going to kick your ass!" The second side included statements from the media critical of alleged racism by the GOP team and concluded with the exhortation "Get to the Polls Before Millner and Skandalakis Get to You." A McCormick staffer observed, "With Mitch threatening to kick Bill Campbell's butt and with Millner running the anti-affirmative action ad, we looked like angry white guys." McCormick did not introduce race into his campaign against Bishop but suffered from a higher black turnout.

Black turnout in the Second District was strong in 1998. Data collected by Georgia's secretary of state shows that blacks cast 31 percent of the votes tallied in the district in 1998, up from 29 percent of the votes cast two years earlier. With blacks casting 90 percent or more of their votes for Democratic candidates in the South, the higher turnout caused McCormick to suffer.[51] (Anecdotally, a person who takes black Albany voters to the polls told a McCormick staffer that he ferried far more people to the polls in 1998 than in the preceding years.)

A seasoned black politician in Albany reported that black preachers' pulpit exhortations to vote were more widespread and urgent than usual in 1998. Reinforcing these pleas were messages on black radio, including one that warned that if Republicans win, "another brother dies, another church burns." Late in the afternoon of election day, black students appeared on street corners with signs urging those who had not voted to go to the polls.

While "voting against" is a powerful lure, Georgia African Americans also had a strong positive incentive to vote. The Democratic statewide ticket included three black nominees, two of whom were locked in tight contests. The victories of former state representatives Thurbert Baker, who had been appointed attorney general, and Michael Thurmond, who ran for the open post of labor commissioner, marked the first time that African Americans had been elected to statewide nonjudicial posts.

Finally, Bishop may have drawn the full reward of incumbency in 1998. In 1996, despite four years of service in the House, he was a new face in four counties and in white portions of five other counties that had been added to the district when it was redrawn. Two years later he was better known.

In winning a fourth term, Bishop reassembled a biracial coalition. He attracted almost all of the black vote—as black Democrats often do in general elections—and about 38 percent of the white vote, the same as two years earlier when he faced a less well-financed opponent. Anecdotal evidence suggests that Bishop's white support continued to include a number of farmers pleased with the incumbent's advocacy of farming issues critical to the economic well-being of the district.[52]

While the 1998 turnout broke records, a multivariate analysis using counties as the unit of analysis and reported in table 4-3 suggests that, to at least some extent, the results of the 1998 congressional election were determined by factors generally operating in this corner of the state. Georgia Republicans rarely attract as much as a tenth of the black vote, and percent black among registered voters is a strong negative predictor of McCormick's vote. Each additional 1 percent black among registrants translated into about a 0.5 percent smaller vote share for McCormick. The racial composition of the electorate was not as big a factor for McCormick as it had been for Ealum two years earlier when a 1 percent change in black registrants reduced votes for the Republican by about two-thirds of a point.

Table 4-3. *Multivariate Models for Republican vote, 1996, 1998*[a]

Predictors	*McCormick*	*Ealum*
Percent black among registrants	–0.546 (–6.181)	–0.660 (–7.688)
Population change, 1980–90	0.325 (3.115)	0.054 (0.529)
Percent work force in agriculture in 1990	–0.035 (–0.133)	–0.143 (–0.556)
Constant	58.848	67.278
Adjusted R^2	0.773	0.763
F	35.045	33.194

a. *t* statistics in parentheses.

Statewide, Republicans have run stronger in growth areas, and the multivariate model shows McCormick faring better in counties that grew during the 1980s. Population growth of 1 percentage point during the 1980s was associated with an additional one-third of 1 percent of the vote. Ealum's performance was unaffected by population change in the county.

McCormick made a concentrated effort to win the farm vote away from Bishop. If he succeeded, then there might be a positive relationship between the percent of the labor force involved in agriculture and support for the challenger. The multivariate analysis showed no relationship (b = –0.004, s.e. = 0.265), repeating the results from 1996 when there was also no relationship.[53] For both McCormick and Ealum, the three-variable model explained more than 75 percent of the variance.

Conclusion

As Canadian folk singers Ian and Sylvia observed in *Summer Wages*, "When you bet against the dealer, the odds don't ride with you." Taking on a House incumbent, like pulling on Superman's cape, is a high-risk activity. Joe McCormick failed to unseat Sanford Bishop . . . but then all but one Republican House challenger came up short in 1998.

Neither the candidate nor his staffers had second thoughts after the loss. A month later Kitchin said, "There's not a thing that we would have changed. We felt good about the election we were in." This was the best-funded effort Bishop has confronted and Kitchin felt that the campaign had sufficient money—even though McCormick ended the campaign with a $30,000 debt. Johnson agreed that the problem was not lack of money—unlike in 1996 when he speculated that with another $100,000, Ealum might have pulled out a win. Both McCormick and Bryce Johnson, who worked up estimates of votes required by county, were pleased that their effort came so close to achieving the support that they thought they needed. Johnson went so far as to say, "I am not sure there were more than a couple of thousand more Republican votes that we could have gotten. It is scary."

Although Bishop has reported raising more money than McCormick, once party expenditures in the district are included, the Republican believes that his candidacy attracted more financial support than did the incumbent. Had turnout and voting patterns been comparable to 1994, the challenger would have eked out a victory. Instead, he lost by almost 19,000 votes.

What McCormick did not anticipate was a black vote tsunami in which Georgia African Americans turned out in record numbers. Democrats learned from their string of setbacks earlier in the decade and designed a massive, stealth get-out-the-vote effort, urged on by a united effort that surpassed GOP efforts. Augmenting the telephone calls and mailings were ads launched by Republicans at the top of the Georgia ticket that the state's blacks saw as hostile. Finally, efforts by congressional Republicans to set Bill Clinton up for impeachment triggered a backlash among African Americans bent on protecting the man whom Nobel Prize–winning novelist Toni Morrison has called America's first black president.

Unexpectedly high black participation for a midterm election, coupled with a strong economy, stopped GOP growth in Georgia dead in its tracks. Earlier in the 1990s, Georgia Republicans had gained seven congressional seats, forty-four state House seats, twelve state Senate seats, a U.S. senator, and six statewide state officials. In the last election of the decade not only did McCormick fail to increase its congressional holdings but the GOP lost one seat in each chamber of the General Assembly and failed to make any further headway among state officeholders, even though the offices of governor, lieutenant governor, secretary of state and labor commissioner were open. In reality, the GOP lost little ground but set against its high expectations for ending more than 125 years of uninterrupted Democratic control of state government, the stagnation of 1998 was bitter indeed.

To win, Joe McCormick needed a strong Republican showing up and down the ticket; instead he was swamped by unprecedented black turnout. He was but one of a large group that included most Republican challengers in Georgia and across the nation, as well as pundits and political scientists stunned to learn that the midterm advantage for the party not controlling the White House is a generalization, not a guarantee.

Notes

1. David J. Garrow, *Protest at Selma* (Yale University Press, 1978).

2. Jimmy Carter, *Turning Point* (Times Books, 1992).

3. On GOP legislative election efforts, see Charles S. Bullock III and David Shafer, "A Party Targeting and Electoral Success," *Legislative Studies Quarterly*, vol. 22 (November 1997), pp. 573–84.

4. During the 1990s, Pennsylvania's First District was the only one in Congress to have a majority black population but a white representative. See Charles Cameron, David Epstein, and Sharyn O'Halloran, "Do Majority-Minority Districts Maximize Substantive Black Representation in Congress?" *American Political Science Review,* vol. 90 (December 1996), pp. 794–812. The authors estimate that by the time a southern congressional district reaches 45 percent black in voting age population, it is likely to have an African American legislator.

5. See Richard F. Fenno Jr., *Home Style* (Little, Brown, 1978).

6. Charles S. Bullock III and Richard E. Dunn, "The Demise of Racial Districting and the Future of Black Representation," presented at the annual meeting of the American Political Science Association, Washington, 1997; and Stephen D. Voss, "Black Incumbents, White Districts: An Appraisal of the 1996 Congressional Elections in Georgia and Florida," presented at the annual meeting of the Southern Political Science Association, Atlanta, 1998.

7. Voss, "Black Incumbents, White Districts."

8. In 1998 Coles won the Democratic nomination for the U.S. Senate and opposed Paul Coverdell.

9. Stuart Rothenberg, "House Outlook: Midterm Fallout," *Rothenberg Political Report,* vol. 21 (September 18, 1998), p. 3.

10 . All quotations in this chapter not cited or attributed to a publication are from personal interviews with the author.

11. McCormick did not include Glenn's picture along with his. When this has been done elsewhere, it has often been considered a racial appeal.

12. David Pace, telephone interview with author, June 15, 1998.

13. A clearer case of racial appeal can be made when the white candidate juxtaposes his or her picture with that of the black opponent.

14. The list of black candidates included two seeking statewide offices, one each in the three U.S. House districts held by Democrats, fifteen candidates for the state legislature, and two who sought local offices. The twenty-two marked a

dramatic increase over the eight black Republicans who ran for the state legislature in 1996. None of the recent efforts has proved successful, although there have been rare black Republican officeholders, most recently the county school superintendent in Douglas County and a member of the council in Columbus.

15. Kathey Pruitt, "Blacks in GOP Blaze Trails in Georgia," *Atlanta Journal-Constitution,* May 5, 1998, p. C1; and Georgia Republicans, "Georgia Leads the Nation in the Qualification of African American GOP Candidates," press release, May 4, 1998.

16. It eventually became clear that Glenn did know many of his contributors and that the only reason they gave was because of their ties to the candidate. Later when McCormick solicited some of these same contributors for his general election effort, they were offended and indicated that the only reason they had given to Glenn was because of their belief in his candidacy. Wayne Partridge, "McCormick Accused of Improprieties in Fund Raising," *Columbus Ledger Enquirer,* September 18, 1998.

17. When David Duke, a former leader of the Ku Klux Klan and organizer of the Organization for the Advancement of White People, faced another Republican in a GOP Louisiana state legislative district, Republicans from President George Bush on down urged Duke's defeat. Duke's past with its racist and anti-Semitic overtones was so unpalatable that GOP leaders called for his defeat in 1990 when he ran for the Senate and in 1991 when he joined former governor Edwin Edwards (D) in surviving the state's open primary. Ethics charges against Edwards were widely known. The unappetizing choice in the second round of elections gave rise to bumper stickers that urged, "Vote for the crook, it's important!"

18. Tim Craig, "Who's the Outsider? Carpetbagging Charge Sticks to Glenn," *Roll Call,* July 15, 1998, pp. 15, 22.

19. David Pace, "A South Georgia Primary Tests White Republican Racial Attitudes," *Associated Press*, June 22, 1998.

20. Craig, "Who's the Outsider?"

21. "McCormick on the Move," Thomasville Debate, 1998.

22. Charmagne Helton, "Gingrich Endorses Black Republican," *Atlanta Journal,* July 8, 1998, p. C4.

23. V. O. Key Jr., *Southern Politics in State and Nation* (Knopf, 1949).

24. The racial characteristics (percent black among registered voters) and votes in these precincts are as follows:

County	*Precinct*	*Percent black*	*Glenn*	*McCormick*
Colquitt	Shaw	81	10	7
Cook	Adel West	91	1	0
Grady	Cairo Fourth	83	8	12
Lowndes	Craig Recreation	87	8	5
Lowndes	Pinevale-Lomax	94	13	5
Mitchell	Camilla North	84	6	7
Taylor	One	81	8	8
Thomas	Harper	84	49	35
Tift	Armory	81	12	3

25. David Pace, telephone interview with author, June 15, 1998.

26. James A. Barnes, 1987 "A Party in Waiting," *National Journal*, September 19, 1987, pp. 2340–45; and Gregory S. Thielmann, "The Rise and Stall of Southern Republicans in Congress," *Social Science Quarterly*, vol. 73 (March 1992), pp. 123–35.

27. Tom Perdue, interview with author, June 1, 1993.

28. Tony Bridges, "A McCormick Hit with Controversy," *Albany Herald*, September 18, 1998.

29. Wayne Partridge, "McCormick Accused of Improprieties in Fund Raising," *Columbus Ledger Enquirer,* September 18, 1998.

30. As of January 22, 1999, McCormick had still not completed work on his postelection FEC report; however, he estimated that he raised about $500,000 during the 1997–98 cycle.

31. Tom Baxter, "A Clinton Referendum? A Poor Bet," *Atlanta Journal,* October 15, 1998, p. E1.

32. *Associated Press* reporter David Pace told the author that he had heard similar criticisms of Ealum. He contrasted the 1996 and 1998 GOP nominees, saying of Ealum, "I think his personality turned some people off. McCormick is smoother. He comes across as a nice guy."

33. Since Kitchin served on the Ealum campaign, he had access to polls conducted in the course of that effort and therefore could compare McCormick's progress with the earlier campaign.

34. Polls done at the behest of candidates often show the purchaser of the poll to be in better shape than do polls conducted for disinterested parties. As far as I can tell, no independent polling occurred in Georgia's Second District in 1998.

35. McCormick arrived at this figure by summing the votes for Democratic and Republican congressional candidates in the thirty-one counties in 1994. As figure 4-1 shows, some of these counties were wholly in the Second District, some were in the Eighth, and some were divided between the Second and Eighth. Thus some of the figures used are votes for Saxby Chambliss and his Democratic opponent. The campaign's in-house number cruncher, Bryce Johnson, expected a somewhat larger turnout and estimated that McCormick would need 62,500 votes to win.

36. Steve Visser, "Counties See Surge in Mail-in Balloting," *Atlanta Journal,* November 5, 1998, p. K8.

37 . Richard Berke, "GOP Begins Ad Campaign Citing Scandal," *New York Times,* October 28, 1998, pp. A1, 21.

38. Bill Orsinski, "Attack Ads Unleashed," *Atlanta Journal-Constitution,* October 31, 1998, p. A10.

39. Charles Walston, "Democrats Tour State on Bus," *Atlanta Journal*, October 29, 1998, p. F4.

40. Elliott Minor, "Agriculture Secretary Glickman Campaigns for Bishop," *Athens Banner-Herald,* October 31, 1998, p. 3B.

41. Amy Frazier, "Gingrich Blasts Ag Secretary for Comments," *Athens Banner-Herald,* November 1, 1998, p. 3B.

42. On broadening a re-election constituency, see Fenno, *Home Style.*

43. Kevin Sack, "In the Rural White South, Seeds of a Biracial Politics," *New York Times*, December 30, 1998.

44. Bill Orsinski, "No Matter Who Wins Race, Conservatism Will Rule Day," *Atlanta Journal-Constitution,* October 11, 1998, p. B4.

45. Ibid.

46. Ibid.

47. McCormick was seemingly happily married throughout the campaign, but his wife left him immediately upon its unsuccessful conclusion. Bishop is divorced.

48. Kathleen Hall Jamieson, *A Weekend Edition,* National Public Radio, October 25, 1998.

49. Although we have no figures on voting by gender in the Second District in 1998, statewide exit polls show no gender gap among white females in the vote for governor or US senator.

50. Earl Black and Merle Black, *Politics and Society in the South* (Harvard University Press, 1987).

51. Charles S. Bullock III and Richard E. Dunn, "The Demise of Racial Districting and the Future of Black Representation," presented at the annual meeting of the American Political Science Association, Washington, 1997.

52. Sack, "In the Rural White South."

53. The same three-variable model used to estimate support for McCormick was used for several other recent candidates and generally percent of the labor force in agriculture is negatively associated with support for Republican nominees (for example, lieutenant governor Skandalakis and attorney general David Ralston) and positively associated with support for Democrats (for example, governor Roy Barnes and Bill Clinton in 1996) when it achieves statistical significance. That this variable bore no relationship to the McCormick vote may indicate success in neutralizing what would often be a problem for a Republican.

CHAPTER FIVE

Kansas's Third District: The "Pros from Dover" Set Up Shop

BURDETT A. LOOMIS

AUGUST 28, 1998. It's just 10:30 on this late August morning, but the air conditioning is already running full blast in the strip-mall office "suite" that houses the campaign of Democrat Dennis Moore. Inside, the press secretary, Mark Nevins, is returning some phone calls and waiting for the candidate to appear—after all, a major debate with Republican incumbent Vince Snowbarger is scheduled for noon a few miles away at the Overland Park (Kansas) Marriott. Sitting across the room from Nevins is Moore's worried campaign manager, Chris Esposito, whose extensive debate preparation with the candidate may go for naught. Moore, the challenger in this most improbable "toss-up" race, is tending to a morning court date that will determine the fate of one of his many clients. Esposito waits, simultaneously confident in his candidate's abilities and concerned that Moore's continuing work as a defense attorney will reduce his effectiveness as the campaign enters its final two

I wish to thank any number of individuals who contributed to whatever virtues this chapter may have. Chad Kniss proved a resilient and reliable research assistant, Heather Hoy has provided her usual excellent assistance, as well as transcribing the BBC interviews. Jeremy Cooper conducted superb and highly useful interviews. Steve Kraske and Scott Canon were excellent sounding boards (and good reporters). And the Moore for Congress campaign, from top to bottom, could not have been more forthcoming. My particular thanks go to Jenny Pechar, Marcia Stoneburner, Chris Steineger, the pros from Dover, and—especially—Stephene and Dennis Moore.

months. But Moore—a stubborn man—will not give up his lucrative criminal defense practice.

The door opens and Moore sweeps in, heading for his Dilbert-sized cubicle in the back, the only private space in the entire office. Esposito follows, ready to assess his candidate's mental state. Moore quickly reappears, asking Nevins to find his income tax returns, which he says he must make available immediately. The returns fail to surface, and his wife, Stephene, is called to check on their whereabouts. The returns are found, the minicrisis subsides. An hour to the debate, and the candidate is pacing around the suite, talking to Nevins and Esposito, more or less randomly.

At 11:15 Moore strides through the office and says, "Let's go." Before anyone can grab the keys, he's at the wheel of his well-used Ford Taurus, ready to head out. Esposito and Nevins hurriedly pick up a bundle of campaign literature and a video camera, and off they go. Zooming down highway 69, cutting across the older suburban core of Kansas's Third Congressional District, Moore reaches for his cell phone and makes a call. He's back practicing law, as he hashes over sentencing scenarios with the morning's defendant. As he weaves in and out of traffic, at least a bit above the speed limit, Moore doesn't miss a beat as he covers a wide range of options and potential outcomes.

The Taurus pulls into the Marriott parking lot. Moore steps out, puts on his suit coat, and keeps talking to his client. The campaign manager and the press secretary lug Moore for Congress signs, literature, and the video equipment across the steamy parking lot. As the cool, slightly humid air of the Marriott engulfs the trio, Moore tosses his phone to Esposito and extends his hand to "meet-and-greet" one of his potential constituents. Esposito watches him plunge into the gathering Chamber of Commerce crowd and frets, "He's on edge, but he's not focused."

The debate itself is standard issue for well-qualified candidates like Snowbarger and Moore.[1] Long statements, reasonably good questions, artfully crafted answers. It's just August, and the race lacks intensity as yet. The candidates are, more or less, "on message," and the surprises are few. By 1:15 the debate is over, and the Chamber members file out. Moore, Snowbarger, and their aides hang around, putting a bit of spin on their performances for a couple of reporters and some local notables. Esposito retrieves the extra campaign literature, Nevins talks with one last reporter, and the Moore campaign moves back into the Kansas heat.

Moore asks for the cell phone, pokes out a number, and even before easing behind the wheel again, he is chatting up a potential client who needs a defense attorney—a conversation that continues all the way back to the campaign headquarters. The Moore staffers wait for their principal, who is scheduled to make some fund-raising phone calls, and they ponder, once again, how they will implement their campaign plan without the benefit of a full-time candidate.

This is the story of the ultimately successful attempt by Dennis Moore to replace Vince Snowbarger as the congressman from the four-county Kansas Third District, which borders Kansas City, Missouri, to its east. It is also the story of three young campaign professionals: Chris Esposito, Mark Nevins, and Larry Jacob, who had never intentionally spent a moment in the Sunflower State before signing on with the Moore organization. And it is, at least obliquely, the story of a Kansas Republican Party whose divisions made a Moore victory (indeed, a Moore candidacy) a legitimate possibility.

Although there are many useful ways to frame these story lines, the Moore for Congress campaign can be best viewed as a test of two distinct, though related, hypotheses. The first question is, was Vince Snowbarger "too conservative" to represent this congressional district, where moderate Republicans prevailed for almost forty years? The second and more important question (at least for this study) is, can a Democratic campaign run by outside professionals and consultants succeed in winning a historically Republican seat in a thoroughly Republican state? In the end, the evidence and the results answered both queries. One, Republican Vince Snowbarger was too conservative to represent a congressional district in which moderate Republicans had prevailed for almost forty years; and two, outside professionals and consultants can run a Democratic campaign to gain a seat in the House and succeed, even a historically Republican seat in a thoroughly Republican state. But the outcome remained in doubt until well into election night.

These hypotheses are not mere academic exercises. The Moore operatives—Esposito, Nevins, and fund-raiser Larry Jacob—viewed themselves as campaign professionals who could employ "scientific" methods to answer these questions (and, of course, win the election). To them, this Kansas seat was important largely because the data indicated that the race could be won—a good place to put their tactics, expertise, and judgment to the test.

The Kansas Third Congressional District

The Third District does not appear, at first blush, a likely venue for a highly competitive congressional race. Composed of four distinct counties, its core (60 percent of the population) lies in the suburban affluence of Johnson County, whose schools and amenities can match those of the wealthiest areas bounding Atlanta, Minneapolis, or Phoenix. In addition, the district includes the Democratic bastion of Wyandotte County (Kansas City, Kansas), the university community of Lawrence (Douglas County), and small, rural Miami County. The district's population is overwhelmingly white (87 percent), although a third of the residents of Kansas City, Kansas, are either Hispanic or African American.[2] The district is home to myriad corporations and major businesses, many of which compete in national and international markets and help fund some of the nation's best public schools in Johnson County.

The post-1990 reapportionment cost Kansas one House seat, but the outlines of the Third District changed only modestly (the addition of Douglas County, the loss of the smaller Lynn County), although its population rose to more than 600,000 (from 470,000). Between 1985 and 1996, Congresswoman Jan Meyers represented the district; a fiscal conservative who was pro choice, Meyers reflected moderate Republicanism long typical of Johnson and Douglas counties. But the Kansas Republican Party was changing, and nowhere more dramatically than in the fast-growing reaches of southern Johnson County.[3] The traditional Republicanism of a Bob Dole or a Nancy Kassebaum had come under attack, in both the state legislature and the party organization. In 1994 social conservatives gained control of the state party, and state senator Todd Tiahrt upset long-time Democratic congressman Dan Glickman in Wichita's Fourth District. In 1996 Tiahrt won reelection, while conservatives Jim Ryun and Snowbarger emerged triumphant in the Second and Third districts, respectively. At the same time, moderate Bill Graves won the governorship in 1994 by an overwhelming margin over a strong Democratic candidate, Representative Jim Slattery. The very success of Kansas Republicans had encouraged a split in the party along a social-issue cleavage line, and this was fought out with a vengeance in Johnson County. Aside from bitter precinct elections and state legislature primaries, the most public airing of Republican differences came in the 1996 primary election that would choose a candidate to run for Jan Meyer's seat.

The 1996 Republican primary witnessed state representative Vince Snowbarger, the House majority leader, defeat the favored and better-funded mayor of Overland Park, Ed Eilert. Despite his advantage in finances and an endorsement from the highly popular senator Kassebaum, Eilert could not match the grassroots efforts of the social conservatives, who worked diligently on Snowbarger's behalf. Moderate Republicans found themselves on the outside of their party, and Democrats hoped to take advantage of the split by putting forth a strong, well-funded candidate of their own.

Democrat Judy Hancock had run a reasonably competitive race against Jan Meyers in 1994, winning 43 percent of the vote and raising $341,000. She continued her impressive fund-raising in the 1995–96 cycle; in the end, her receipts totaled $840,000—far more than Snowbarger's $466,000. Hancock sought to depict Snowbarger as too conservative for the Third District, but her 45 percent performance seemed to demonstrate severe difficulties for even a well-funded Democrat in this seat. As *The Almanac of American Politics* concluded in its 1998 edition, "Given Hancock's money advantage and the [generally favorable] coverage in the local press, Snowbarger showed considerable strength in winning this seat, and must be considered the favorite to hold it in 1998."[4]

Nevertheless, there were some favorable portents for Democrats as they eyed a contest against the first-term incumbent. First, Bill Clinton had actually carried the district in 1992, and home-state favorite Bob Dole had won by just 8 percent (50 percent to 42 percent) in 1996. Hancock had demonstrated that an attractive Democratic candidate could raise real money, and Snowbarger had proved himself an indifferent fundraiser in both his primary and general campaigns. Democrats in Washington and Kansas would keep close tabs on the size of his campaign war chest in 1997. Finally, Snowbarger had won only 50 percent of the vote in 1996 (two other candidates received the outstanding 5 percent), and moderate Republicans remained lukewarm, at best, in their support. In sum, the hypothesis that Snowbarger was too conservative for the district stood open to further examination.

Dennis Moore: Deciding to Run

In recent years strong politicians—the heavyweights—who could mount a tough challenge to incumbents have tended to vanish from the electoral scene, in most cases leaving the task of defeating sitting congressmen to unknown, untried politicians.

Linda L. Fowler and Robert D. McClure, *Political Ambition*

Few American electoral politicians are as secure as incumbent representatives, who win reelection at a rate of well over 90 percent. The dearth of "quality candidates" to mount a challenge tends to make the lack of competition a self-fulfilling prophecy.[5] Nevertheless, in most congressional districts there exists a handful of individuals who *could* make a strong run; only infrequently, however, does one of these individuals decide to make the sacrifices required to construct a credible effort.[6]

In the Kansas Third, no prospective challenger was stronger than Dennis Moore, a moderate Democrat who had three times won election as Johnson County district attorney, who had narrowly lost a race for state attorney general in 1986, and who had twice won a seat on the board of the Johnson County Community College (an institution with tremendous facilities, almost 20,000 students, and a central place in this affluent suburban community). After Hancock's disappointing defeat in 1996, Democrats in both Kansas and Washington made a series of attempts to interest Moore in running. Absent from serious politics for almost a decade, Moore had many good reasons to dismiss these entreaties. He had built up a strong, financially rewarding criminal practice to the point that running would be a true sacrifice. Moore observed that when he first considered the race, "I thought it might cost me thirty or forty thousand in my law practice in lost opportunities and what I'd have had in income. As it's turned out, I think it's well over $100,000 . . . compared to what I made last year."[7]

Becoming a candidate would not only cut into his income, but it would also open him up to attacks on his defense of some truly despicable characters—including the defendant in a high-profile murder case. Furthermore, Moore had been divorced twice and married three times—and was loathe to expose his present "Brady Bunch"–like family to potential attack.

At the same time, the fifty-two-year-old Moore retained his political ambitions, which had been sidetracked in the 1980s, and he saw a real possibility of contributing a moderate voice to the shrill partisan debates of post-1994 Capitol Hill. Such a motivation fed directly into his campaign style and his campaign theme and message. As the candidate noted, "you continually have to think about . . . how do I get enough people to win this election when I'm in the minority party? That means making a successful appeal to . . . moderate Republicans, and independents, unaffiliated voters . . . as well as Democrats." By August 1997, Moore had tentatively decided to run, but he was a long way from announcing his candidacy.

As Moore felt his way toward becoming a candidate, two key sets of facts were pushing him in that direction. First, in September 1997, the Kansas Democratic Party hired the Cooper and Secrest polling firm to conduct a survey that would demonstrate to Moore that the seat was winnable. Finance director Larry Jacob recounted that "Dennis was in Italy, and he figured he'd get back and the poll would show that he was way behind, that there was no real chance." Instead, the September numbers demonstrated, remarkably enough, that "*Dennis Moore enjoys greater raw popularity than Vince Snowbarger*" and that in a head-to-head trial heat "*Moore holds Snowbarger far below 50 percent* and . . . ties Snowbarger at 39 percent (22 percent undecided)."[8] The Cooper-Secrest report concluded that the Third District represented a great opportunity, one of the best in the country, "*assuming a sufficiently funded campaign warchest.*"[9]

Upon returning to the country and assessing the survey results, Moore took his first—and perhaps most important—step in becoming a congressional candidate. On October 7, 1997, he hired Jacob, a young Trinity College graduate who had cut his teeth on several other campaigns, to begin raising funds for a potential Moore for Congress effort. Jacob took his job seriously as he built on Moore's wide friendship and professional circles in Johnson County.

In less than three months, Jacob had raised almost $84,000, with virtually all of the contributions coming from individual donors. Moore's December 31, 1997, Federal Election Commission report showed $68,837 cash on hand. Snowbarger reported about a thousand dollars less ($67,757) in current accounts. This was the second key piece of information. Moore and his nascent campaign now had an enticing story to tell: Moore was tied with the incumbent in the polls and a bit ahead in fund-raising, even before he had formally announced his candidacy.

Remarkably, the Snowbarger campaign seemed not to view these finance figures with much serious concern. During the next three and a half months, Representative Snowbarger raised less than $34,000, most of which ($21,000) came from political action committees (PACs). Conversely, Jacob and Moore kept on going—raising $143,675 by the April 15 reporting date. As of mid-April 1998, Moore had $184,538 on hand—to Snowbarger's $73,250. By then, Washington political handicappers Charles Cook and Stuart Rothenberg, as well as the Capitol Hill newspaper *Roll Call*, had taken note of the disparity. Moore and his fund-raising operation had put the Kansas Third in play.

"The Pros from Dover" Land in Kansas

In the movie *MASH,* crack surgeons Hawkeye Pierce and Trapper John, the self-proclaimed "pros from Dover," are set down near the Korean front and proceed to practice the medicine that they had learned in the finest American medical schools, all with a sense of humor and an unceasing desire to depart as soon as possible. Especially in retrospect, it is tempting to see Esposito, Jacob, and Nevins in such roles, as they practiced their campaign craft in a Kansas strip mall, a stone's throw from a busy interstate highway and seemingly a million miles from the Washington Beltway.

What Esposito, Jacob, and later Nevins brought to the Moore campaign was a sense of by-the-book professionalism. For them, this was a job—and one that could be accomplished. Jacob noted that he could have gone to San Diego for a campaign and lived in a beach house, "but I was going to lose, even though I'd be getting a tan." The Moore race was different: "I came here [from a Missouri fund-raising job], I looked at the polling, I looked at the district, I looked at Vince Snowbarger . . . and really decided I wanted to take this guy out."

For Esposito, in a year of few competitive races, the Moore-Snowbarger race stood out as a rare chance to make a mark. After all, it was a Republican district, so a win would be a real upset—a feather in his cap. In November 1997, Jacob had called Esposito to alert him to the Moore effort; Esposito got in touch with the would-be candidate and eventually went through a formal interview process, in which six prospective managers were interviewed by both Dennis and Stephene Moore, as well as the candidate's so-called kitchen cabinet, made up of long-time friends and advisers. Jacob remained out of the decision process but was pleased to have his friend land the job and start work in February.

With the hiring of a manager, the campaign began to take shape. Given a reasonable financial base, the campaign pros could put together a plan—one that they came very close to implementing. For Esposito, the plan began with television:

> You want to buy a minimum of 1000 points of TV in the final two–three weeks of the campaign. So you're able to quickly understand what the budget is by looking at the television market. I mean six full weeks of TV in this district is approximately $700,000 . . . at a minimum Larry and I would have known that we need $700,000 to pay for TV in isolation of everything else in the budget . . . payroll isn't counted, fund-raising expenses . . ., communications expenses . . . , research expenses like polling, none of that is counted.

At the start of the campaign, Jacob and Esposito speculated that they could raise $900,000—an amount that would give them, just barely, $700,000 for television.

The Consultants Come on Board

With the hiring of a manager, the campaign could begin to contract for the professional consultants who populate most competitive-seat races. Esposito, Jacob, the Moores, and the "kitchen cabinet" auditioned various pollsters and media consultants, all of whom paid their own way to the Kansas City suburbs to make their pitches. In the end Cooper and Secrest won the polling job, and Seder, Legens, and Hamburger became the media consultants. This proved a strong core team, in that both the campaign professionals and the consultants had some prior working relationships. For Esposito, it meant that he had reliable allies in his bid to control as much of the campaign as he could; he and the D.C. consultants would usually be on the same page—and could present a united front if the candidate and his local advisers should offer differing opinions on tactics and strategy.

Almost immediately the campaign commissioned its first two important expenditures—an opposition research package from Andrew Kennedy of Washington-based MTR Research and an initial baseline poll from Cooper and Secrest. Jacob commented that the opposition research did its job—lots of "bite lines" derived from Snowbarger's past votes, positions, and statements—the raw material for shaping Moore's messages and some of his comparative (or less charitably, negative) ads. Kennedy also compiled a full research work-up on Dennis Moore, so that the campaign could be ready for any attacks. In the end, Jacob concluded, "Kennedy did a great job on Dennis and Vince—we didn't get surprised by anything in the campaign."

The baseline survey also provided a lot of bang for the buck (polling expenses amounted to about $50,000 for the campaign). Many key campaign decisions—on message, target groups—came directly from the April poll, which confirmed the September 1997 findings of an evenly divided Third District electorate. This was the most extensive survey of the campaign (which did not poll again until early October), and it helped set Moore's issue agenda: to save Social Security, provide more support for (public) education, and emphasize public safety, including strongly opposing "concealed carry" laws for handguns. Only reform of health maintenance organizations (HMOs), which emerged later in the year as a major issue, did not flow from the polling results. These messages blended easily with Moore's moderate tendencies to accentuate the overall campaign theme—one of getting things done to improve people's lives.

Two other consultants were hired in the spring—Ed Peavey for direct mail and Bob Doyle for national fund-raising in Washington. Given the campaign's reliance on television and on local fund-raising, these individuals proved less important than the core professional staff and key consultants.

The Campaign Strategy: Organization Meets Message

> *In this district they haven't elected a Democrat in the last forty years. And the local view is because we haven't had the right candidate talking about the right ideas. That's a very naive view. I mean the reality is you haven't had a good candidate that's run an aggressive campaign, that's had money for television, and has had a strong message to compete against an incumbent. Period.*
>
> Campaign Manager Chris Esposito

In the wake of the 1998 Third District race, Snowbarger opined that the Moore strategy came straight from the Democratic National Committee's playbook. The DNC was not the direct source, but the congressman had a point, one with which the Moore campaign professionals would have readily agreed. Indeed, the Snowbarger observation identifies the basis of the campaign's second belief: that outside professionals can come to virtually any competitive district and organize a winning campaign. Esposito offered the basic mantra: "There is a proven, tested historical formula for winning elections. It's a strong candidate, . . . it's good fund-raising, it's good polling, and it's strong organization, . . . and it's a message." All the pros, Esposito, Jacob, and later, Nevins, saw Moore as a strong candidate who personified the raw material that could support the "scientific" campaign they sought to run. Armed with a good candidate, the pros from Dover then viewed their job as adapting the basic plan to the Third District and executing it to a tee.

The generic strategy was fleshed out by an emphasis on making sure the Moore candidacy reached the last six weeks of the campaign in a position to win. That meant raising enough money for adequate mass-market television and establishing a thorough get-out-the-vote (GOTV) effort. This is congressional campaigning 101, but that makes it no less true. The baseline poll also provided two elements of the overall strategy in helping frame, first, the core message (Social Security, education, health, public safety) and, second, the weaknesses in the Snowbarger record (Social Security, the environment, concealed carry of handguns, and education).

As the initial messages were being crafted, Esposito laid out the basic campaign organization, which also reflected the modification of a generic plan. The basic organization consisted of (another Esposito mantra): overall administration, including relations with parties and other groups; fund-raising; communication, both paid and free; research (including opposition, defensive, and ongoing); and field, both securing the electoral base and maximizing pro-Moore turnout. Again, there are no surprises, but the basic outlines were clear; and creating the organization—"expanding like an accordion" as the election neared, in Esposito's words—remained the continuing problem to be solved.

The Hidden Campaign: Fund-Raising and Questions of Control (May to July)

After the April survey, the Moore campaign—the Moores, Esposito, Jacob, and several members of the kitchen cabinet—went on a retreat to establish the core strategy for the final five months of the race. The pros already knew what they wanted to do, but campaigns are about control, and that issue had not been decided—indeed, it may not have been completely decided by the election. Approximately twenty-five years older than Esposito, Moore was a successful lawyer who got things done as a district attorney and in private practice; moreover, he had won election five times in Johnson County. "He served the public well," Esposito noted. "He's very demanding, very impatient. There are fundamental components of a campaign that are incompatible with his personality. He hates to wait for anything, and in a campaign you have to wait for certain things." Simply put, the campaign pros saw their boss as a "control freak" who could not realistically hope to control the campaign.

At the same time, Esposito's role was to maintain as much control as possible over the campaign. That might mean fighting it out over advertising or deciding not to buy cable television instead of major market spots, but more than anything, for Esposito, it meant getting everyone on the campaign to perform their particular tasks. This was the ultimate control. Esposito observed:

> My job is to keep people focused. . . . I never want Larry making phone calls to the field until the final three to five days, because if he's making calls to volunteers, he's not raising money . . . I guess my job really boils down to the nine times a day Dennis will come to me . . . with ten ideas probably in a day. Nine of them will have some merit, but will not be relevant to our campaign plan. So I need to say, good idea, but we don't have time to execute that, here's why we need to stay focused.

Between April and August, the campaign experienced a sporadic series of struggles for control. The candidate never completely gave in, but Esposito did manage to keep him and the campaign reasonably well focused, especially in the wake of the May campaign retreat. In a sense, Dennis Moore needed some control over his own affairs, and practicing law gave him that—especially as he kept swimming in a sea of political uncertainty during the hot Kansas summer. It was truly difficult to demonstrate much progress, even though Moore spent occasional hours during the week and lots of weekends making public appearances—all with no clear measure of any impact.

Fund-raising was different. One of the first things a visitor noticed in the Moore headquarters was a large sheet of white paper that tallied how much money had been raised to date. This was Larry Jacob's domain, and he was relentless. If Esposito provided the focus, it was because he remained completely confident that Jacob—and Moore, with Jacob's continual prodding—could raise enough money to carry out the campaign plan.

In addition, fund-raising could be easily measured. The white sheet told the story, day by day. Jacob had begun raising money in earnest only two years earlier, in a New Hampshire campaign in which he worked his way into directing the finance operation. The keys, Jacob argued, were "setting up the systems . . . and kissing a bunch of ass." The systems were important—the callbacks, the follow-ups, the right people to ask for the right amounts. And some sucking up has never hurt a fund-raiser either. But Jacob's true talent came in his utter persistence, in pushing himself and his staff and in cajoling as much fund-raising from the candidate as he possibly could. Like almost all candidates, Moore despised fund-raising: "I absolutely hate asking people for money. And I'd rather ask strangers than my friends." Few strangers write $1,000 checks to Democratic challengers in Republican districts. So Jacob's first and most important targets were Moore's friends, especially in the legal community. Then came Stephene Moore's friends, many of whom were doctors, Jacob noted, and "that's a group that had probably never given to a guy like Dennis, or to anyone at all." Former Senate candidate Jill Docking provided her list of maxed-out ($1,000 per campaign) contributors, which helped. Less useful were the lists provided by former representative Jim Slattery, the state Democratic Party, and Kansas Insurance Commissioner Kathleen Sebelius, which included lots of overlapping names.

And what of Judy Hancock, the 1994 and 1996 Democratic candidate, who had raised $840,000 in 1996? "We got 'in-kinded' her list from a former staffer and we used it early on," Jacob recounted, "but a couple of her friends got called and complained, so we stopped right away."

Although the lists were important, what counted most, perhaps, was Moore's willingness to get on the phone. In 1986 during Moore's statewide attorney general race, his campaign raised $450,000, and Moore never had to make a call. As Jacob pointed out, once the databases are set up, showing whom to call or call back, "then it's [a matter of] calling them. Dennis averaged ten-to-twelve hours a week of calling and [even so] raised the kind of money he did. . . . That says something about his history here with voters." Moore simply could not make calls for more than two or three hours a day, but Jacob was persistent to a fault, and Esposito made more than his share of calls for the campaign. Then Jacob and his assistants followed up, both with individuals and labor union personnel. And the checks kept coming in.

Between April 15 and July 15, the Moore campaign raised $166,725—almost $2,000 a day. A new pattern in giving was beginning to emerge. Individuals still gave most of the money ($91,320), but interest groups—and especially labor—were climbing on board with substantial contributions—almost $75,000. Local unions must decide to back a candidate before the national organizations will write large checks. "Without local support, it's very rare that we ever see national support," Jacob pointed out, adding, "We've had luck with local support."[10] Jacob knew, however, that it had little to do with luck and everything to do with persistence. "For each of those union contributions," he stated, "I'll bet I made thirty to forty phone calls. I'd call and they'd say, 'Oh, it's you again.' Finally, we wore them down."

A few blocks away, the Snowbarger camp was finally starting to raise some serious money. Indeed, in the April–July period, the Snowbarger campaign pulled in a bit more than the Moore organization ($172,258, with $102,057 coming from individuals and $70,201 from PACs and other committees). Remarkably, Moore outraised the incumbent in funding from groups, and he retained his substantial advantage in cash on hand ($254,538 to $155,562). If fund-raising in American politics represents the "wealth primary," Moore stood $100,000 ahead of Snowbarger as of July 15—less than four months before election day.

With no data from polls and only modest newspaper coverage, the campaign could at least take the measure of its bank account—an indicator that could give both the candidate and the pros from Dover a bit of satisfaction. Still, the pros were working for a candidate who continued to practice law almost full time. "A full-time attorney and a part-time candidate," according to one staffer. If Jacob had pressured Moore into becoming a decent fund-raiser, he and Esposito could not move him into adopting the candidate role as his only job. The battle for control was not over yet.

Defining Dennis Moore (August)

Kansas primary elections are held in the sunny, dusty days of early August, a date that almost ensures low turnout and modest interest in all but the most hotly contested campaigns. Moore did have a primary opponent—Dan Dana, a relatively unknown employment mediator. Representative Snowbarger, with an uncontested race and a shortage of cash, was expected to sit on the sidelines and keep an eye on the Democratic race. The Moore campaign anticipated no trouble in defeating Dana; virtually no resources were directed at the primary, except for an increase in personal appearances by the candidate. Indeed, Moore won the primary election with 74 percent of the vote, and he honed his set of messages, initially crafted in the spring.

The Kansas primary did affect the Third District congressional campaign, however, in two ways, both of which worked to the disadvantage of Snowbarger. First, the incumbent got caught in the middle of a bitter internal fight between the social conservative and moderate factions of the state Republican Party. Conservative David Miller (from Eudora, a Third District town) had resigned the GOP party chairmanship to run in the gubernatorial primary against popular moderate incumbent Bill Graves, in a race that attracted national attention. Snowbarger, a conservative who had served as majority leader of the Kansas House under Graves, was criticized for not endorsing Miller and working for him.[11] Subsequently, for the remainder of the campaign, Miller disappeared from the Kansas political scene after his overwhelming (73 percent to 27 percent) defeat in the primary. At the time, Snowbarger did not seem to suffer from the Graves victory; after all, he would have an incredibly popular governor at the top of the ticket. In November, Graves did come through, winning the election with 73 percent of the statewide vote, and incumbent Republican Senator Sam Brownback won reelection in a similar landslide. But Snowbarger had to fight against losing his own moderate Republican supporters, many of whom would be tempted to vote for the Graves-Moore combination. Indeed, of November's Graves-Moore voters, fully 77 percent held a negative view of the incumbent.

Although the gubernatorial primary did not seem, at first glance, to hurt Snowbarger, it did set the stage for a lack of enthusiasm among both moderate Republicans (who foresaw a general election sweep) and conservatives (who reacted badly to Miller's trouncing). Much like Moore, Snowbarger would have to create his own excitement and produce his own turnout, even in the ordinarily Republican environs of the Johnson County suburbs.

If Snowbarger was placed in a no-win situation by the Graves-Miller contest, he was his own worst enemy in the second important episode of the Kansas primary. To the astonishment of almost everyone, the Snowbarger campaign mailed out a series of three postcards that sought to affect results in the *Democratic* primary. These cards, sent to Democrats and independents, compared Snowbarger, Moore, and Dana on three specific questions, with the final mailing asking: "Which of these candidates for Congress makes a living defending murderers, rapists, drug dealers, and child molesters?" The answer, of course, was Moore, and the mailings, which cost approximately $45,000, were directly attributed to the Snowbarger for Congress campaign.

The tactical reasoning behind these postcards was murky at best, but the result was to take a routine primary and create both news and an outpouring of anti-Snowbarger editorial opinion.[12] Beyond the editorials, which called the mailings a "smear campaign," the Snowbarger postcards redounded to the Moore campaign's benefit in two distinct ways.[13] First, they demonstrated that Snowbarger truly was worried about the Moore challenge, despite the incumbent's seemingly relaxed attitude toward the race. For those in the Moore organization, this was one more concrete indicator they could place before potential contributors and Washington opinion shapers. Second, the early attacks on Moore as a defense attorney, and their lack of impact, demonstrated to his campaign that the candidate could respond effectively to charges that he represented unsavory individuals. In fact, one of Moore's most effective advertisements played directly off this theme—that he had fought hard for his clients and that he would do the same for the citizens of the Third District. In the end, Moore's profession worked—through his fund-raising contacts and his district attorney credentials—to his advantage, despite his criminal defense practice.

Early August brought more than the Kansas primary and its shaping of Moore's image in the Third District. It also marked the arrival of press secretary Nevins, the campaign's third outside professional. Nevins, a veteran of Senator Dianne Feinstein's staff and a graduate of the George Washington School of Political Management, proved a valuable asset to the campaign, as he removed the press relations responsibility from Esposito's portfolio. Nevins saw real opportunities in the Kansas City media market, despite some misgivings about moving to the middle of the country:

> I had some serious concerns . . . I lived in Los Angeles, I lived in Washington D.C., I had some concerns about coming to Kansas, frankly. But for the most part this is a good place to be. I mean I work on press, so it's a good media market, the Kansas City market. It's big enough where it's a challenge, there are four TV stations, plenty of radio, several different newspapers to work with, but small enough that they won't just tune you out. There is not so much going on around here that they won't pay attention to the campaign, so from a purely personal perspective on working with

> the press it's been a good place to be. . . . This is a close race, it may be one of four or five races in the country that are this close, for us personally [the pros from Dover] it's a huge resume builder.

Coming on board last, with just three months to go in the campaign, Nevins had to learn how to work with his two control-oriented bosses—Moore and Esposito. With Esposito, the professional campaign manager, the transition seemed to go smoothly; after all, Nevins's presence enhanced his ability to focus on running the overall campaign. But the Nevins-Moore relationship took longer to work out, in that the new press secretary was not from Kansas and one more person whose job it was to tell the candidate what to do. The Moore-Nevins bond grew stronger all through the campaign, and by the end, Nevins had skillfully orchestrated the linkages between free and paid media. Moreover, he had earned Moore's trust.

Planning the Air Wars: The Pros Take Charge (September)

Central to the campaign plan was the decision to go on television early (mid-September) and stay on through the election—six weeks of significant television buys in a market whose coverage extended to parts of four congressional districts. Advertising was not cheap, but it did get the job done—the entire Third District watched Kansas City television. As the summer progressed, Larry Jacob and Dennis Moore had done their fundraising jobs—the campaign had the resources to begin its television buys in early September. Esposito recounted:

> One of the key decisions . . . was to get on TV early. . . . raise a lot of money early so that we'd be in a position . . . to start buying television. And you're always faced with two ways to buy. You can buy week six which is September 21, or you can buy back from election day, week one and week two. We decided to spend approximately $236,000 the day after Labor Day and buy week one from election day back and then buy week two. When we did that, the rates were cheaper than [they would be in October]. And we saved a substantial amount of money, which then allowed us to buy week six, then we were able to buy week five, then we were able to buy week four, then buy week three. . . . Something we didn't assume was that our opponent wouldn't raise enough money early to get on

> TV at the same time. . . . We were on the air for two and a half weeks, and he was nowhere on the air. That is a major advantage for us. Particularly a challenger versus an incumbent. It's very rare that a challenger outraises an incumbent, and it's extremely rare to run more television ads than an incumbent.

Buying early had another benefit—at least in the eyes of the Moore professionals. Jacob saw a competitive advantage in this tactic. He noted, "We're not only competing against Vince Snowbarger, we're competing against the Republican National Committee . . . [and] the Senate campaign [Bond-Nixon] next door in Missouri." In the end, better placement meant more viewers, including the campaign staff and the candidate. This was especially important for Moore, who was "pumped up" throughout the last weeks of the campaign by seeing his commercials or getting an endorsement or having a lively crowd response. For the pros from Dover, having an enthusiastic, happy candidate made their jobs a bit easier and a lot more enjoyable.

Once solving the problem of buying air time, the campaign still had to address the questions of ad content and presentation. Enter the Washington firm of Seder, Legens, and Hamburger, which would produce the advertisements. The consultants from this firm, along with the Cooper and Secrest polling organization, had talked at length with Moore and his staff in terms of developing themes and message, and Martin Hamburger had come to Kansas on a couple of occasions, including a trip to organize Moore's candidacy announcement in April. The consultants and staff also talked in frequent one-on-one conversations and in regularly scheduled conference calls.

By September 1, the rough footage for the campaign commercials was in the can; although Moore would spend one more day (in Washington) shooting some additional footage, the raw material for the seven advertisements that would eventually run had been produced. And on September 14, Cooper and Secrest conducted two focus groups in Overland Park to assess the mood of the electorate (including attitudes toward Bill Clinton in the wake of his August 17 admission of "improper relations" with Monica Lewinsky), reactions to Moore's core messages, and the impact of ten prospective Moore television ads.

The focus group research accomplished several things for the Moore campaign. The two groups of participants (one all men, the other all women) generally confirmed why Moore—with his experience and low levels of partisanship—was a strong candidate and why he could defeat Snowbarger. Furthermore, the April survey findings on key issues continued to hold, and the consultants' report noted, with an almost audible sigh of relief, that the Clinton scandals and the "family values" catchphrase were not at the front of voters' minds.

One significant finding was that men and women viewed the race, candidates, and issues in very different ways. Although Moore would mute his partisanship on the air, the consultants urged him to pitch his ads to men and women with distinct, if overlapping, messages. This approach was exploited throughout the campaign and started with the "introductory" Moore ad that ran in late September. Daytime audiences (disproportionately female) saw a version of the ad that emphasized Moore's support of a women's shelter, while evening ads emphasized his crime-fighting record as district attorney. The most important gender gap implications for campaign came on the "public safety" front, where consultants Dawn Legens and Hamburger created a powerful, highly emotional antigun ad, which the Moore professionals kept in reserve until the last few days of the campaign.

Finally, on one key issue—Social Security—the focus groups demonstrated the continuing importance of the issue, as well as the need for Moore, or any candidate, not just to say that he would "save" it but to inspire confidence that Social Security indeed could be saved. The campaign's opposition research paid off, as it came up with a key Snowbarger quotation, which was that he might consider a "phase-out" of Social Security. Far more than any other single Snowbarger statement, this one came back to haunt the incumbent—even though he tried to deflect the Moore attacks with a counteradvertisement.

Although the candidate and his kitchen cabinet of friends and supporters (including loyal and reasonably sophisticated individuals) reviewed the ads and offered their views on voice-overs, the campaign pros and the consultants, working in tandem, had achieved most of the control that they had sought from the start of the campaign. Ironically, the person most responsible for this ceding of power was the candidate himself. Despite his apparent desire for day-to-day control and flashes of impatience, sometimes laced with temper, Moore had consciously hired outside professionals to run virtually every aspect of his campaign; intellectually, if not emotionally, he was willing to hand over most of the organizational control to his professional staff and consultants. Moore recounted, "When my kitchen cabinet was interviewing different applicants for the position of campaign manager, at one point Chris [Esposito] told me I would have three vetoes during the campaign at different times and after that, all the decisions would be his. I told him then, veto, veto, veto, to get it out of the way. And then I said to get on with it."

As the campaign progressed, however, Moore said no—or tried to—much more often than three times, but on the big decisions he deferred, even when, at the time, he was noticeably unhappy about the choice at hand.

Moore could feel at ease with his staff and consultants because, by September, they had done what they said they would—that is, through fund-raising and media buys, placed him in a position to unseat the incumbent. And the pros from Dover knew they had won the war over control—not just because they had raised enough money, but because they had done their jobs in the Kansas context. Larry Jacob put it best:

> The phrase all three of us have heard nonstop since we've been here is: "You're not from around here, you don't know how it is here." I've been in eight states since I graduated from college and I've heard the same thing everywhere I went and you know what? It's been exactly the same. You have people who produce and people who don't. You have candidates that melt down and candidates that melt down more . . . People tell me you're not going to be able to do this, you're not going to be able to do that. That nobody around here has money. . . . *I know the donors of the 3rd District better than probably anybody in this district* does because nobody is paid to sit there eighteen hours a day and study this stuff and I've done it for thirteen months. *Chris knows the voters here better* . . . because nobody in this district has sat down and studied the voting patterns . . . as much as Chris has. And that's what they don't get. They think: we're not from here, we don't get it. *We do get it, but we get it from a more objective point of view.* And we're then able to take that kind of data and apply it to what we need to do to win. And that's I think the fundamental tension between staff and candidates and people surrounding the candidate. Dennis is an attorney . . . but I would never walk into his law practice and say, "Dennis, you are not doing this right because I saw this somewhere else," whereas people feel completely comfortable doing that in our career.

That struggle for control was—more or less—over. The poll numbers (at least as of early October) and the finance figures had put it behind them. Moreover, the organization for the final "ground war" was well on its way to coming together, and finally the candidate had sharply reduced his time commitments to his law practice. For the last six weeks of the campaign, the pros from Dover would have what they had long desired—a full-time, highly motivated candidate.

The Moore campaign professionals' interim success also gave them some time to mollify one other important organization—the national party. The Democratic Congressional Campaign Committee (DCCC) can overwhelm a candidate's organization with its monitoring, both from field operatives and the Washington staff. Although Esposito and the other pros talked regularly with DCCC personnel, they could demonstrate to them that the campaign was not in need of any extra help, aside from whatever funds could be directed toward the Kansas Third. The manager observed that the DCCC "has tried to provide resources to us, money, people, advice, etc. But they haven't tried to manage this campaign by any stretch of the imagination." So the Moore organization had insulated itself from another source of intervention—as well intended as the proposed help might have been.

This stage of the race ended on an upbeat but cautionary note. First, Cooper and Secrest conducted its initial tracking poll in early October (6–7), and the results were heartening if not totally positive. The Moore ads had been up for two weeks, with no Snowbarger response, and the head-to-head results continued to show the two candidates in a dead heat. That was not necessarily encouraging, but it was not bad news, since the survey demonstrated how difficult the political context had become for Moore. The Cooper-Secrest narrative summarized: "The face of this electorate has literally changed (thank you, Mr. President) with Democrats simply 'opting out' for the time being . . . [And Governor] Graves could not be more dominant."[14] Across the Third District fewer voters in every county were identifying themselves as Democrats, and the undecideds were disproportionately Republican and independent.

At the same time, Snowbarger remained extraordinarily weak for an incumbent one month from the general election. In many ways, Moore's efforts had kept the race about where it had been in April—although the national political landscape had changed considerably since then. The Clinton scandal had few first-order effects in the Third District, but it had caused the voters to view the race in more partisan terms, and that was bad news for any Democrat, even an attractive candidate with plenty of money for television exposure.

The survey results suggested various minor modifications in tactics, but the overall strategy remained in place—to hit Snowbarger on his weak points (for example, Social Security) and to prepare for a massive ground-war effort to get Moore voters to the polls. Although "almost certain voters" gave Snowbarger a five-point advantage, the "probable" voters (10 percent of the electorate) chose Moore by a two-to-one margin (46 percent to 23 percent). As Cooper and Secrest concluded, "Turnout matters . . . a lot."[15]

Into the highly competitive, increasingly Republican context came the initial pro-Snowbarger ads, not from the incumbent's campaign but from the Republican National Committee, the first of a series of its extensive media buys that would run through the general election. The RNC ad specifically questioned Moore's record of being tough on crime. Most important, it demonstrated that the national GOP was not going to let Snowbarger go down without a real fight, especially in an election year that included no more than twenty or so truly competitive races by early October and only a handful of endangered Republican incumbents. The battle had truly been joined.

The Visible Race Intensifies: Air Wars, Free Media, and Outside Money (October)

> *Dennis Moore looked into the camera and played his ace. "I'll vote to use the entire budget surplus to save Social Security. . . . Vince Snowbarger opposes this plan, and he actually said that we should, quote, phase it out.". . . It is the oldest weapon in the Democratic arsenal, an appeal to one of the party's most faithful constituencies, but executed with a 1998 twist.*
>
> Howard Kurtz, *Washington Post,* October 28, 1998

> *[Dennis,] you needed a wedge issue, something to scare people, especially those senior citizens. Get them off their duffs and into the polls. And by golly, Social Security is always a handy club.*
>
> Steve Kraske, *Kansas City Star,* November 7, 1998

There were, to be sure, other issues and other advertisements as the Third District race entered its final month, but Social Security, that old reliable, was on the top of Moore's agenda—for two, related reasons. First, his early October tracking poll had demonstrated continuing power, and Representative Snowbarger had stated on the record that Social Security might possibly be phased out, at least for some portion of the population. During the entire campaign, the candidate, the pros from Dover, and the media consultants capitalized on that phrase; as political reporter Steve Kraske noted in a bitter postelection column, this was not necessarily Moore's finest hour as a responsible citizen-candidate. But for the Moore campaign, including the candidate, the Social Security issue was a no brainer: it worked for Democrats generally, and it worked specifically against the incumbent in this race, given his unfortunate statement.

Indeed, Moore's paid media and his free (or earned) media strategies coalesced around the Social Security issues, as they did on public safety (with a visit by gun control advocate Sarah Brady) and education (with a visit by Secretary of Education Richard Riley). But these topics paled before the Social Security albatross that the Moore campaign kept hanging around Snowbarger's neck. Aside from running advertisements that continually mentioned "saving" Social Security, Moore used the "phase-out" quotation in almost every stump speech and debate. This attack culminated in the last debate of the campaign at Johnson County Community College—an otherwise indecisive October 18 encounter that was televised throughout the district.

Although the format called for a no-holds-barred "Lincoln-Douglas" debate in which the candidates would question each other, the confrontation was little more than a practiced repetition of set-pieces. Still, Snowbarger demonstrated the extent to which the Social Security issue had crippled him—and his essential inability to respond effectively. After the usual Moore attack, the incumbent admitted that he had said he might look at phasing out the program, and he went on to scold Moore for misrepresenting his overall position. Moore's professionals immediately seized this opportunity. The Moore campaign had neither the time nor resources to cut a new Social Security television ad, but the media consultants did a quick turnaround on a radio advertisement that played extensively during the last ten days of the campaign. Thus, on the air, Snowbarger could be heard admitting to his "phase-out" statement. In no way did this bit of tactics decide the election, but it demonstrated the ability of the Moore organization to stay on a message and tweak its content from the beginning of the campaign to the end.

In addition, the initial outside money to be spent on advertising came from organized labor, as the AFL-CIO spent a modest amount ($500,000 in twenty congressional districts, including the Kansas Third) in late September to link a Republican tax-cut proposal to the shortfall faced by the Social Security program. Such spending did not approach the hundreds of thousands spent in 1996 by labor and other outside groups in the Third District, but it did reinforce one of Moore's core messages.

By mid-October, the Moore-Snowbarger air wars had escalated to the point that each campaign was spending approximately $100,000 a week on Kansas City television. In addition, the Republican National Committee continued to run its anti-Moore ads. Labor had not returned to television, but it had begun to send extensive mailings to its members and lend its weight to an impressive GOTV effort.

The Advertising Strategy

The Moore and Snowbarger advertisements were a study in contrasts; the incumbent produced only three ads, and all attacked Moore. Snowbarger never appeared in any of his own ads, as opposed to Moore, who came across to his focus groups as an effective advocate. In a telling quip, Snowbarger commented, "I've got a face made for radio."[16] By not appearing in his own spots, Snowbarger gave Moore the chance to define him—and the challenger's campaign took full advantage. Nor did Snowbarger have much luck with the advertisements produced by his campaign. Not only did they fail to frame the incumbent in a positive light, but one ad generated negative free media coverage. The *Kansas City Star* series on the race included an article, with a front-page, above-the-fold color picture, that depicted the Snowbarger media consultants shooting a Social Security ad in which an elderly Washington-based actress repeatedly flubbed her lines and mispronounced Snowbarger's name but eventually stated her intention to vote for Vince Snowbarger. The Moore campaign could scarcely control its glee when the article ran, four days before the election.

The footage for the Moore commercials—shot in Kansas in late August, with one extra day (October 3) in Washington—offered the consultants a wide range of options in crafting individual ads. The core themes—Moore's moderation and experience as a prosecutor, Social Security, public safety, HMO reform—were emphasized. Focus groups impressed on the consultants that Moore was his own best spokesperson when he addressed the camera directly, much as he had done with juries for more than twenty years. The consultants and campaign pros were completely dispassionate about advertising tone and subject matter. Their job was to win an election, and as long as the truth was not completely violated, any subject, any presentation was fair game, as long as it worked.

The key illustration of this attitude was an antigun–public safety ad that Seder, Legens, and Hamburger had produced in early September; its message was communicated by a seedy looking gunman prowling the outside of a playground—a "this could happen here" theme that ostensibly related to Snowbarger's votes and positions on gun control. This ad worked with women in the focus group, and there was no question that the pros intended to use the commercial near the very end of the campaign, but only, they decided, during the daytime hours. In response to a BBC television producer's questions, as part of a documentary on the campaign, Nevins, Esposito, and Jacob demonstrated how much they were all on the same page when it came to media strategy.

Producer: You were pressuring the candidate to go negative?

Nevins: There is no such thing as negative, because you can only compare and contrast. . . . It has to be based on fact. . . . [Even] the gun ad is about Vince Snowbarger's public record and that ad is entirely based in fact.

Producer: But when you wrap it up . . . in your gun ad, people would say that was not exactly negative, but was very emotional.

Esposito: They're wrong. I mean that ad is about Vince Snowbarger's public record and that ad is entirely based in fact and if it's negative that's not our problem.

Producer: But Vince Snowbarger didn't send a guy with a gun into a playground.

Esposito: Well, he voted for laws that would have allowed it.

Nevins: It could have happened because of votes he cast.

Esposito: I mean we're framing it for the public.

Producer: Was it a controversial decision to use that ad?

Nevins: Not for me.

Jacob: I didn't think it went far enough.

Esposito: Well, yes and no. . . . there was broad agreement that the gun ad was effective. There was some disagreement—more local-based versus the three of us—that it should be highly charged, very emotional with visuals and sound effects. And in the end the good guys [the pros from Dover] won. The bottom line is we always

> knew we would use this ad, but the question was what was the right time and that gets back to your campaign plan. We knew . . . we still needed to attack. And when we looked at one of our targets, women, we knew that this ad was particularly powerful with them. We decided to make some final changes and put it on the air.

Moore and the kitchen cabinet often resisted going for the jugular, but their attitudes, as with the gun ad, changed during the campaign, often in response to Snowbarger's negativism, real and perceived (and framed for the rest of the campaign by the pros). For instance, when House Minority Leader Dick Armey (R-Tex.) came to Kansas for a Snowbarger event, Nevins drafted a press release, "Dick Armey and Vince Snowbarger: The Extreme Team." Moore felt uncomfortable with the "name-calling," so Nevins dropped the "extreme" references. Subsequently, the Snowbarger campaign produced an ad that linked—far more dubiously than the Armey-Snowbarger combo—Moore to Ted Kennedy, with the obligatory black-and-white photo of an overweight Kennedy and the tag line of "the extreme team." With such "I-told-you-so" evidence, Nevins continued to lobby for being as tough as possible, but observed that "it took until the last two weeks of the campaign . . . to get Dennis on board."

To leaven the comparative/negative ads, Hamburger, Legens, and the campaign staff produced a purely positive, even "corny," commercial that stood distinct from the contrast ads that dominated the campaign's repertoire and the generally negative ads that appeared on Kansas City television. This piece, entitled "Guitar Lessons," drew on Moore's genuine talents as an amateur guitarist-singer.[17] Hamburger recounted how he and the Moore pros had desired to do something with Moore as a musician and finally wrote a script over lunch on the last day of shooting in Kansas. "We actually had to talk Dennis into doing the ad. He said he didn't want to look foolish." In the ad, Moore performs a few different types of guitar licks and then ends with the tag line on "pickin'"—that voters should pick him to go to Congress. Although some focus group participants and many viewers considered "Guitar Lessons" hokey, it served as a valuable counterpoint to the tougher Moore commercials, especially the gun advertisement, in the last few days of the campaign. Furthermore, the ad was both an artistic triumph—winning a postcampaign award—and a political success, with 10 percent of Moore's voters spontaneously mentioning the ad in a postelection survey.

In sum, the Moore campaign produced enough ads, with enough themes, and enough different kinds of delivery, to have a wide selection of offerings to modify and run over the important late October period, when the campaign was spending at least $133,000 a week on Kansas City television (1,000 points of advertising exposure a week). And the campaign could respond effectively to the findings of its second tracking poll, conducted October 24 and 25, fewer than ten days before election day. Cash on hand was adequate to add substantial cable television buys in Lawrence (where some of the audience watched Topeka stations); even though the pros found cable not especially significant, they had the means and the products to extend their reach over the last ten days of the campaign. Overall, the air wars were being conducted according to the campaign plan, but this only softened up the district for the ground war of the final days—where the election outcome was likely to be determined.

Independent Expenditures: Dogs That Don't Bark, At Least Not on Television

The 1996 Third District campaign witnessed the wholesale purchase of television time by outside groups. The Hancock-Snowbarger race was one of the thirty to forty top targets of labor's $35 million effort (about $22 million was spent on media), and the shadowy Triad Management firm spent $287,000 on behalf of the Snowbarger campaign.[18] Both Democratic and Republican party entities (state and national) purchased advertising time. The resulting cacophony meant that no one could get much of a handle on what source said what; the labor spending was notably unsuccessful in moving the Third District electorate toward Judy Hancock's candidacy; and the spending on all sides was viewed as excessive. Still, most observers braced themselves for repeat performances, given the small number of competitive races across the country.

In 1998, however, not much independent spending went for media. After labor's bit of early advertising, it focused on ground war tactics. Triad never surfaced, in part, perhaps, because of a bizarre advertisement, broadcast widely in Kansas, that attacked Koch Industries and Triad, its alleged conduit for independent funding. The Sierra Club did purchase some radio, but the only major outside funds to be spent for broadcast advertising came from the Republican National Committee. Estimates vary widely as to the amount of RNC expenditures, but it spent at least $450,000 on advertising, along with additional funds on mailings and automated phone calls, one of which featured a recorded message from Bob Dole. The RNC ads, which attacked Moore as soft on crime, were in sync with the basic Snowbarger message. In the end, independent expenditures did not muddy the waters of a Moore-Snowbarger debate that did allow, generally speaking, voters to distinguish between the two candidates.

For the Moore campaign, this was a real bonus. It could shape its messages within a "one-on-one" context, not having to worry about extraneous messages (for or against Moore), and maintain as much control as possible in a competitive campaign. If the overall partisan tendencies of the district worked against the Moore candidacy, at least the campaign could communicate a consistent set of messages, more or less according to plan.

Earned Media: The Politics of Endorsements

The Third District has several daily papers, most notably the *Kansas City Star* and a major set of suburban weeklies (the *Sun* chain). Neither political scientists nor campaign professionals ordinarily give much weight to endorsements, yet candidates and campaigns (Moore's included) work hard to obtain the nod from the major papers. Without question, endorsements from both the *Sun* and the *Star* were up for grabs in 1998. To make a long story short, Moore won both, with the *Sun*'s coming on October 14 and the *Star's* on October 28. Although the campaign reprinted the respective editorials (an edited version for the not totally positive *Star*) and distributed them widely, the principal advantages of the endorsements were to energize the campaign, and especially Moore, and to include the fact of the endorsements in the last week's television advertising.

The *Sun* endorsement was also important because its author, publisher Steve Rose, spoke directly to a key Moore constituency—Republican moderates. Rose tied his dissatisfaction with Snowbarger directly to the disastrous gubernatorial-primary candidacy of conservative David Miller. For the most part, the issues of the social conservatives and the religious right, with the partial exception of the concealed carry of handguns, were absent from the campaign debate, but Rose placed them front and center—emphasizing Moore's superiority in terms of the "American values that include tolerance, respect, and compassion."[19]

How many votes were these endorsements worth? Relatively few in all probability, but they surely gave an emotional boost to Moore and his troops, and in the last two weeks of the campaign, that counted for a lot.

The End Game: Grinding It Out on the Ground

> *We recommend pursuing all viable options for maximizing Democratic turnout (phones/mail). You have done virtually everything you can do to prepare for the final week and for victory. If Hurricane Mitch stays away, you have as good a chance at victory as does Snowbarger, something few challengers can say. Be proud.*
>
> Cooper and Secrest, "Findings," October 24–25 survey

So began the final week of the Moore campaign. Although there was a bit of last-minute tinkering on television ads, including the gun spot, attention shifted, as was long anticipated, to the ground war—getting out the vote. Hurricane Mitch did not hit land-locked Kansas, but the weather was truly terrible for the last few days of the race, and low turnout remained a great concern for the Moore campaign in a district in which Republicans traditionally succeed in getting out the vote.

Off-year elections draw low levels of voter interest, of course, and Kansas politics in 1998 did little to attract much attention. There was no major competitive statewide race, nor were there any truly "hot" issues in a year of economic satisfaction and general disaffection with politics. For Moore to win, his organization, the Democratic Party, and their allies (labor, environmentalists) would simply have to obtain a disproportionately high level of turnout from Democrats, independents, and cross-over Republicans.

The Moore campaign's professionals, consultants, and DCCC field operatives all understood the importance of getting out the vote in any close race, and especially in a district where the natural Republican constituencies—most notably pro life forces and evangelical Right churches—effectively turned out their own, with only modest help from individual candidates. In June, the Moore organization hired state senator Chris Steineger, from Kansas City, Kansas (Wyandotte County), as its field director. With the need for a huge turnout from this heavily Democratic county, Steineger's appointment made a lot of sense. His ties to organized labor, popular Wyandotte chief executive Carol Marinovich, and the party organization would help with an integrated effort on behalf of Moore—whose race represented the only major contest on the ballot. Steineger himself did not face a reelection contest.

The Moore campaign, with its overwhelming commitment to paid media, could not provide for the bulk of the GOTV effort. Rather, the Democratic Party and the local labor movement would have to do the heavy lifting. Such a prospect could simply not be reassuring to Moore. The district's Democrats and unions were scarcely imposing forces, and their recent track record was less than sterling. Still, the Democratic Coordinated Campaign would be central to any successful GOTV effort. Esposito estimated that Moore needed to come out of Johnson County with at least 45 percent of the vote—so that Democrats and labor, mostly in Wyandotte, but also in Douglas, could overcome the Johnson County Republican edge. In reality, that edge came in the southern half of Johnson County, where conservative Republicans held sway; the Moore campaign and its allies did very little in this area, as they focused most of their efforts in the older parts of Johnson County as well as Wyandotte and Douglas.

If there was a secret to Moore's ultimate success, it was the coordinated GOTV efforts of the Democrats, labor (and to an extent, the environmentalists), and the Moore campaign. Esposito and other Moore staff helped raise more than $100,000 of the coordinated campaign total budget of $400,000, and labor acted on its best chance to win the seat in forty years. Aside from post hoc, "the proof is in the pudding" assessments, it is difficult to judge the effectiveness of GOTV efforts, but the extent of the Third District Democratic Coordinated Campaign's work is worth examining. Between September 20 and November 3, the Democrats made, through telephone and direct mail, 424,927 contacts with prospective Moore voters.[20] Many individuals received eight to ten calls. Although the coordinated campaign fell short in early efforts to contact its targeted number of voters, the last- weekend GOTV efforts demonstrated the Democrats' energy in the final days. The coordinated campaign had established a goal of making 37,899 GOTV calls between October 29 and November 3 (election day). Remarkably, party and campaign personnel—volunteer and paid—made 62,533 calls in this period—including check-back contacts from both the coordinated campaign office and Moore headquarters until 6:30 in the evening of November 3, half an hour before the polls closed. Labor and environmental groups made their own GOTV calls.

This was no accident. Ten days before the election, consultant Martin Hamburger noted that he had "talked to Chris [Esposito] about GOTV. I went over everything, and every question I raised he had an answer for. The phone calls were coordinated, we had everything maxed." The campaign had done all it could to win this seat, except perhaps, in Jacob's and Esposito's eyes, raise more funds for post–Labor Day television, and convince Moore that he should become a full-time candidate earlier in the campaign.

Overall, however, the candidate did his part to the end. Buoyed by the last tracking poll and the *Star's* endorsement, Moore put on a strong, energetic, highly focused push in the final week. He spent Friday, Saturday, and Sunday before the election in Douglas County, with Monday and part of Tuesday being dedicated to Wyandotte. If the margin in Johnson County was not too great, he had placed himself in a situation in which he could, even should, win.

November 3, 1998: The Third District Goes Democratic

The first returns, which came in about 7:30 P.M., were encouraging—Moore trailed Snowbarger by only a bit more than 1,000 votes in Johnson County's advance voting. This was considerably better than Hancock's performance two years earlier, and although he did not say anything at the time, Esposito concluded that his candidate would win. During the next hour, Chris Steineger worked his cell phone to keep tabs on the four county-seat election-return centers. With half the Johnson County vote in, things appeared promising. Wyandotte then began to report majorities of better than two-to-one for Moore, and Douglas looked good in the early going. Suddenly, almost all the Johnson County vote was in, and Moore was well over the 45 percent threshold (he would end with 48 percent). Wyandotte's majority totaled 13,561 votes (of 30,555 cast, or 71.5 percent for Moore), more than enough to overcome Snowbarger's 7,109-vote edge in Johnson County (see appendix table A-1 to this chapter). In the end, the Third District's turnout came to 49 percent, and Wyandotte County's 42 percent turnout performance helped provide the Moore margin. [21]

After spending the evening at the home of kitchen-cabinet member Mike Buser, close to the campaign's "victory party" location at the (public) St. Andrew's Country Club, Moore joined the party at 8:50 P.M. but remained cautious—Representative Snowbarger was not yet conceding defeat. By 9:50, however, Moore was ready, and at 10 P.M., right on time for the late-night news, Moore stepped to the podium to declare victory—live—on all the Kansas City television stations. Jacob and Esposito each grabbed a champagne bottle and hugged everyone in sight. Mark Nevins moved his new congressman from one interview to the next; he could celebrate only after the last reporters got their quotes, close to midnight. A thousand Moore supporters, including the Overland Park mayor Ed Eilert, defeated two years earlier in the Republican primary, joined with the guitar-plucking candidate to sing "This Land Is Your Land."

When the votes were counted, the tally came to 102,299 for Moore and 92,801 for Representative Snowbarger. With an almost 10,000-vote margin (52 percent to 48 percent), Dennis Moore had won the Third District race—one of just six challengers (five of them Democrats) to gain a seat in the 106th Congress.

Conclusion: The Two Questions Revisited

> *This is a big race and a big [prospective] win because a Democrat has not won in this district for forty years and if we win we probably get some undue credibility. People will think Mark did awesome press, Larry did great fund-raising and, you know, I was the manager who made everyone work together and we ran a great race. That may be true, but it may also be untrue. We might have just gotten lucky.*
>
> Chris Esposito, October 30, 1998

In many ways, professional campaigners and consultants resemble political scientists. Both groups gather data, perform analyses, and reach conclusions. Of course, campaign pros and consultants must act on their conclusions, often within days, if not hours. They do not, however, have to publish their results and can move on to the next race, the next state.

The Kansas Third in 1998 was a single case, so any findings are limited. But the evidence appears to confirm both initial hypotheses—first, that Snowbarger was too conservative for a district that had historically been represented by moderate Republicans. But few would argue that Snowbarger's social conservatism represented a fatal flaw. In a status quo year, there is little reason to think that he should not have survived, if only by a narrow margin.

For the purposes of this study, the second question is more intriguing. Could three outsiders, all under thirty and utterly foreign to Kansas, come in and apply their "scientific" campaign principles to win a difficult, but not impossible, race? Given an attractive, articulate candidate who would help raise funds and a weak incumbent, the pros from Dover saw from the start a solid chance to win the Third District seat. As Esposito noted, this district represented a real opportunity, which evolved as the campaign developed:

> In January . . . Larry and I thought we could raise close to $900,000 . . . in fact we've exceeded $900,000 (tables A-2 and A-3 in the appendix to this chapter), which is something Larry and I probably thought we could do, assuming x, y, and z fell right along the way. . . . I mean strong polling numbers, and we've had the race tied from day one. We've out raised the incumbent in every reporting period. . . . [other candidates across the country] have fallen off the funding map and we've gotten some additional money that a candidate in California might have been getting three weeks ago . . . we've raised more money in October than Larry and I expected.

Indeed, on election day, thousands of dollars were still coming in. With a look of disbelief, Jacob recounted how he talked a person out of giving $500 that the campaign could not use (and the sum would have been a sacrifice for the donor).

Representative Snowbarger opened the door by not raising enough funds to keep Moore out of the race. Once in, Moore put together an effective, professional campaign. As the pros acknowledged, it was Moore's name on the ballot. He was the one who suspended his lucrative law practice and placed his family in the spotlight. More important, he was the one to hire the pros from Dover who came to Kansas and demonstrated how Democrats could run a marginal-seat campaign in a hostile environment. And, in Moore's words, "I think we . . . won because we were able to put together . . . the coalition of moderate Republicans and Democrats and independents, who believe in the issues as I do."

Three days after the election, Mark Nevins and Chris Esposito have driven off, to well-deserved rest and new career opportunities.[22] Larry

Jacob has moved his computer into Dennis Moore's basement. He has agreed to stay on for a while, and his whiteboard registers a new goal: $100,000 by February 1, 1999. A new cycle has begun.

Postscript, November 2000

Representative Dennis Moore completed his two-year congressional cycle with a 3 percentage point victory over an aggressive, conservative Republican challenger, state representative Phill Kline. Marked for defeat by Republican strategists and various interest groups, Moore survived by returning to the Third District almost every weekend, compiling a moderate voting record (to the point that the Business Roundtable ran a pro-Moore campaign advertisement in the wake of his pro-China trade vote), and raising almost $2 million to fund a campaign that emphasized his record and that remained, generally speaking, positive. In the end, Moore demonstrated that even in a Republican district, he, as a moderate incumbent, could take advantage of the significant advantages accorded sitting members of Congress. And the Republicans in the Third District helped him, given their nomination of a highly conservative, albeit energetic and reasonably attractive, challenger. Still, the Moore organization had little choice but to begin preparing immediately for the 2002 race. For a Democrat, at least, this seat does require a permanent campaign.

Table 5A-1. *Election Results, Third District, 1994–98*

Year	*Candidate*	*Number of votes*	*Percent of vote*
1994	Judy Hancock (D)	78,401	43
	Representative Jan Meyers (R)	102,218	57
1996[a]	Judy Hancock (D)	126,848	45
	Vince Snowbarger (R)	139,169	50
1998	Dennis Moore (D)	102,299	52
	Representative Vince Snowbarger (R)	92,801	48

a. Others: 13,296 (5).

Table 5A-2. *Moore for Congress Budget, Unofficial, as of Election Day*

Thousands of dollars, percent in parentheses

Item	*Funds*
Receipts	$982,000
Individual contributions	646,000 (66)
PACs and party contributions	336,000 (34)
Labor	230,000 (23)
Other	106,000 (11)
Democratic Party	50,000 (5)
Congressional leaders	30,000 (3)
State/local	10,000 (1)
Nonaffiliated business	10,000 (1)
Expenditures	950,000
Approximate allocations	
Radio/TV time purchase	625,000 (66)
Staff salaries, expenses	10,000 (12)
TV/radio production	70,000 (7)
Polling	50,000 (5)
Research	25,000 (3)
Field (printing and other expenses)	20,000 (2)
Paid phone banks	15,000 (1.5)
Fund-raising costs	15,000 (1.5)
Administration (phones, rent, and so on)	15,000 (1.5)
Miscellaneous	5,000 (0.5)

Source: Moore for Congress Campaign.

Table 5A-3. *Campaign Contributions and Cash-on-Hand, Third District, 1997–98*

	Funds raised (cash-on-hand)	
Reporting period	*Dennis Moore*	*Representative Vince Snowbarger*
July 1–December 31,1997	$ 83,895 (68,838)	$ 137,863 (67,757)
January 1–March 31, 1998	143,675 (184,538)	33,896 (73,250)
April 1–June 30, 1998	166,399 (254,538)	172,258 (155,562)
July 1–September 30, 1998	312,898 (24,002)	337,938 (258,228)
October 1–November 23, 1998	280,362 (32,713)	301,533 (29,944)
Total	944,377	1,003,807
Individuals	623,243	437,592
Political action committees	324,633	537,113

Source: Federal Election Commission, December 31, 1998.

Notes

1. In Fenno's terms, both Snowbarger as an incumbent (and former state legislator) and Moore as a former district attorney have easily surpassed the standards of basic qualifications. See Richard F. Fenno, Jr., *Home Style* (Little Brown, 1978), pp. 57ff.

2. Philip D. Duncan and Christine C. Lawrence, *Politics in America* (Washington: CQ Press, 1998), p. 571.

3. Peter Beinart, "Battle for the 'Burbs," *New Republic*, October 19, 1998, pp. 25–29.

4. Michael Barone and Grant Ujifusa, *Almanac of American Politics 1998* (Washington: National Journal/Times Books, 1998), p. 589. It should be noted that there were two other candidates in the 1996 general election, and Snowbarger won a bit less than 50 percent of the total vote.

5. Gary Jacobson, *The Politics of Congressional Elections* (Longman, 1997), pp. 34 and following.

6. Linda L. Fowler and Robert D. McClure, *Political Ambition* (Yale University Press, 1989).

7. All quotations not footnoted are from personal interviews with the author or from a transcript of BBC interviews conducted by Jeremy Cooper, November 2, 1998.

8. Cooper and Secrest polling advisory, February 26, 1998, p. 1 (emphasis in original).

9. Ibid., p. 3 (emphasis in original).

10. Scott Canon and Steve Kraske, "Money and Its Sources Talk in Snowbarger-Moore Race," *Kansas City Star*, September 28, 1998, p. 1. Canon and Kraske wrote a series of detailed articles on the campaign, with Canon gaining excellent access to the Moore organization and Kraske doing the same for the Snowbarger camp.

11. With 20-20 postelection hindsight, the right wing of the Republican Party harshly criticized Snowbarger for not presenting himself as a true-blue social conservative—which they interpreted as costing him the election. Snowbarger backed off few of his conservative positions during the campaign; rather, he campaigned as the conservative he always was, one who could get along with a range of factions. Democratic exit polling demonstrated that a conservative fall-off in votes did not cost Snowbarger the election. On the other hand, conservative activists did not put the energy into the Snowbarger race that they had exhibited in many other recent Kansas races.

12. The received explanation was that the Snowbarger campaign wanted to see what effect the ads would have in holding down Moore's primary vote, which could be compared to Judy Hancock's primary totals two years earlier.

13. "Smeared Issues," *Olathe Daily News*, Wednesday, August 5, 1988, p. 12.

14. "A Survey of Voter Attitudes in Kansas 3rd Congressional District." The poll included the staggering finding that Republican incumbent Graves was leading challenger Tom Sawyer 55 percent to 31 percent among Democrats. On election day Democrats rallied to give Sawyer a bare majority of their numbers.

15. Ibid., p. 2.

16. Steve Kraske and Scott Canon, "Seeds of Bitterness Sown in 3rd District Long before Election Harvest," *Kansas City Star*, October 5, 1998, p. A1.

17. From his district attorney days on, Moore had performed with a group called "Dennis and the Doo-Dahs." One of the Doo-Dahs was Mike Buser, an attorney, colleague, and long-time friend, and perhaps the most important kitchen cabinet member. Moore could be abrupt and impatient, but his musical side effectively softened a sometimes hard-edged image.

18. The Triad Management Company purchased ads that supported several conservative Republicans in Kansas in 1996, including Representative Snowbarger. The sources of Triad's funding were secret but included in-laws of Senator Sam Brownback and members of the Koch family, which controlled Wichita-based Koch Industries, the second largest privately held corporation in the United States. Among a series of *Kansas City Star* articles, see James Kuhnhenn, "Political Funds of Kansans Examined," *Kansas City Star*, October 4, 1997, p. A1. See also Allan J. Cigler, "The 1998 Kansas Third Congressional District Race," in David B. Magleby, ed., *Outside Money* (Rowman and Littlefield, 1999), pp. 77–92.

19. Steve Rose, "The America I Choose," *Sun Newspapers*, October 14, 1998, p. 1.

20. "1998 Kansas Coordinated Campaign Timeline for 3rd CD," undated document.

21. Based on figures from the Kansas secretary of state's office, turnout in the Third District was 49.1 percent of registered voters and 40.8 percent of eligible voters in the district.

21. Esposito subsequently signed on with the Moore office as press secretary but then moved to the DCCC as a regional director for the 2000 election. Nevins took a position with Senator Frank Lautenberg and also ended up with the DCCC. Jacob stayed with the Moore campaign for a couple of months but then took a job with a nonprofit organization in the Kansas City area and anticipated going to graduate school in American studies.

CHAPTER SIX

Brian Baird's "Ring of Fire": The Quest for Funds and Votes in Washington's Third District

JAMES A. THURBER
CAROLYN LONG

MOST ELECTORAL BATTLES for a congressional seat involve two primary campaigns; one for money and one for votes. This was certainly the case in 1998's highly competitive, open seat for Washington's Third Congressional District.[1] This case study uses this congressional race to examine whether a symbiotic relationship exists between political consultants and a candidate in the development of a winning campaign strategy, theme, and message. Additionally, we explore the role of money in the pursuit of votes and address how campaign conduct influences broader questions of representative democracy.

Our analysis examines the world of congressional campaigning using in-depth interviews and participant observation. We gathered information from candidates, campaign staff, campaign consultants, party strategists, journalists, and other participants involved in this congressional contest. We also accessed internal campaign documents, opinion surveys, and campaign budgets both public and private to explain the development and execution of the strategy, theme, and message common to congressional campaigns.

Overview of the Election

When Brian Baird, a psychology professor at Pacific Lutheran University, decided to run for Congress in 1996, neither major party took him seriously. The Democrats thought incumbent Republican Linda Smith

Table 6-1. *1996 Primary and General Election Results in Washington's Third District*

	Total votes	Money spent
1996 Primary election		
Linda Smith (R)	69,291 (52 %)	
Brian Baird (D)	62,778 (48 %)	
1996 General election		
Linda Smith (R)	123,117 (50 %)	$1,216,368
Brian Baird (D)	122,230 (50 %)	718,322

Source: Office of the Secretary of State, Olympia, November 1996.

was unbeatable in southwest Washington's Third Congressional District. The Republicans agreed, giving little notice to the college professor who had never served public office. However, two important events between late 1996 and the spring of 1997 changed the minds of party leaders. First, in 1996 Baird was declared the winner over the incumbent Smith, who had outspent him by nearly half a million dollars. Then, after spending nearly a week in Washington to attend orientation for new members of Congress, meeting party leaders, and setting up his congressional office, Baird found out that his victory was nullified by absentee ballots, which had been added to the count (table 6-1). The second contributing event was Smith's decision to run for the U.S. Senate in May 1997. Suddenly, Baird was in the race for an open House seat, and he quickly became the Republican's number one target. There was national attention paid to his candidacy, and Brian Baird was paying attention to the Third District. Baird said he remembered the importance of money (or lack of it) from his close defeat in 1996 and the significance of absentee voting, and he took the early steps necessary to secure an advantage in the race. Baird spent the next two years traveling the district, building grassroots support, learning the needs of constituents, and sharpening his political message and campaign skills. Above all, Baird said he made a conscious choice to focus his time on fund-raising nationally and in the district.

The Third Congressional District

Washington's Third Congressional District lies in the southwestern corner of the state of Washington.[2] It starts from Olympia in the north, reaches the crest of the Cascade Mountains, south to the Columbia River and

Vancouver, west across the coastal range to the mouth of the Columbia River and the Pacific Ocean, and north to Grays Harbor. Timber dominates the economy, but maritime and high-tech industries are also essential. Forty-four percent of the voters in the district live in Clark County (Vancouver), and almost 30 percent of the voters come from Thurston County (Olympia). The remaining 26 percent of the population is scattered among the five rural counties that make up the rest of the district.

Vancouver, an industrial and high-tech center, has seen its population grow rapidly in the past two decades. It is Washington's fourth largest city and the main population center of Clark County, the fastest growing county in the state. The top employer in the county is Hewlett-Packard, followed by Southwest Washington Medical Center and the James River Corporation, a wood products industry. The politics of the county has changed as it has increased in population. In 1996 Republicans had a slight edge, having elected the very conservative Smith in two cycles after a succession of Democrats.

Olympia, the state capital, and the surrounding suburbs, located in Thurston County, is also one of the fastest-growing metropolitan areas in the country. The county, which includes a number of individuals working for the state, adds to the Democratic voter base at the northern end of the district. The more politically conservative and rural counties of Lewis, Cowlitz, Skamania, and parts of Klickitat make up the remainder of the district. These counties rely heavily on timber, fishing, dock work, and some tourism for their economic base. There is also a strong presence of organized labor with workers concerned about how environmental regulations will affect jobs. The district is almost evenly split between Republicans and Democrats, with the populous Vancouver and suburban Clark County playing the key role in the outcome of most national elections.

The district has produced mixed results in recent congressional elections. Liberal Democrat Jolene Unsoeld was elected in 1990 and 1992, and ultraconservative Republican Linda Smith in 1994 and 1996. Bill Clinton carried the Third District in 1992 and 1996 as had Michael S. Dukakis in 1988.[3] Republican Smith barely beat Unsoeld in 1994 and Baird in 1996 in two tough battles. But as these returns suggest, the Third District is politically competitive, making it a key target for both parties. Once considered a Democratic stronghold (it elected a succession of Democrats to Congress from 1958 until 1994 when Smith won), the Democrats wanted to regain the seat, and Republicans wanted to demonstrate a permanent shift to the GOP column.

The Primary Election

Even before Linda Smith announced her candidacy against Senator Patty Murray in the 1998 election, several congressional hopefuls were eyeing a run for the Third District. Brian Baird was the first. He began unofficially campaigning for the seat a few weeks after his disappointing 887-vote loss. In December 1996, he enlisted Cindy Gibson, the Clark County Democratic Party's vice president and volunteer for his 1996 campaign, to organize a task force for the 1998 election. Baird then spent the next several months crisscrossing the district, meeting prospective voters, and canvassing state and local politicians for support. When asked about the 1996 loss, Baird put a positive spin on the experience, noting that the extra time allowed him to meet more people and learn more about the issues important to voters in the district. "I didn't go into a funk at all from the outcome of the election," he said. "What we accomplished was pretty remarkable, and I feel proud about that."[4]

By the time he officially announced his candidacy in May 1997, Baird had collected endorsements from the nine Democratic county chairmen in the district and two former members of the U.S. House of Representatives—Don Bonker and Jolene Unsoeld. He also received the early backing of the House Democratic Congressional Campaign Committee (DCCC) and Democratic leaders at the state and federal level. Baird then quickly assembled his campaign team, which included several professional campaign consultants. These endorsements and organization provided Baird with significant momentum in the search for early campaign funds. Coupled with a core of district supporters, he effectively dissuaded others from challenging him in the primary and tapped into the flow of campaign money essential to winning the general race. It was an entirely different story for the Republicans as four candidates emerged to retain Smith's seat for the party (table 6-2).

Two of the four candidates led the GOP pack: Don Benton, an incumbent state senator and businessman who owned a sales and management company, and Pat Fiske, Linda Smith's former chief of staff. Benton was a political newcomer. He first entered politics in 1994 with a win to the state house in a year many Republicans were swept into office at the state and national level. In 1996 he defeated an appointed incumbent to move up to the state senate. Benton was well known as an aggressive, active member of the Republican-controlled state senate, and he sponsored or cosponsored more than 300 bills during his tenure in office. Fiske had

Table 6-2. *1998 Primary and General Election Results in Washington's Third District*

	Vote total	Percent of vote	Money spent
1998 Primary			
Brian Baird (D)	63,979	47.9	$ 100,000[a]
Don Benton (R)	29,153	21.9	262,200
Pat Fiske (R)	21,564	16.1	112,292
Rick Jackson (R)	12,970	9.7	130,114
Paul Phillips (R)	5,755	4.4	135,794
1998 General			
Brian Baird (D)	120,364	54.8	1,602,473
Don Benton (R)	99,855	45.2	755,022

Source: Office of the Secretary of State of Washington; Federal Election Commission, November 25, 1998.
a. Compiled by authors as estimated from newspaper reports.

more political experience: he represented the Skagit County district in the state legislature from 1982 to 1986 before moving to Clark County in 1986. In 1992 he was the GOP nominee for the Third Congressional District, a race he lost to Jolene Unsoeld. In 1994 Fiske successfully managed Representative Linda Smith's write-in campaign and later worked as her chief of staff in Washington, D.C. for three years. He was well regarded as a political operative able to work with party insiders and other members of Washington's congressional delegation. The other two candidates, Paul Phillips, a fifty-five year old chiropractor and Rick Jackson, a family practice medical doctor and country western singer, were political novices with little name recognition and limited campaign funds.

The primary campaign was uneventful up until the last two weeks before the September 15 election. Unopposed, Baird spent considerable time raising funds and increasing his name recognition in the district. By the time of the primary election, he had more than a half million dollars in his campaign coffers. He spent little before the primary, preferring to wait for the general election before starting an aggressive campaign. Baird focused his campaign theme on education, health care, crime, care for the elderly, free trade, and a careful balance between environmental protection and economic prosperity (jobs). The race between the four Republican candidates was more competitive, but was fairly tepid, in part because of their strong similarities. The four candidates ran as social and fiscal conservatives. Each opposed abortion, gun control, managed care, and affirmative action. The candidates also held similar positions on the need to cut taxes, reduce the size of government, overhaul the Internal Revenue Service, and eliminate the Department of Education and return the schools to local control. Joel Connelly of the *Seattle Post-Intellegencer* noted, "All are staunch conservatives, and the only competition among them seems to be to see who is more steadfastly anti-abortion, who can more enthusiastically champion the rights of gun owners, and who has the darkest prediction about how federal power is choking Americans' initiative."[5] However, the tone of the discussion between candidates was civil and respectful. Each adhered to the Republican Party's eleventh commandment to not publicly attack one another in a way that would injure the GOP candidate in the general election. As a result, the focus of debates and public forums usually centered on how poor economic conditions appeared in the district and the country.

In the end, each Republican candidate focused on one or two local issues that distinguished his campaign from the others. Fiske emphasized his political experience and ability to build a consensus. He also garnered the support of the five major newspapers in the district, which mentioned him as the candidate most likely to appeal to moderate voters and beat Baird in the general election. Benton, the most conservative contender, heralded himself as a fiercely independent-minded, experienced businessman and legislator who was the taxpayers' greatest friend.

Benton's candidacy was also aided by the support of outside individuals and groups. Supporters of national term limits campaigned heavily against Fiske, who chose not to sign a self-imposed pledge to leave after six years in office, and the National Rifle Association strongly supported Benton, a member. Benton also won endorsements by other Washington State politicians, such as state Republican John Pennington, speaker pro tempore of the House. Pennington actively campaigned on his behalf.

Because of the parallels among the Republican candidates, the outcome of the primary race turned on money and name recognition. As an incumbent state senator who would retain his seat if he lost, Benton held an advantage over his competitors in name recognition and fund-raising from both individuals and groups. Between January and the time of the primary election, he raised and spent $262,200, approximately $70,000 of which came from political action committees (PACs). Benton ran a more visible campaign than his opponents. More than $50,000 was spent on radio and television ads that went unanswered by his lesser-financed competitors. He also distributed a number of direct mailings that highlighted his legislative successes and support of American families widely across the district. The other Republican opponents were limited to less visible forms of campaigning, such as funding lawn signs and purchasing lists of absentee ballot voters to target.

After campaigning nonstop for eighteen months, Baird had mustered a great deal of momentum, going into the primary as the clear Democratic nominee. However, because Washington State has a late open primary, his margin of victory would be closely watched in order to assess his position over the eventual GOP nominee. The Baird campaign was running smoothly until two weeks before the September 15 primary, when the national Republican Party joined the race with an influx of "soft money" and issue ads.

In early September, the National Republican Congressional Committee (NRCC) announced that it would be launching Operation Breakout, a $37 million effort to target approximately fifty-two competitive swing districts with hard-hitting issue advocacy ads using unregulated "soft money." Financed and coordinated by the NRCC and state party organizations, the ads were tailored to address issues sensitive to each particular contest. The first series targeted Democratic House candidate Shelley Berkley of Nevada. On September 8, NRCC Chair John Linder (R-Ga.) announced that the party intended to make Brian Baird Operation Breakout's second target, despite the fact that the state primary had not yet been held. Linder reasoned that it was a competitive seat, and the GOP needed to act preemptively to stop Baird's momentum. The first NRCC ad portrayed Baird as soft on crime and depicted him as opposing prosecuting even the harshest juvenile criminals as adults. When asked why the ads focused on juvenile crime, Linder responded that the issue was important to the district. "This guy has views that are out of step with the views of the people in the Third District." Linder stated, "Why juvenile crime? That happens to be in polling data, high on the list of people's concerns."[6]

The NRCC's issue ad attacking Baird for being soft on juvenile crime was based on a "nonanswer" to a question on a Project Vote Smart questionnaire that the candidate answered in 1996. The questionnaire included inquires about ways to reduce crime. Baird left one question, which asked whether he would "prosecute youths accused of murder as adults," blank. He elected not to check the box, since it would indicate his agreement with the question, and he did not wish to give an all-or-nothing response.[7] However, he did write a comment in the margin of the questionnaire about how judges need some discretion deciding which juvenile criminals should be tried as adults. According to Project Vote Smart's rules, "If a candidate does not select a response it does not necessarily indicate that the candidate is opposed." Baird chose not to respond to the question.

The Republicans, however, interpreted this nonanswer as Baird's agreement not to prosecute youths as adults.[8] The ad that was produced accused Baird of being soft on crime. The television ad stated, in an ominous tone, "Our streets are dangerous, even deadly places. Violence confronts America's children—in their neighborhoods and in their schools. So it's hard to believe anyone wouldn't support stronger penalties for violent crime by juveniles. But Brian Baird wouldn't. Brian Baird wouldn't support trying even the most violent juveniles as adults."

On September 9 the Baird campaign formally complained that the ad was false and misleading and called on Project Vote Smart to address the appropriateness of the ad. The next day PVS issued a press release stating, "Project Vote Smart does not substantiate the basis of the attack and in fact finds the attack false. This kind of negative campaign activity is precisely the kind of misinformation that the Project attempts to counter with its factual database."[9]

In response to complaints of the Baird campaign, an ABC television affiliate, KATU in Portland, pulled the ad.[10] Another station, KOIN, the CBS television affiliate, initially delayed airing the ad but elected to air it several days later. The NBC television affiliate, KGW, continued airing the ad. However, in response to the complaints, the NRCC retooled the ad and rereleased it on September 14, a day before the primary election.

Baird continued to express displeasure about the inappropriate and misleading ad, and asked Benton to have the ads pulled or to disavow the ad. Benton publicly responded that his campaign had no control over the ads and no role in producing or scripting them. Later, Benton's campaign manager, David Castillio, stated that the campaign had asked the NRCC to stop airing the ads, but that the committee refused to do so. By the time of the primary election, the NRCC had spent more than $300,000 in television ads in the Portland media market, which covers Vancouver. This amount was modest compared with the amount spent in the general election.

Despite the NRCC's attack ads, Baird won the open primary handily with 63,979 votes, 47.95 percent of the total. Benton placed second with

29,153 votes, 21.9 percent of the total. Although Baird's margin was large, his campaign still worried that he had not won the open primary with more than 50 percent of the vote, and that the combined Republican vote gave the GOP a 5,462-vote edge over the Democratic nominee. Yet, given that Baird spent little money in the primary, it was still a significant win. Following the election, all the Republican nominees endorsed Benton's candidacy. Baird complimented Fiske, Jackson, and Phillips for running a positive campaign, and he pointedly omitted Benton from his praise, noting instead that he ran a "less constructive and less honest campaign."[11] Although Baird had not been elected to public office and Benton had several times, Baird seemed to know much more about how important it is to have a professional group of campaign consultants and staff along with significant money to fuel the campaign. Baird understood the importance of the key players in his battle to gain a seat in Congress.

Candidates need money to formulate a clear strategy and message and to communicate and mobilize voters. To achieve these objectives, congressional candidates use professional consultants, paid staff, and volunteers to conduct press relations, issue and opposition research, fundraising, polling, media advertising, get-out-the-vote (GOTV) drives, and legal and accounting support. Successful congressional campaigns for open seats require sophisticated staff organizations that are often temporary and pieced together just before a declaration of candidacy. The campaign organization, therefore, is a complex mix of the candidate, consultants, paid staff, volunteers, party activists, and interest groups, all striving to win a plurality of votes. This case study focuses on the key players in the Baird campaign. The political context is analytically important to the case. To fully understand the case of Baird versus Benton, it is important to describe the background of the candidates, the issues of the campaign, and the general political environment of the race.

The Candidate and His Issues

Brian Baird was raised in western Colorado by a father who was a political activist and a teacher and a mother who owned a small business. His father once ran for local office and lost a very close election, something Baird said had a major impact on him. He said he never forgot that elections can be very close, a fact that hit him in his first bid for a seat in Congress. Baird spent his childhood in a small town fishing, hunting, hiking and mountain climbing, and playing sports. After graduating from high school, Baird attended the University of Utah where he earned a B.S. in psychology (1977), and later he earned an M.A. (1980) and Ph.D. (1984) in psychology from the University of Wyoming. After receiving his degree, Baird worked as a licensed clinical psychologist in private practice in medical centers at Veterans Administration psychiatric hospitals and at community mental health clinics. After several years in private practice, Baird accepted a position as a psychology professor at Pacific Lutheran University, where he served as departmental chair.

Baird's 1998 campaign focused on the same four major issues from his unsuccessful 1996 campaign: education (his top priority), health care, crime, care for the elderly, and foreign trade. After being questioned by labor leaders in the district, Baird said he was careful to advocate both environmental protection and economic prosperity (jobs), a tough balancing act in the Third District, home of the timber industry and new high-tech, environmentally conscious employees. Baird projected himself as a commonsense, pragmatic, back-to-basics candidate who could connect with people in the district and work with individuals from both political parties. "People ask, Are you a liberal, a conservative or a moderate?" stated Baird. "I say I'm a problem solver."[12]

Successful competitive campaigns for public office usually have a clear strategy, theme, and message. The development of Baird's strategy, theme, and message emanated from the views of voters in the district and from his own ideas of what was important to Washingtonians. The candidate spent considerable time in the district and felt in touch with voters. "Candidates who are active, and in the field, either on the phones or talking to voters are conducting a focus group a day. You have to go into an election and listen to what's important to the voters and address those concerns, so that's what I am trying to do."[13] Baird also concluded that candidates have to "follow their guts a little bit" and "push for issues they can relate to." Most of the issues Baird focused on reflected his life experiences.

> If you look at the issues that I am pushing hardest about in this campaign, they are issues that come rather easily and naturally to me because that is what I happen to have dedicated my life to. So, sure the polls say education is important, but I'm an educator, so it's pretty

> natural that I would care about education. The polls say HMO reform is important, and I've worked with HMOs as a psychologist. I've dealt with the whole billing process, and the denial of care, so that's pretty natural.[14]

Baird's campaign was assisted by visits from Vice President Al Gore, House Minority Leader Richard Gephardt, former U.S. senator Bill Bradley, and former Texas governor Ann Richards. Strong support from the Democratic Congressional Campaign Committee (DCCC), the Democratic National Committee (DNC), the Washington State Democratic Party, Washington State Governor Gary Locke, and other prominent Democrats in the state was provided as well.

A hands-on candidate, Baird involved himself in every aspect of the campaign, which included a strong commitment to improving campaign conduct. He wrote a code of ethics for staff and volunteers working on the campaign, and he issued guidelines requiring everyone to conduct themselves with "integrity, responsibility, honesty, sensitivity, compassion, intelligence and thoughtfulness and to give everything we can to earn the right to win this election and represent the people of this district." Baird noted that the code stemmed from his professional background as a psychologist. Eight principles, referred to as the Baird Code of Campaign Conduct, served as guidelines for all campaign staff and volunteers:

—Treat everyone who works on the campaign in any capacity with respect and caring.

—Treat all constituents with attention and respect.

—Support and encourage the efforts and successes of others and look for the good things each person is doing.

—Maintain professionalism and remember that the campaign and our candidate will be judged by how each individual staff member conducts themselves at all times.

—If problems arise, withhold judgement or criticism until you have seriously asked yourself if you understand the situation from the other person's perspective, if you have listened. Do not respond until you have thought carefully about what you need to say and how best to say it so the results will be constructive.

—Maintain confidentiality about all aspects of the campaign.

—Remember why we are doing this and what is at stake.

—Ask yourself constantly, "Am I doing something right now that is consistent with our campaign principles and that will help strengthen this team and help us win?"[15]

The Opposition

Baird's opponent, Don Benton, was a self-made businessman from Pleasant Valley, a small town located in Clark County. At nineteen he and his sister cofounded his first business, a temporary employment agency, CEO Santa Clara Temporaries. In 1983 he was hired as the district manager for the Farmers Insurance Group, and in 1988 he founded and served as CEO of the Benton Group, a Washington State advertising and management sales agency. In 1994 he won a seat in the Washington State House of Representatives and was elevated to the state senate two years later. His bid for the Third Congressional District came in the middle of his senate term, allowing the opportunity to return to the state senate in the event of a loss.

While in the state house, Benton was widely regarded as a "shoot from the hip" type of legislator, a partisan known for his bombastic style and social conservative views. He characterized politics as war between the forces of good and evil. This style sometimes put him at odds with colleagues. One editorial mentioned, "He often prevents progress through partisan stonewalling. He revels in this take-no-prisoners absolutism." A profile in the *Columbian*, Vancouver's local paper noted,

> The state senator from Pleasant Valley is not Washington's most charismatic speaker, meticulous policymaker or visionary leader. What makes Benton, 41, stand out is his intense drive and focus, along with his natural ability to connect with people on taxes, crime and other gut-level issues. His most controversial ideas, shackling criminals together into roadside chain gangs, forcing sex offenders to take powerful drugs to squelch their sex drives, have earned him newspaper headlines. They have also provoked outrage from those who see Benton as a publicity hound with a salesman's penchant for self-promotion.[16]

Because the open seat was highly competitive and nationally visible, Benton's campaign was aided by the strong presence of the NRCC through its funding of televised issue ads, and visits from House Speaker Newt Gingrich, House Majority Leader Dick Armey, former U.S. senator Bob Dole, and the wife of former vice president Dan Quayle, Marilyn Quayle.

Fund-Raising and Campaign Expenditures and the "Ring of Fire"

A key "player" in any successful campaign for an open seat in Congress is money, how much the candidate has and how he or she uses it. Fund-raising is a campaign activity that requires a candidate's commitment, skill, and connections. Baird had all three of these, and he never lost sight of the importance of money in a successful congressional campaign.

A campaign consultant's dream is a candidate like Brian Baird, who was aggressive and indefatigable in his fund-raising. Most congressional candidates dislike fund-raising and often try to avoid it, but it is a costly mistake to do so in a competitive race. Baird began soliciting contributions in January 1997 and stayed on task throughout the entire campaign. Although tired of the time, effort, and indignities associated with soliciting funds, Baird did it very successfully, eventually exceeding his fund-raising goals. "I knew I had to raise the money to stay ranked and I also knew the drill," Baird stated. "I knew they (the big party and PAC givers) were going to give me some hurdle to hit. I said to myself, 'I'm going to hit it.' We exceeded every single hurdle every time." Perhaps nothing showed Baird's drive more than the "ring of fire": a term Baird coined for one approach to telephone solicitation of campaign funds. The campaign would rent an apartment for Baird and his staff for the sole purpose of making calls. The ring of fire was created when three staffers surrounded Baird in a circle. The staffers would dial potential donors, speak to them briefly about the campaign, and then pass the phone to Baird, who would make the final pitch for a campaign contribution. Sometimes he would do this for six straight hours without a break. "The ring of fire is fun because it is busy. Because you have three people dialing, and they hand you the telephone and you say thank you and go on to the next. It is quick. You're doing it with your $50 to $100 givers—not the big donors. But you can rock. You can make two to three thousand dollars on a good ring-of-fire night." However, much of the fund-raising was a chore for Baird, especially at the beginning. "I remember distinctly one Sunday afternoon when they were saying you needed $50,000 in the bank and I had one thousand. We were supposed to have two dialers and nobody shows. Not a single friend was willing to help me. I open the office and it is sweltering hot. I sit down at one o'clock in the afternoon and start dialing because I have no other way to raise money. I call until five o'clock and I talk with three human beings. Nobody is home. Who is going to be home on a nice Sunday afternoon? Many days the entire challenge is not to quit."[17]

Raising Money

The Baird campaign set a goal to raise $1.4 million to fund his second attempt for the House seat—twice as much money as he raised and spent in 1996. Baird began raising money days after his 1996 loss, and by the end of 1997, he had raised $311,000, leaving the fund-raising goal for 1998 at $1.1 million.

Baird's overall fund-raising strategy was to raise at least two-thirds of this amount from individual donors. This strategy was based, partly, on his 1996 campaign, which raised $710,000 from approximately 4,600 donors. Of this amount, $237,000 (33 percent) came from PACs, and $466,000 (66 percent) from individual donors, most of whom resided in Washington State. Baird took pride in the fact that his 1996 campaign had more individual donors than any other Democratic candidate, including incumbents, for the U.S. House. His campaign's intention was to duplicate these percentages in 1998 and raise $350,000 from political action committees (33 percent) and $700,000 from individual donors (66 percent) to reach the 1.1 million dollar goal for 1998.

The PAC fund-raising took place from the campaign headquarters. The campaign used in-house expertise to raise the PAC funds, rather than hire an outside consultant, which is common in congressional campaigns. As noted in the Baird for Congress 1998 finance plan, "In exploring what consultants have to offer versus what they charge, it is of much benefit to us not to pay outside consultants. We have the knowledge, connections, and staff to take care of it in-house." However, his campaign in the end had a combination of paid professionals and experienced in-house campaign staff. A key ingredient to the campaign's PAC fund-raising plan, for example, was its decision to hire a representative of the local AFL-CIO as a labor liaison responsible for raising at least $250,000 of the $350,000 from labor PACs. The PAC fund-raising drive was organized around Baird's two trips to Washington, D.C., in the spring of 1998 and after the primary election in September. These personal visits were supplemented by biweekly and later weekly phone calls and faxes to possible PAC donors.

Four fund-raising strategies were used to raise money from individual donors: fund-raising events, direct mailings, phone solicitation, and contributions from individual members of Congress. There were three categories of fund-raising events; low-dollar grassroots fund-raising events, mid-dollar fund-raising events, and high-dollar fund-raising events. Although using these types of events to raise money for campaigns is costly and time consuming, the campaign believed it was critical to use a variety of fund-raising approaches as different donors respond to different fund-raising tactics.

The low-dollar grassroots events took place primarily in the form of house parties, coffees, and desserts held in a supporter's home. Party hosts were responsible for invitations, decorations, and catering, and the deputy finance director would provide any needed technical assistance. A target of one hundred house parties, including a "house party extravaganza" was set for 1998 with the goal of raising \$95,000. Other low-dollar events, including a "summit team" funding program orchestrated by volunteers and events hosted by young Democrats and senior citizens and events outside the district, were intended to yield an additional \$20,000. Mid-dollar events planned by the Baird campaign such as constituency events around target groups such as psychologists, mountain climbers, and environmental groups, and "pivot point" campaign events such as the primary victory and the candidate's birthday were expected to raise a combined total of \$30,000. High-dollar events featuring high-profile politicians and individuals stomping on Baird's behalf such as Vice President Al Gore, former House speaker Richard Gephardt, and former Texas governor Ann Richards were expected to bring in approximately \$160,000.

A second fund-raising strategy to target individual donors was direct mail solicitation. The campaign began with a database of approximately 60,000 names, which was tapped in March and April for a mailing to prospective donors. The campaign resolicited these donors later in the campaign, with the goal of raising between \$120,000 and \$140,000.

The third fund-raising strategy, which cost the least in real dollars but the most in Baird's time and effort, was "cold calls" to prospective donors, or as Baird called it, "dialing for dollars." The goal was to raise \$250,000 between February and November. Baird was scheduled to be on the phone soliciting individual donors at least 12.5 hours a week,

Table 6-3. *Proposed Budget: Paid Political Consultants, January to November 1998*

Consultant	*Cost*
Campaign manager	$ 66,000
Deputy campaign manager	19,000
Finance director	38,400
Deputy finance director	13,827
Additional finance director	20,000
Field director	2,500
Polling firm	2,500[a]
Direct mail firm	3,000[b]
Media firm	6,000[c]
Labor liaison	17,000
Total	181,227

Source: Baird for Congress Campaign, November 1998.

a. This figure does not include the fees for the benchmark or the two tracking polls, proposed at $38,600.

b. This figure does not include fees for persuasion mail pieces, proposed at $125,250, or fund-raising mail, proposed at $38,800.

c. This figure does not include any payment that was a percentage of a television buy, proposed as $600,000 for television and $50,000 for radio.

which was anticipated to bring in $500 an hour ($6,250 a week, $25,000 a month). Baird "cold called" virtually every individual whose name was involved in the last campaign, on his Rolodex, in party lists, PACs, party committees, members of Congress, other elected public officials, friends, colleagues, and any donor list he could acquire. Besides Baird's calls, the campaign allocated $22,000 for telemarketing to assist the candidate in his telephone solicitation.

The fourth fund-raising strategy was solicitation of current members of Congress and money raised from "walk-ins," people who came by the office to voice their support and drop off a check.

The campaign was able to achieve its finance goals in most instances, and the actual cost of each fund-raising effort generated a high return (tables 6-3, 6-4). Baird raised $321,000 from PACs, $131,000 from direct mail solicitation, $432,589 from fund- raising events, and $256,878 from direct calls. He also generated nearly $200,000 from a variety of other sources such as contributions from members of Congress, professional telemarketing activities, and unsolicited (walk-in) donations.

The campaign was also able to come close to its goal of the 2-1 ratio of individual donors versus contributions from committees. Also significant is the comparison to the Benton campaign, which raised almost equal amounts from individuals and PACs. In total, Baird collected

Table 6-4. *Baird Finance Goals, Cost and Return, 1998*

Item	*Goal*	*Cost*[a]	*Return*
PAC donations	$350,000	$ 2,450 (blast fax) 1,700 (misc. postage) 4,150 (total)	$ 321,000
Direct mail solicitation	120,000–140,000	24,000 (direct) 19,800 (resolicited) 43,800 (total)	131,000
Fund-raising events	95,000 (house party including extravaganza) 20,000 (summit and misc. low-dollar events) 190,000: (mid- and high-dollar events) 305,000 (total)	12,250 (house party) 7,500 (low-dollar events) 2,750 (summit) 59,250 (mid- and high-dollar events) 81,750 (total)	432,589
Candidate and staff telephone calls	250,000	2,500 (phones/calls)	256,878
Congress member donations			28,000
Professional telemarketing		22,000	28,000
Unsolicited donations (walk-in-door)			123,000
Total	1,045,000	132,200	1,320,467

Source: Baird for Congress Campaign, 1998 finance plan, November 1998.
a. Does not include staff salaries and office overhead.

almost 1.7 million, more than twice as much money as Benton's $804,684 (table 6-5).

Budget Expenditures

The campaign budget for January 1998 to November 1998 for Baird's second run for Washington's Third Congressional District reveals what is found in most political campaigns: the largest campaign expenditure is for media, primarily television advertising (table 6-6).[18] The second largest expenditure is fund-raising efforts.[19] Other significant expenditures include polling and research, followed by field operation and expenditures for staff and overhead. In the last eleven months of the race, Baird

Table 6-5. *Baird versus Benton Fund-Raising*

Candidate	*Net receipts*	*Individual contributions*	*Contributions from other committees*	*Candidate support*	*Net distribution*	*Cash on hand, December 31, 1998*
Baird	$1,671,658	$1,138,040	$472,575	$4,579	$1,602,437	$70,827
Benton	804,684	430,076	395,780	0	755,022	2,007

Source: Federal Election Commission, November 1998.

spent approximately $755,500 (45 percent) of his overall budget on paid media, most of which, $640,000, was devoted to television advertising. Only $50,000 went to radio advertising. Moreover, most of the paid media expenditures were spent in the last two months of the campaign. In September, $150,000 was allocated to television advertising, and in October, the campaign spent $400,000 and $50,000 on television and radio advertising respectively. Production costs and expenses complete the picture. Besides paid media, a significant portion of the budget went to direct mail. Most of the money for direct mail was spent in the final three months of the campaign. Combining expenditures for paid media and direct mail together, in the last three months of the Baird campaign, 47 percent of the entire budget went to advertising and literature designed to appeal to possible voters.

The second largest expenditure in the 1998 Baird campaign budget reveals a related story about money and congressional campaigns: how

Table 6-6. *Proposed Campaign Budget, January 1998 through November 1998*

Expense	*Cost*
Polling and research	$ 75,000
Paid media	755,500
Direct mail	129,150
Field operations	51,000
Fund-raising	228,927
Staff expenses	122,000
Office expenses	45,600
Total[a]	1,415,277

Source: Baird for Congress Campaign, November 1998.
a. An additional $150,000 of soft money was used to fund the campaign school.

much it costs to raise money. The campaign spent $228,927 (14 percent) of its budget on fund-raising efforts. One-third of this amount was spent on salaries (for example, finance director, the deputy finance director, and a finance assistant). Another third of this overall amount was allocated for financing fund-raising events, and the final third was allocated toward direct mail to prospective donors and resolicitation mailings, call time, blast fax, and travel expenses.

The third largest campaign expenditure, $75,000, was spent on polling and research for the Baird campaign. One-third was allocated for a baseline poll, one-third for research and fees to the polling organization, and one-third on focus groups and several tracking polls.

The amount allocated for field operations for the Baird campaign was comparatively low at $51,000, which was used primarily for literature, phone costs, the voter file, lawn signs, and paraphernalia. However, the amount budgeted does not tell the complete story. Baird further contributed approximately $150,000 of soft money to fund a campaign school, which trained students to organize the field operation for all Democratic candidates in the Third Congressional District and to coordinate volunteers for the GOTV effort.

Staff and office expenditures came to approximately $124,200 and $47,700, respectively, fairly standard overhead costs for a political campaign. The expenditure for campaign staff is slightly higher, reflecting the hiring of an additional finance assistant, and Baird's choice to add a labor liaison, a position dedicated to coordinating labor fund-raising and events with labor unions in the district.

The Consultants

The Baird and Benton campaigns and their relationship with their political consultants were dramatically different. Baird had the experience of running for Congress in 1996, and he understood the importance of money and professionals in a campaign to mobilize votes, communicate with the media, and finance the activities that political parties and volunteers bring to campaigns. Baird carefully selected his nationally known and tested consultants, and he made sure they understood the strategy, theme, message, and tone of his campaign. Benton, however, chose a campaign manager and consultants from the local talent, and he allowed the NRCC to have a significant impact on the strategy, theme, and message of his campaign. For example, the NRCC focused on national issues of tax cuts, smaller government, and deregulation, rather than issues important to the district, such as education, health care, and jobs.

The central control of authority in the Baird campaign was clearly with the candidate from the beginning.

> If I had a piece of advice for candidates, it would be, hire slow, and fire fast. Do not get pressured into hiring. Every media consultant says, 'you've gotta have me. I've got the contacts with the DCCC. I will win the election for you, blah, blah, blah. They all worked for the DCCC. Everybody's got personal contacts. But as a new candidate, you don't know that. So I did a lot of homework. I called former clients, I called members, and I called the DCCC.[20]

Baird personally interviewed several nationally known campaign consultants in Washington, D.C., by telephone and in person, and he asked the "finalists" to visit the district to meet local volunteers and party leaders. "I insisted that my consultants come to my district at the start of the race," Baird said. "I insisted that they meet with my county coordinators, that they listen to them, that they hear from the people in each county, the rural counties, and the cities; what they thought was important in a race, who they thought they were working for, how they thought the race should be run."[21] After "field testing" the campaign consultants, he selected media strategist Will Robinson of MCSR, pollster Lisa Grove Donovan of LGD Insight, and Bob Creamer and Jerry Morrison of the Strategic Consulting Group, which ran the campaign school for field organizers. Baird oversaw all of the consulting activity and found compatible and knowledgeable professionals that fit into his organization and the dynamic of the district. Later, the campaign consultants helped Baird select a professional campaign manager, Paige Richardson.

After selecting the professional consultants, Baird asked them to spend time with local party leaders and volunteers to discuss campaign strategy.

> They all sat around in a little Carpenter's Union hall in one of the most rural towns we have, in Centralia, and we spent a day with our volunteer field coordinator, and the county coordinator. I wanted there to be communication. I wanted the county coordinator to know the role of the consultants, and I wanted the consultants to hear what the county coordinators said. Because it was real important for me, that the people working for me to know

that I respected their opinions and knew that I wasn't going to hire a bunch of DC consultants without listening to the local folks.[22]

Baird believes the outside consultants benefited from this interaction. "They listened well, and they discussed things well," he stated. "They listened to the local folks. They would say, 'Help me understand this.'" One of the greatest advantages of this interaction, Baird noted, was that it allowed the campaign to plan its strategy early in the campaign and defuse differences of opinion. For instance, he explained, a field coordinator "may place a high priority on newspaper advertising and yard signs while a consultant will look more at broadcast media. Having that dialogue beforehand can at least reduce to some extent the potential friction between the various strategies."[23]

Baird concluded that this careful attention to the consultants hired for the campaign was instrumental to his success. Previously, he was unable to attract top consultants because no one expected that he would win, and he had few funds to pay them. "It's not as if national pollsters and media and manager people were knocking down my door to want to run on this total long shot who's going to get no money."

Polling and Opposition Research

Candidates often integrate a polling strategy into their campaign that draws on a body of knowledge about voters, using demographics, survey data, and opposition research. For the Baird campaign, such polling and much of the opposition research was conducted by Lisa Grove Donovan of LGD Insight, a Portland polling organization that she started in December of 1996. Before opening LGD Insight, Donovan had eleven years of polling experience, much of it as the vice president and managing partner of the Mellman Group, a prominent Washington, D.C., survey research organization. She was familiar with the Pacific Northwest, having worked on polls for numerous candidates and ballot initiatives in Oregon and Washington. Moreover, Donovan was born in Tacoma, and she lived in Portland for a number of years before moving to Washington, D.C., so she passed the Baird "field test" easily.

There were four phases to LGD Insight's research strategy: background "opposition research" on Baird, use of focus group analysis of persuadable voters in Clark County early in the summer, a benchmark poll at the end of June, and several tracking polls conducted between the end of September up to the election in November. (See table 6-7 for tracking poll results.)

The first phase, the background research on the candidate, which Donovan called "total immersion," took place before any surveys or focus groups. During this period Donovan conducted an extensive examination of opposition research on Baird and his 1996 and 1998 campaigns, including a review of all past and current campaign materials such as survey data, direct mail, media ads, public statements, and endorsement questionnaires. She also reviewed media files on Baird and his opponents and held interviews with the candidate and his family, friends, professional colleagues, staff from his current and former campaign, and key consultants and political supporters. Donovan also participated in two retreats with Baird, the other consultants, and key political supporters. One retreat included Baird's county coordinators, who reflected on their grassroots perceptions of the pulse of the community. This examination phase provided Donovan with enough information to generate possible strategies, themes, and messages for the campaign, as well as the opportunity to evaluate the strategies used in the 1996 campaign and to test any assumptions the candidate might bring to the campaign.

Donovan emphasized that LGD Insight was not "molding" Baird into a particular type of candidate, something Baird would not allow. Rather, her involvement was to determine which of the things Baird did and believed that were most likely to bring in voters, because a candidate must feel and believe his or her own message. She noted, "The premise I have is that Brian Baird thinks of a lot of different things, has done a lot of different things, and cares passionately about a lot of different things. [I take] all of those ideas and conclude which two or three or four of those are going to resonate with the voters."[24]

The second phase of the voter research plan was the use of two focus groups: one of persuadable male voters and one of persuadable female voters from Clark County. The county, which has 44 percent of the district vote, was chosen because of its strategic importance, and because, in 1996, Baird did not do as well as previous Democratic candidates in this county.

Both focus groups were conducted in the early part of the summer, 1998. The participants discussed issues they believed were important to the district and reflected on their feelings about the candidate and his issues after watching videotape from Baird's media training session. One theme detected among the participants was a sense of nostalgia, particularly for

Table 6-7. *Baird for Congress Trait and Issue Research, September through October 1998*

Trait or issue	*September*			*October*			*September to October difference*
	Baird	*Benton*	*Baird ads*	*Baird*	*Benton*	*Baird ads*	
Has common sense	3.06	2.96	0.10	3.02	2.92	0.10	0.00
Cares about people like you	2.91	2.86	0.05	2.89	2.82	0.07	+0.02
Will work to reduce and prevent juvenile crime	2.63	2.87	**–0.24**	2.93	2.78	**0.15**	**+0.39**
Represents your point of view on the issues	3.04	2.63	**0.41**	2.63	2.68	**–0.05**	**–0.46**
Will work to improve the quality of education	2.95	2.79	0.16	2.96	2.79	0.17	+0.01
Will stand up to the special interests in Washington, D.C.	2.43	2.61	**–0.18**	2.58	2.58	**0.00**	**+0.18**
Shares your values	2.76	2.67	0.09	2.76	2.71	0.05	–0.04
Is too liberal/conservative	2.04	2.33	**–0.29**	2.09	2.02	**0.07**	**+0.36**
Out of touch?	1.84	2.05	**–0.21**	1.89	2.01	**–0.12**	**+0.09**
Is being too negative in his campaign	1.73	2.16	**–0.43**	1.89	2.14	**–0.25**	**+0.18**

Source: Baird for Congress Campaign, November 1998.

Note: One of the biggest issues in the campaign became state senator Benton's record of missed votes in the legislature. An illustration of this were questions about his missed votes in the October survey. The mean ranking in October for this issue was 2.56.

The numbers in **bold** indicate the traits or issues that show the largest shifts in attitudes from September 1998 to October 1998.

the old days. Donovan observed, "We found that Brian can talk in value-laden language that really comes from the heart, and the way he was brought up—its not like it was written into his speech, it's who he is—right from wrong, golden rule, a man is only as good as his word, resonated with the voters. It goes back to [this] nostalgic longing."

A benchmark poll taken at the end of June was the third phase of the polling plan.[25] Its purpose was to determine the level of name recognition and support for Baird and his opponents. (See table 6-8 for June.) It also tested which messages resonated with the voters in the district and by how much. The poll explored some of the candidate's strengths and weaknesses, as well as the strengths and weaknesses of his opponents. Donovan remarked that as a social scientist, Baird was very involved in the construction of this poll, which made it longer than most benchmark polls.

The poll revealed that while Baird enjoyed an advantage over possible Republican challengers, a substantial number of voters in the district were still undecided. The results indicated that Baird had 42 percent of support in the district, compared with 29 percent of support divided among four Republican challengers. Significantly, 39 percent of those polled were undecided. Also important was that Baird had positive name recognition with only 38 percent of those polled, despite having almost won the seat in 1996 (table 6-8).

The fourth phase of the plan consisted of three trend or tracking polls that monitored voters' attitudes as the campaign progressed. The tracking polls were conducted in late September, mid-October, and late October. Donovan noted that she held off until the last possible moment to conduct the tracking polls because she wanted to wait until the campaign was ready to spend resources communicating to voters. A carefully timed tracking poll could help the campaign detect successes or failures in its campaign strategy.

The first tracking poll, taken on September 25 and 26, compared Baird's support with that for Don Benton, who won the open primary for the Republican Party. Baird had the support of 39 percent of those polled, compared with 27 percent for Benton. The percentage of undecided voters decreased from 37 percent in the benchmark poll to 33 percent. Significantly, Baird's name recognition increased from 38 percent to 54 percent, a sixteen-point positive change, and his favorable rating increased from 27 percent to 37 percent, a ten-point positive change. However, there was also an increase in Baird's unfavorable rating, from 11 percent

Table 6-8. *Washington's Third District, Favorable or Unfavorable Ratings, June to October 1998*
Percent

	June	*September*	*October*	*June–October Change*
Brian Baird				
Name identification	38	54	54	16
Net favorable	27	37	37	10
Net unfavorable	11	17	17	6
Don Benton				
Name identification	32	41	47	15
Net favorable	16	25	29	13
Net unfavorable	16	16	18	2
Bill Clinton				
Name identification	94	96	94	0
Net favorable	59	46	44	–15
Net unfavorable	35	50	50	15

Source: Baird for Congress Campaign, November 1998.

in June to 17 percent (table 6-8). This increase was likely because of a number of negative ads aired against Baird at the beginning of September. By this point in the general election season, the Republican Party's Operation Breakout campaign had spent approximately $440,000 in attack ads on the issue of crime.

There were few changes in the third tracking poll taken on October 17. The only significant shift was a decrease in the percentage of undecided voters, which declined five points from 33 percent to 28 percent. This change was split between the two candidates; Baird's support increased two points to 41 percent, and Benton's support increased three points to 31 percent. Baird's favorable and unfavorable ratings remained the same, at 37 percent, and 17 percent, respectively. His name recognition also remained the same at 54 percent.

The final tracking poll conducted at the end of October revealed no change in these numbers. Overall, the tracking polls illustrated that while Baird made some positive gains in name recognition among the electorate and had made minimal gains in his favorability ratings, a significant percentage of the voters in the district remained undecided until election day.

According to Donovan, her strategy was to ensure that the campaign was defined in such a way that it touched the interests of voters in the district, and it maintained this focus. She described the campaign theme as, a "common sense candidate guided by the lessons he has learned in life, and the voters he has listened to." Donovan noted that Baird's campaign emphasized the values that he found important, and, "some of them sound really hokey, but he was a person that came to us with them. [They] were all Brian Baird values that he brought to this, and how he looked at life."[26]

One significant challenge faced by the campaign was the minimal change in the tracking polls from September to the end of October. Twenty-eight percent of the electorate was still undecided two weeks before the election. This affected the campaign's strategy. The large percentage of undecided voters and the minimal change in the polls proved both a blessing and a curse. It was a blessing, Donovan noted, because the Republicans were unable to get traction with the negative ads. However, it was also a curse because Baird was unsuccessful in getting traction. Because of this, Donovan recommended that Baird continue to spend money on advertising in the final days of the campaign to "break through" to the electorate. She also suggested that the campaign not air multiple ads, which might confuse weary voters inundated with advertising from races across the river in Portland and Salem, which are in the same media market. As Donovan explained, "This discipline was critical to our success. We had to just stay on it. And not communicate too many different messages. We had to stay very focused on our strategy and put a ton of money behind a single ad in order for it to cut through."[27] The ad selected for broadcast showed Baird in a classroom talking about basic values. Baird himself had direct control over the final version of this ad. The campaign also continued to air a second ad that emphasized how Benton missed multiple legislative votes while in the state legislature.

The strategy of a campaign is often revealed by the way a candidate spends his time. Baird's time was spent primarily on fund-raising. As with most congressional election campaigns, constructing a schedule that permits the candidate to juggle multiple demands on their time is a challenge. Further, a schedule must be flexible enough to accommodate last minute changes and possible crises. In an interview Baird emphasized the challenges he faced as a candidate.

> The level of multi-tasking is prodigious. This scenario has actually happened. I'm in the middle of making fund-raising phone calls,

> [and] the press calls, and the press has an off-the cuff—the other side is hitting me on something, and I have to respond to that. We finish the press call, I get a rough draft of a fund-raising letter that is going out, I have to work on that, and then a critical staff issue arises that my manager and I have to deal with. All of that can happen in a 20 minute span, and you have to be able to shift gears completely. You might be having a big fight with somebody on the campaign, or yelling at your consultants, and then your next minute, touching bases with the press. And if you mix up those emotions, you're dead.[28]

To visualize how much time Baird spent on various activities during the campaign, we analyzed his daily activities in fifteen-minute increments for the last four months of the campaign (July to October) (table 6-9).[29]

The most striking fact uncovered from this examination of Baird's schedule is the time he spent fund-raising rather than meeting voters and groups or participating in campaign rallies. This was a campaign of hustling money first and foremost. For the final four months of the campaign, the highest percentage of Baird's total scheduled time was dedicated to fund-raising calls: 33 percent in October, 41 percent in September, 28 percent in August, and 22 percent in July. In real time Baird averaged well over thirty hours a week on the phone in August, September, and October. Baird's approach to fund-raising calls was reflected in his dedication to the task and drive for winning office.

> When I first ran in '95 people told me I would not want to do this, that I would spend my whole life fund-raising. They wanted to put me in a nice room with a mini-bar, some paintings, a comfortable chair . . . I told them, shut up. You are wasting time, you are wasting money. I don't want to raise money to pay for a damn minibar. I want you to get me a phone, and get me good lists, and let's go to work. They said I would hate this. And I told them, yes, but I hate a lot of stuff, and I do it. And I do it well because what matters is not whether I like it. What matters is what's important. You know, did I love hauling garbage to get through college? No, I made the best of it. Does it feel good to want to puke your guts out and have a pack hanging onto your neck, and realize you can fall and get killed when you're climbing Mount Rainer, no. But you did it because it is important and it matters to you. So I do it.[30]

Moreover, the scheduled call time only tells part of the story. Baird and his finance assistant confirmed that he made calls during at least half of his scheduled travel time, the activity that consumed the second largest percentage of Baird's daily activities. The only time Baird would be off the phone was when his cell phone was out of range. Baird also often made phone calls to possible donors during much of his "personal time," which was time scheduled to eat lunch and dinner and brief rest periods before the four public debates. If one conservatively estimates that at least half of the average travel (16 percent) and personal time (16 percent) was also used for call time fund-raising, the average amount of time Baird spent "dialing for dollars" jumps from 32 percent of his time to 48 percent of his time during the final four months of the campaign.

The fourth category that constituted a noticeable percentage of the candidate's time was meetings with individuals, groups, and visiting politicians for the purpose of raising funds. In July and September, most of this time was concentrated in three-day trips to Washington, D.C, when Baird met with a number of PACs. Other scheduled activities throughout the four months included meeting with rank-and-file labor members during shift changes at local union businesses and meeting with individual donors. The average percentage of Baird's time dedicated to meetings with individuals, groups, or visiting politicos in this four-month period was 12 percent. Miscellaneous fund-raising activities accounted for an additional average of 3 percent of his time. Adding this additional 15 percent of time dedicated to fund-raising to the above 48 percent of time scheduled for fund-raising calls brings the total amount of time scheduled for fund-raising to 63 percent, almost two-thirds of Baird's scheduled time.

However, the average time spent on public meetings over the last four months of the campaign was only 8 percent. The average time spent with voters was also low; 7 percent, with most of this time concentrated on the days before the primary and general election in September and late October.

The schedule for the last four months of the Baird campaign reflects a tremendous amount of time dedicated to fund-raising calls, other fund-raising activities, and traveling, which included fund-raising calls on the road in the large Third Congressional District of Washington State. The time scheduled for voter contact and public events for visibility in the district pales in comparison. This was a campaign about soliciting money as much as it was a campaign in search of votes.

Table 6-9. *Analysis of Candidate Brian Baird's Schedule, Final Four Months*

	July		*August*		*September*		*October*		*Totals*[a]	
Activity	*Hours*	*Percent*	*Hours*	*Percent*	*Hours*	*Percent*	*Hours*	*Percent*	*Hours*	*Percent*
Fund-raising call time	54.50	22	81.50	28	135.25	41	126.25	33	397.50	32
Other fund-raising	10.50	4	9.50	3	8.50	3	7.50	2	36.00	3
Meeting with individual, group or politico	55.25	22	17.50	6	44.50	14	28.75	8	146.00	12
Public event	31.25	12	14.00	5	15.75	5	35.00	9	96.00	8
Meeting with media	4.50	2	0.50	1	5.50	2	20.50	5	31.00	2
Voter contact	5.00	2	13.00	4	19.25	6	52.00	13	89.25	7
Meeting with staff	17.00	7	23.00	8	11.00	3	7.75	2	58.75	5
Travel	40.75	16	38.75	13	55.50	17	68.25	18	203.25	16
Personal time	32.00	13	97.00	33	33.00	10	39.50	10	201.50	16
Totals	250.75	100	294.75	100	328.25	100[b]	385.50	100	1,259.25	100[b]
Total hours per day	8.9		9.5		10.9		12.4		10.2	

Source: Computerized Schedule, Baird for Congress Campaign, November 1998.

a. November time analysis is omitted because the month consisted of only three days of campaigning. However, the candidate's time mostly consisted of voter contact—November 1: 10.75 hours, November 2: 9 hours, November 3: 13.50 hours

b. Due to rounding, some percentages do not add exactly to 100 percent.

Relationship with the Consultants and the Campaign Manager

Throughout the campaign, the professional political consultants, Will Robinson, of MSCR, Lisa Grove Donovan of LGD Insight, and Bob Creamer and Jerry Morrison of the Strategic Consulting Group, which ran the campaign school, worked closely with Baird's campaign manager, Paige Richardson, who oversaw the local office staff and dozens of volunteers. The consultants shared ideas and strategy with Richardson, who characterized the relationship as a "two-way" street. Communication between the paid professional consultants and the Baird campaign staff was frequent and constructive. Moreover, Baird was often involved in these conversations. According to Donovan, Baird was an "entrepreneur of ideas," and he frequently bounced ideas off of her. She also complimented his involvement and interest in the polling, including the wording of the questions, and stated that he frequently made inquiries, because of his statistical knowledge, about how the polls were being conducted. "He is a very strategic person, so had more involvement as a strategic big thinker than most candidates." Moreover, she was impressed with how the Baird group ran a positive campaign and resisted the urge to go negative, even in light of the barrage of negative ads from the NRCC. It is important to note that the selection of Paige Richardson, a professional campaign manager, was made by Baird after he hired his professional consultants and with their input and support. They effectively selected Richardson in coordination with Baird, which led to a well-integrated campaign organization.

The Use of the Internet

In this rapidly growing information age, the use of websites is becoming increasingly more common in election campaigns. Both Brian Baird and Don Benton constructed websites listing their biographies and issue positions, breaking news, calendar of events and key directories of headquarters, and staffing information. Moreover, Baird additionally used an issue-specific website in an innovative way to highlight his opponent's shortcomings. The site recorded all of Benton's missed votes while he was a state legislator in Olympia.[31] Five weeks before the general election, the Baird campaign began a humorous television attack ad that pointed out that Benton missed more than four hundred votes while serving in the

Washington State legislature. The website's address was featured prominently in the television ad. The site was also featured in campaign literature. Baird also referred to the Internet site in his debates with Benton and in several press releases. Although the actual site did not generate a substantial number of "hits," the press covered the ad extensively, and the website was used as a source for stories. Several editorial endorsements in the district referred to the site, and there was national media coverage of the site. Later, the site received an American Association of Political Consultants award for the best campaign website in 1998.

Overall, however, the Internet was not effective in fund-raising or getting volunteers for the Baird campaign. Baird's staff thought it was most effective in communicating within the campaign and with journalists. There was little evidence that it had a major effect on the voters in the Third District contest.

The Ground War: The Campaign School and Getting Out the Vote

Field work or the "ground war" involves voter registration and GOTV-drives, mailings, distribution of pamphlets, and placing yard signs. It also includes candidate rallies, parades, speeches to groups, door-to-door campaigning, candidate appearances, and other grassroot activities. Baird contracted with professionals for much of the ground war using the campaign school. The school was formed to benefit all Democratic candidates in the Third Congressional District, as well as the GOTV effort on behalf of Senator Patty Murray, who was running for reelection against Linda Smith.

Bob Creamer and Jerry Morrison of the Strategic Consulting Group (SGC) from Chicago, Illinois, created the campaign school in 1997. It was first used for the candidacy of Jan Schakowsky, a Democratic state representative from Evanston, Illinois, in a three-way primary for a seat in the Ninth Congressional District for the retiring Representative Sidney R. Yates. Creamer, Schakowsky's spouse, and Morrison, her campaign manager, formed the campaign school to simultaneously provide training for students seeking a career in electoral politics and to aid Schakowksy in her field operation. The message of the school was straightforward, stated Creamer:

> Come to Chicago where politics is serious business, and freeze your ass off during the winter. The deal is real simple. You agree to

> devote the next thirty-two weeks to the campaign, fifteen hours a day, seven days a week. We'll train you by some of the best political people in the United States, we'll give you seminars on every area of politics, you'll get assigned a turf for which you are responsible to develop the organization and bring out the vote.

After the successful Schakowsky campaign, the Strategic Consulting Group decided to replicate the school in other areas of the country for the 1998 election cycle. Baird elected to pay for the campaign school after meeting a graduate, Jessica Robinson, from the 1997 program. The Baird campaign paid for the school, which cost approximately $100,000, through Washington State's Coordinated Campaign to benefit all party candidates in the district.

Robinson was selected to supervise the school as field director. The effort was divided into five phases. In the first phase of the project, which began the second week of July, campaign school interns arrived at the campaign site to attend a series of workshops, taught by professional consultants, about every aspect of a political campaign. In the second phase, interns embarked on a five-week effort to recruit volunteers to help build the field organization. To recruit volunteers, the field operators held coffees, attended by one of the Democratic candidates, where interns encouraged people to volunteer for the field organization. Interns also worked mass locations such as parades, malls, bookstores, commuter bus stops, and candidate forums. After the recruitment of volunteers, interns moved to the third phase of the project: voter identification. Several operation bases were established outside regular field offices for phone banking and literature drops in order to identify Democratic voters in the district and to create a voter file for the later GOTV effort. This phase, which started in August, was complicated by the fact that Washington does not have party registration or primary voter information. The identification effort began with lists of preidentified voters from the state party and county party organizations in the district.

Identification of voters was followed by phase three, the creation of the GOTV universe. Interns separated voters into four categories in order to focus their effort. One category included likely Democratic voters, a second listed voters with a history of voting less than 100 percent of the time, a third identified voters living in 65 percent Democratic precincts with a history of voting less than 100 percent of the time, and a fourth targeted individuals who voted Democratic 65 percent of the time or more but who vote less than 100 percent of the time. Given the highest priority for GOTVcontacts, these categories reflected Creamer's GOTV philosophy:

> The fundamental premise is that political campaigns are only about two universes of voters. Persuadable voters who are going to the polls and are undecided, and the second group are people who would vote with us if they went to the polls, but won't. So our two goals are persuading the persuadables and motivating the mobilizables. And that's all. And we have to convince people that we don't care about people who are for the other guy, we don't care about people who are for us. We care about people who are undecided and [those] who are not going to the polls. We just care about those two groups.[32]

The fourth phase of the campaign, voter contact, took place before the primary and general elections. Although it primarily consisted of phone contact, it was also supplemented by door-to-door canvassing and other forms of visibility such as yard signs and a campaign presence at public events. Interns and volunteers called voters to persuade them to vote for Democratic candidates and, in some instances, to inoculate them against negative ads airing against Baird. The early generic script included information about the Democratic candidates on the ticket, in which the caller would remark that he or she was phoning on behalf of the Democratic Party to inquire whether or not the caller supported Baird, Murray, and the legislative candidate in the district. Later, issue-oriented scripts contained answers to some of the negative ads aired against Baird.

The final phase of the project included the field operation for election day. Campaign school interns recruited 1,100 volunteers to assist in targeting voters to get to the polls. Training sessions were conducted the week before election day to review relevant election laws and lay out the final GOTV push. On election day, volunteers were assigned to precincts to retrieve data on voters, which were then sent to regional headquarters where interns would coordinate phone and door-to-door efforts to contact those who had not yet voted.

The Campaign School, the Baird Campaign, and the Party

The relationship between the campaign school and the Baird campaign was informal but effective. Robinson periodically attended staff meetings in order to schedule time with the candidate, and Baird's campaign manager, Paige Richardson, occasionally visited the campaign school's Sunday evening meetings to brief the campaign's progress and to solicit feedback on what the interns were hearing from the voters in the district.

The campaign school was aided in its effort to create a voter file and to coordinate the field efforts of the Democratic Party county chairs throughout the district. The goal of the school was to complement and integrate the efforts at the county party level. To this end, interns obtained voter files from the county chairs and state Democratic Party to aid the voter identification effort at the beginning of the project. Although the strategy for the campaign school and the county parties was the same—to get as many voters as possible to the polls on election day—differences in style led to some tension in the relationship between the two groups. The interns at the campaign school, for example, were more aggressive in their identification of voters, often asking people specifically whether they would vote for the Democratic candidates, while party members used a more neutral approach, usually dropping off literature about the candidates and reminding them to vote on election day. Some party organizers criticized the interns for not respecting the culture in the Northwest. They believed questions about whether a person would specifically vote for a candidate was intrusive, especially for the independent-minded voters in Washington, which does not list party identification. However, as the election approached, the field school and the county parties aligned their efforts to coordinate the final push to get out the vote.

The efforts of the Democratic Party Central Committee of Clark County, considered the best-organized county in the district, aided interns significantly in the creation of the voter file and GOTV plan. For the previous four years, Dan Ogden, a former Washington State University political science professor, chaired the county central committee, making a concerted effort to build the party organization. Disciplined in his approach, Ogden regularly held monthly meetings with good attendance by the executive board members. He successfully placed precinct officers in a majority of the 315 precincts in the county, as well as hosted regular fund-raising activities on behalf of Democratic Party candidates. He revitalized the party organization. The county central committee provided equipment and headquarters space for the candidates and ran six "common" ads, which listed all the Democrats who were running for office. As the election neared, Ogden's party staff and volunteers integrated the county's GOTV effort with the campaign school. The county's coordination with the Baird campaign, while informal, was aided by the fact that Cindy Gibson, Baird's office manager, was the vice chair of the central committee.

Media Strategy

Within the Baird campaign staff, Dave Field, the press secretary, oversaw the media strategy. A journalist before becoming involved in politics, this was Field's second congressional race. He previously worked as press secretary on behalf of Judy Olsen, who lost to Republican George Nethercutt for Thomas Foley's seat in eastern Washington. Field's primary role in the campaign was to schedule interviews with the media and to issue press releases. Field ended up spending a great deal of time engaging in damage control when the Republican National Committee started to air negative television ads against Baird. He was vigilant in issuing press releases denouncing the ads and in following up with phone calls to the broadcast and print media to express the campaigns' concerns. He found this the most difficult part of the job. Using candidate Bill Clinton's "War Room" approach, he noted, "You have to raise a stink every time it happens." And, with an estimated $1 million spent by the RNC on this race, he was on the phone often. However, Field stated that the Baird campaign did not change its advertisement or campaign strategy in light of the attacks. He said, "We have a plan. We're gonna stick with it. Its like in a game . . . you don't change your game plan."

Field also used two other strategies to raise interest in the Baird campaign: press releases and phone calls to prompt the media to attend public events. For instance, he issued press releases trumpeting Baird's policy suggestions, such as loans for part-time college students, and he aggressively pursued media coverage of a planned event where Baird voted by absentee ballot. After the election, Field stated that he had a great deal of difficulty generating media attention about the race. For instance, aside from a thirty-second blip on one of the television stations, the impact of absentee voters was not covered by the local press, despite the fact that Baird lost by 887 votes when the absentee ballots were counted in 1996. Ironically, the *Washington Post* covered the event in its national section. The *Washington Post* also ran a prominent story, accompanied by a sizable picture of the candidate, on the NRCC's Operation Breakout campaign, which announced that Baird was its second target.

The Baird campaign was also very successful with the earned media, newspaper endorsements. It received endorsements from the *Olympian, Seattle Times, Colombian, Seattle Post-Intelligencer, Chinook Observer, Tacoma News Tribune, Oregonian,* and *Longview Daily News.* He received endorsements from every newspaper except for the *Bulletin's Frontrunner.*

Conclusions

House contests for open seats are usually highly competitive, and Washington's Third Congressional District was no exception. Campaign funds, field operations, media coverage, and candidate strategy, theme, and message have a major impact on these competitive races. In 1996 Baird lost his first bid for this district by 887 votes. He was outspent, and he did not focus on absentee ballots. He learned a hard lesson that paid off in his 1998 contest. Money to fuel a professionally run campaign and an effective operation are essential in competitive races. Baird beat his opponent by more than 8 percent in the 1998 general election (table 6-10). As a contestant for an open seat, Baird brought in and spent significant sums of money (more than three times that of this opponent). He hired experienced professional campaign consultants and campaign staff, a characteristic of open seat winners. Baird knew better than to hire amateurs. He ran on a strategy, theme, and message that often went against his national party but was effective with voters in the district. He hired and built an effective grassroots operation to register and get out the vote. He attracted favorable media coverage. He was immediately responsive to negative advertising from the opposition and effectively fought off a massive flood of issue ads from outside groups and the opposition national party organization. Both Baird and his campaign organization knew how to defend themselves against party and interest group advocacy ads and how to incorporate party-financed voter mobilization efforts into this campaign strategy. Issue and opposition research was important to the Baird campaign. Baird's conclusion about the race summed up the importance of money in a competitive congressional seat: "Because I have sacrificed my life to raise money for this race, we are able to roughly match the attack ads from the Republican Party."[33] He also effectively used opposition research about Benton's absenteeism while a state legislator to create an important issue in the campaign and to reinforce it through the innovative website on missed votes. Baird disseminated this message through

Table 6-10. *Vote in Washington's Third District, June through November 1998*
Percent

	June	*September*	*October*	*November 3*[a]
Brian Baird	34	36	35	54
Don Benton	18	25	26	46
Undecided	48	41	39	. . .

Source: Baird for Congress Campaign, November 1998.
a. Turnout in the general election was 62 percent, and turnout in the primary was 35.3 percent of the eligible electorate.

debates, interviews, campaign literature, and by encouraging reporters to go to the website, which they did. The local party organization helped Baird, but the national party organization in Washington played an important supporting role through coordinated expenditures for the grassroots operation organized by the campaign school, by helping Baird hire professionals for the campaign organization, and by offering campaign services and sending campaign funds directly to his organization.

The Baird campaign was typical of contemporary congressional contests. It was candidate centered. It drew on the expertise of professional grassroots organizers, mass media experts, professional pollsters, and a professional campaign manager and experienced staff. Baird did not depend on the parties or interest groups to carry out most of his campaign activities, although they were helpful—especially the fund-raising the local labor liaison provided. He created a paid professional campaign organization that was loyal and responsive to him and no one else. In the end, the contest with Benton was lopsided because Baird worked very hard to raise funds, which established a bigger campaign budget that allowed him to hire some of the best professional campaign consultants in the business. As the Baird case confirms, successful campaigns for open seats in the twenty-first century need money and professionalism.

Notes

1. Paul S. Herrnson, *Congressional Elections: Campaigning at Home and in Washington* (CQ Press, 2000), p. ix.

2. Note that Richard F. Fenno includes this district in his analysis of Congressman Donald Bonker's home style in *Home Style: House Members in Their Districts* (Little, Brown and Company, 1978).

3. Clinton earned 48 percent in 1996, beating Dole by 11 percentage points.

4. Jeff Mize, "Narrow Loss to Linda Smith in 1996 only Re-energized His Quest," *Seattle Times*, October 11, 1998, p. A1.

5. Joel Connely, *Seattle Post-Intellegencer,* September 10, 1998, p. B1.

6. "NRCC Ad Campaign Moves In," *AP The Bulletin's Frontrunner*, September 9, 1998, p. 1.

7. Interview with Brian Baird, October 28, 1998.

8. This tactic was also used against Moore in the Kansas Third Congressional District race in 1998. See chapter 5.

9. Peter Callaghan and Joseph Turner. "Election 98: The Campaign Trail: TV Station Turns Down Attack Ad," *News Tribune,* September 11, 1998, p. 1.

10. The ad was also pulled in the Kansas Third Congressional District race, and the station had aired the thirty-second spot on two occasions before canceling it. See chapter 5.

11. Jeff Mize, *Colombian*, September 16, 1998, p. A1.

12. Peter Callaghan, "Congress' 3rd Congressional District: Both Parties Have Much at Stake in Battle for 3rd District Position; Democrat Baird, who almost won in '96 faces GOP's Benton," *News Tribune,* October 21, 1998, p. A1.

13. Interview with Brian Baird, October 28, 1998.

14. All nonfootnoted quotations from Baird are from on-the-record interviews with him by the authors. This passage is from an interview with Brian Baird, October 28, 1998.

15. Principles reprinted directly from the code supplied by Baird campaign staff, October 1998.

16. Jeff Mize, "Don Benton-Profiles in Determination," *Colombian,* October 11, 1998, p. A1.

17. Interview with Brian Baird, October 28, 1998.

18. See Gary C. Jacobson, *The Politics of Congressional Elections,* 5th ed. (Longman, 2000), pp. 81–82.

19. Jacobson, *The Politics of Congressional Elections,* pp. 40–46.

20. Interview with Brian Baird, October 28, 1998.

21. Ibid.

22. Ibid.

23. Ibid.

24. Interview with Lisa Grove Donovan, November 15, 1998.

25. Benchmark polls are the initial poll conducted by campaigns. They provide a baseline of the important issues in the race, district sentiment, candidate name recognition, and other variables important for developing a campaign's strategy, theme, and message.

26. Interview with Lisa Grove Donovan, November 15, 1998.

27. Ibid.

28. Interview with Brian Baird, October 28, 1998.

29. The coding of the activities began with the first scheduled event and ended with the completion of the last event on the schedule. We then divided each activity into percentages of total campaign time for each month. Nine major activities were coded: call time, travel, meetings with individuals, groups, and receptions with visiting politicians, public events, voter contact, other fund-raising

activities such as house parties and events, staff meetings, meetings with the media, and personal time. Time not specifically scheduled during the day was listed as personal time. For instance, if Baird was scheduled to take the day off, it was recorded as eight hours of personal time. The remaining coding of personal time consisted of lunch and dinner breaks. However, as is noted in the text, Baird often worked during this period that was scheduled for personal time. All data came from the Baird campaign's computerized schedule.

30. Interview with Brian Baird, October 28, 1998.

31. www.missedvotes.com.

32. Interview with Bob Creamer, November 1998.

33. Interview with Brian Baird, October 28, 1998.

CHAPTER SEVEN

Wisconsin's Second District: History in the Making

DAVID T. CANON

THE SUBTITLE TO THIS chapter may sound a bit melodramatic, but voters in the Second Congressional District of Wisconsin truly participated in making history. It is not very often that voters have a hand in producing two historical firsts: Tammy Baldwin was the first woman elected to the U.S. House of Representatives in Wisconsin's history and the first openly gay candidate in the nation to win a House campaign as a nonincumbent (and the first openly gay woman in Congress).

In many regards this campaign was worthy of its historical stature. Baldwin and Republican opponent Josephine Musser held twenty-eight joint appearances and debates in the fifty-six-day general election campaign. Media coverage of the campaign was extensive, and the candidates clearly articulated their policy views. Turnout was high—more than 60 percent in some parts of the district—and 48 percent districtwide. Perhaps most significant, Baldwin's campaign energized the electorate in a manner rarely seen in electoral politics. Her grassroots field campaign was modeled on the strong parties of an earlier era, and it worked! In short, this appeared to be exactly the type of race promoted by the advocates of reforming campaign conduct.

Paradoxically, the campaign also epitomizes everything that is wrong with today's political campaigns: massive amounts of money (more than $4.5 million spent by the candidates in the primary and general election; the total for the election including outside groups approaches $6 million) that required both candidates to spend substantial time "dialing for dollars" rather than talking to voters, floods of money spent by outside groups on soft-money negative ads, poll-driven messages that shied away from tough issues such as entitlement reform, and hard-hitting ads that turned off many voters.

This chapter will examine the Second Congressional District in Wisconsin to gain insight into the conduct of modern House campaigns. What role do political consultants play in shaping House campaigns? How are decisions made at the critical junctures of the campaign? What impact does campaign conduct have on broader questions of political participation and representative democracy? These questions go to the heart of the role of elections in democracy. Do elections continue to provide the ultimate check of political accountability, or has the process devolved into a cynical, poll-driven manipulation of voters that lacks substantive content and democratic meaning?

Overview of the Election

The Second Congressional District in Wisconsin is primarily composed of Madison and its surrounding suburbs in Dane County (72.6 percent of the district's voters in 1998 were in Dane County). Madison is the state capital and home to the University of Wisconsin. It also has a large number of white-collar jobs based in the insurance and biotech industries, as well as some blue-collar jobs, such as the ones at the Oscar Mayer factory on the east side of town. In the surrounding rural counties, tourism and farming are key.

In the 1960s and 1970s, Madison had a reputation of being extremely liberal as one of the centers of opposition to the Vietnam War. This reputation produced the labels "The People's Republic of Madison" and "twenty-three square miles surrounded by reality." However, in terms of population, Madison has never dominated the district. Madison constituted roughly a quarter of the district in 1950–60 and then increased to just over a third in 1970, where it has remained. The population in the outlying rural areas has fallen substantially while the Madison suburbs have grown by ninefold in absolute terms and nearly sixfold in relative terms since 1950.

Most political observers have concluded that the political complexion of the Second District has changed along with the growth of the suburbs, largely because a moderate Republican named Scott Klug held the seat between 1991 and 1999. His mix of relatively liberal social views (he was pro choice) and conservative fiscal views proved extremely attractive. However, the view that the district is more conservative now than it was a generation ago is simply wrong. While the relatively conservative suburbs have grown, this has been at the expense of the equally conservative rural areas rather than the more liberal city.[1] The district was much more conservative before 1963 than it has been since then, largely because Waukesha County, which contains the suburbs to the west of Milwaukee, was removed in the 1960s round of redistricting. The district delivered large majorities for Dwight D. Eisenhower in 1952 and 1956 and gave Richard Nixon 54.9 percent of the vote in 1960. That was the last time that a Republican presidential nominee carried the district, though there have been some close calls (George McGovern and Walter Mondale both won 51 percent of the district vote as the Democratic nominees in 1972 and 1984, respectively). Recently, Democrats have been racking up larger margins, with Michael Dukakis winning the district by eleven points in 1988, and Bill Clinton winning by 18 percent in 1992 and 22 percent in 1996. Klug demonstrated that it was possible for Republicans to win in the Second District, but the district still has a strong Democratic tilt.

The Primary Election

When Klug announced on February 23, 1997, that he would not seek a fifth term, it marked the first time in forty years that the seat would be open (the previous incumbent, Robert Kastenmeier, held the seat for thirty-two years, and Klug defeated him in 1990). The open seat stimulated a flurry of activity in both the Democratic and Republican parties. However, the Democrats appeared to be the big winners in the recruitment sweepstakes. Three of the biggest political names in the district, state senator Joe Wineke, county executive Rick Phelps, and state representative Baldwin, all announced that they would run.[2] Phelps was perceived as the front-runner by most political observers. He had the largest political base (all of Dane County), and ideologically he was somewhat to the left of Wineke and to the right of Baldwin (though there were not many issues that separated the three). The Democratic candidates and contributors sensed this was their seat to win, as evidenced by the sixfold fund-raising advantage that the three Democrats held over the first three Republicans in "early money." In 1997 the Democrats raised

$551,983 among themselves, compared with only $92,099 for the Republicans (as reported by the Federal Election Commission).

The Democratic primary was a relatively low-key affair in which the candidates all stuck to the issues and ran on their records. There were many candidate forums and for the most part, the candidates refrained from attacking one another. The most intense exchanges typically occurred on the issue of campaign finance, when Wineke and Phelps would point out that Baldwin was the only candidate who refused to sign a pledge that would have limited the amount of money spent in the primary to $250,000 and limited the percentage of contributions from outside the district to 40 percent. Baldwin did not sign the pledge for obvious reasons: she was the only candidate to raise substantial money from outside the district, and she led the field in overall fund-raising. All three candidates raised huge sums of money for the primary (Baldwin raised $738,567, Phelps $587,820, and Wineke $345,981). The campaign got a little tense in the week before the primary when Phelps sent out a letter attacking Baldwin and Wineke, both of whom said the charges were misleading and inaccurate.[3] Nonetheless, all three of the leading Democrats signed a "unity pledge" in the week before the primary, noting that they shared the same basic values and positions on most issues.[4] Baldwin squeaked through the primary with a narrow 1,513-vote win over Phelps.[5] One central explanation for her win, according to Baldwin's campaign manager, Paul Devlin, was that she was able to define herself as an "issues person." "We knew that we had to give people a reason to vote for her. Health care and the women's issues, such as comparable worth, played to our advantage. We also played the angle that Tammy was the only woman in the race, which helped us as well," said Devlin.[6] Another important development was removing the media-given suffix that had appeared with Baldwin's name, "the first lesbian member of the state assembly." In the early part of the campaign, nearly every reference to Baldwin mentioned that she is a lesbian. Devlin called the newspapers every day, arguing that this information was not relevant for the campaign. He said, "I would tell them, 'You don't point out that Rick Phelps is a converted Jew every time you mention his name, so just drop the lesbian stuff.'" After a month or so of badgering them, it worked. The references to Baldwin's sexual orientation still appeared in some articles, but it lost its status as the unofficial suffix to her name.

On the Republican side there was even more activity, with six candidates entering the fray, but none was well known in the district. Don Carrig, a wealthy beer distributor, was the first to get into the race in July 1997. He was followed by Jo Musser (the state insurance commissioner), Meredith Bakke (a chiropractor), John Sharpless (a University of Wisconsin history professor), and Nick Fuhrman (a former congressional aide). Some party activists were privately grousing that they lacked a big-name candidate. This general malaise among Republicans prompted a tongue-lashing from Scott Klug, who told them to "quit the whining and get to work."[7]

The relative quiet of the campaign was shattered when Ron Greer exploded onto the scene. Greer was an African American firefighter and part-time minister, who had recently been fired for his anti-gay activities on the job. This incident was front-page news for several days right around the time that he announced he would run for Congress. The media started paying attention to the campaign when a Greer-Baldwin match-up looked like a real possibility.[8] At first, most observers dismissed Greer's campaign. However, he quickly gained national attention, including a segment on ABC news, a visit and endorsement from All-pro Green Bay Packer defensive lineman Reggie White (who had his own controversies concerning anti-gay statements), and endorsements from James Dobson, president of Focus on the Family (a Christian Right organization) and 1996 presidential candidate Alan Keyes. Four of the Republicans (all except Fuhrman and Greer) signed a letter rejecting Greer's gay-bashing tactics.[9]

Carrig and Musser lavishly funded their own campaigns, with Carrig pumping in more than $400,000 of his own money and Musser putting up $300,000. Carrig was also the most active of the Republican candidates, logging more than 40,000 miles in his red pickup and attending more than 800 events. However, it was Musser's careful, targeted campaign that prevailed. "We made an important decision to get on TV early, and this really paid off," said David Welch, Musser's media consultant. "Jo was the perfect candidate in the primary. She always came up with the money we needed to do things right. In many ways, it was a textbook campaign. We targeted likely voters with a direct mail campaign and had an extensive phone campaign through which we identified 12,000 supporters and 7,000–8,000 leaners." Klug also commented on the shrewd primary campaign, noting, "It was a good move for Musser to

Table 7-1. *Primary Election Results and Campaign Finance, Second District*

Candidate	*Vote total*	*Percent of vote*	*Money spent in the primary (dollars)*	*Total expenditures (dollars)*
Democrats				
Tammy Baldwin	24,226	37	738,567[a]	1,342,785
Rick Phelps	22,713	34.7	587,820	587,820
Joe Wineke	17,446	26.7	354,981	354,981
Patrick O'Brien	1,036	1.6	300	300
Republicans				
Jo Musser	10,269	21.2	414,135[a]	858,862
Ron Greer	9,874	20.2	213,932	213,932
John Sharpless	8,488	17.5	75,568	75,568
Don Carrig	8,337	17.2	712,525	712,525
Nick Fuhrman	6,731	13.9	151,548	151,548
Meredith Bakke	4,829	10.0	247,151	247,151

Source: Compiled by the author from official election returns and the Federal Election Commission.

a. Primary spending figures for Baldwin and Musser are from the Federal Election Commission report, September 30, 1998. This overstates the level of primary funding because it includes some money that was spent on the general election.

identify herself as the Thompson candidate in the primary. Most of the candidates were using my name, but I think the difference for Jo is that she was seen as Tommy's candidate by virtue of being in his cabinet." The base of supporters proved critical in the late stages of the campaign when Carrig attacked Musser's position on partial birth abortion with a direct mail piece in the last week of the campaign. However, Musser responded with thousands of phone calls to her supporters, and the damage was limited. The stunning part about the Republican primary was not Musser's win (she was seen as the front-runner relatively early in the primary) but Greer's strong showing. He finished second, only 395 votes behind Musser. Carrig, who spent the most money in the Republican primary, finished a distant fourth, behind John Sharpless (table 7-1).

The 28 percent turnout of registered voters was the highest ever recorded for House primary elections in the Second District; this turnout was a small taste of what was to come in the general election.[10] Voter interest was high, but the candidates had their work cut out for them. For one thing, the parties were deeply split. Welch told me that he reminded Musser the day after the election that 79 percent of the Republicans in the district had not voted for her. Baldwin needed to close the party's ranks behind her as well, given that she drew just over one-third of the Democratic votes. Fund-raising, opposition research, polling, strategy, forming the general election team, and cutting new ads all had to quickly get into high speed. The few days after a primary often place a campaign on the track to success or failure. This is especially true in campaigns with late primaries. After a couple of fits and starts, Baldwin was off and running, but Musser's campaign limped away from the starting line. As one party insider put it, "By early October, Musser's campaign was a car going down the hill with the wheels coming off." John Nichols, the editorial page editor at the *Capital Times*, continuing the automotive analogy, described the campaign in these terms, "Musser's campaign was spinning its wheels, stuck in the mud, while Baldwin cruised right through in four-wheel drive." What can explain the difference?

The General Election Campaign

The first difficulty for the Musser campaign was something that she had no control over. Greer, who had been a loose cannon throughout the primary, considered calling for a recount and then when he finally decided against it, he publicly weighed a write-in campaign. He even made a trip to Washington, D.C., to meet with Christian Right leaders to see if there would be financial support for his write-in campaign. He ultimately decided not to run, but this activity was a major distraction to Musser and hindered her attempt to unify the party. In contrast, Baldwin quickly moved into the general election with a unified party. Musser says that the degree of Democratic unity may have been exaggerated because she had "boatloads of Phelps and Wineke supporters," but she conceded that the Greer distraction and the reluctant conservative base caused her problems that Baldwin did not have to deal with. Eventually, four of the other five Republican candidates (all except Greer) attended a "unity rally" hosted by Klug and endorsed Musser's candidacy.[11] However, the meeting was nearly two weeks after the primary, whereas Baldwin's unity meeting occurred the day after the primary.[12] The second critical juncture was Baldwin's ability to define her opponent before Musser had an opportunity to define herself. Baldwin stuck to her message on health care reform, while defining Musser as an agent of the insurance industry and therefore someone who could not reform the health care industry. Baldwin had some tough contrast ads, but about three weeks into the campaign neither candidate had gone strongly negative. Musser's campaign took an aggressive turn at this point with an ad that showed two elderly people being literally covered with mud from a Baldwin ad. The ad struck many as an overreaction, but Musser told me that they were anticipating a *very* negative Baldwin ad that they had been told would be running soon. In this ad (which never ran and the Baldwin people say never existed), a distraught woman tells how her husband was denied approval for the treatment he needed by his health maintenance organization (HMO) while the insurance commissioner (Musser) refused to intervene on his behalf. In tears, she relates that her husband died while waiting for treatment. Welch, Musser's media consultant, doubts that the ad ever existed, or if it did, he thought Baldwin's campaign would not run it. He said, "I've been in this business a long time and I can't imagine anyone running an ad like that. It just didn't sound right." However, the mud ad was hastily put together from some old footage that Welch had from an Illinois state senate race, and they started running it the next week, even though the "Musser is a murderer" ad did not appear. Welch stands by the ad, saying, "I loved that ad. I thought it was a good defense against mud-slinging and injected some humor into the campaign." Ruth DeWitt, the campaign manager, however, said, "In retrospect, I think we overreacted." A Republican Party insider concurred, "If they would have asked me about the ad, I would have told them not to run it."

The campaign took on a more negative tone from this point, and things went from bad to worse for Musser. In an editorial board meeting at the liberal-leaning *Capital Times* early in October, Musser described her credentials as a moderate Republican. She noted that she had not even been a Republican until fairly recently (she had been an independent) and that she often voted a split ticket. She also spoke passionately about the unfairness of the flag burning and partial birth abortion ads by the Republican nominee in the U.S. Senate race, Mark Neumann. She was then asked if she would vote for Neumann, and she said she was not sure. A few minutes later, she was asked whether she would vote for Russ Feingold, the Democratic incumbent in the Senate race, and again she said she "really didn't know." John Nichols said, "She was very impressive and effective. She knew exactly what she was saying, and she clearly was trying to appeal to our relatively liberal editorial board. Many of us walked out of that meeting saying that we could be comfortable with her as our congressperson. At that point I didn't have any idea about the firestorm that would follow. We didn't even think it was that big a story. We sat on it for about five days because we didn't view it as hot-breaking news."

The firestorm erupted a few days later when Nichols wrote a story noting that Musser might not support Neumann. Republican Party leaders and conservative talk show hosts Charlie Sykes and Mark Belling went berserk. Belling even endorsed Baldwin on the air (which, to give it some perspective, would be like Rush Limbaugh endorsing Bill Clinton) saying, "Tammy Baldwin is an honest left-wing crackpot. Jo Musser is a duplicitous left-wing crackpot. I'll go with the honest one."[13] David Decker, the Republican chair of the First Congressional District, called for a cutoff of all party funds to Musser, as required by the Republican Party platform that was adopted in the summer of 1998 (the platform says that candidates who support partial birth abortions may not receive money from the party).[14] Musser beat a hasty retreat that ended up angering everyone. She said that her comments had been mischaracterized, which made the moderates lose faith in her. At the same time, her conservative base was further alienated by her stand on partial birth abortions. Nichols argues that this outcome was completely unanticipated. He said, "My guess, when I wrote the article, was that the political fallout would be a wash. She would gain some moderate Republican voters who shared her reservations about Neumann and would lose a few more conservatives. In fact, I had one Democratic consultant call me the day the column appeared and say, 'Gee thanks. You just delivered the election to Musser.'" However, when she backed down, she lost all political advantage from the comment. "This completely threw us for a loop," said DeWitt. Musser downplayed the significance of the incident, saying that "not that many people read the *Cap Times* anyway." However, the fallout of the comment went far beyond the readership of Madison's liberal paper.

The next week Musser bounced back a bit with favorable press coverage of an experience that Musser said was the best thing that ever happened to her. She was reunited with her son for the first time since giving him up for adoption twenty-nine years earlier when she was in high school.[15] The media liked the human interest angle, and the conservative editorial page of the *Wisconsin State Journal*, the largest circulation newspaper in the district, pointed out the implications of the story for the abortion debate: "Musser made the right choice," the editorial said. It was not clear how many pro-life Republicans this story may have brought back into the Musser camp, but it certainly helped the campaign to have a positive story on the front page.

Throughout October, the Musser campaign never hit its stride. Musser said, "Everywhere I went I was on the defensive. I didn't have a message. I failed to define myself and I failed to define my opponent." The drift in the campaign was evident to party leaders who urged a more aggressive campaign. In the last ten days of the campaign a "coup" removed Welch from his position and brought Scott Klug in to attempt to save the campaign. It proved to be too little too late. Baldwin carried the election by slightly more than 13,500 votes, 53 percent to 47 percent. Very heavy turnout in Madison made the difference. Districtwide, about twenty-five precincts ran out of ballots. Some voters waited in line for two and a half hours after the polls closed to get a chance to vote. Campaign workers from the Feingold and Baldwin campaigns bought pizza for hungry voters who had not eaten dinner before coming to the polls (this could have been seen as an illegal attempt to influence voters, but given the circumstances, nobody complained)!

The Key Players

While there were dozens of people who played key roles in both campaigns who will not be mentioned here, the central figures are the candidates, the consultants, and the campaign managers.

The Candidates

Baldwin served for three terms in the state assembly, one year on the Madison city council, and eight years on the Dane County board before being elected to the House. She was one of the more liberal members of the state assembly, but she also had a reputation for pragmatism and working with Republicans. John Nichols said, "Some observers have underestimated Tammy Baldwin. She is a very good, effective politician, combined with backbone and idealism. She has been watching politics for nearly twenty years, even if she is still relatively young [36]. She knows where the land mines are and how to avoid them."

Baldwin's real strength as a politician is her ability to connect with people. She is not a spell-binding speaker or a great communicator on television, but in person she exudes a warmth and empathy that is immediately obvious and also very real. Nichols develops this point in more detail:

> Tammy provides humanity that is usually missing in politics. She has a real ability to connect with people. She cares about people, and this is one reason hundreds of people were really committed to her campaign. One example will illustrate this point. The Sunday before the primary was the "Taste of Madison" down on the square. Tammy was out campaigning, shaking hands, meeting voters. As she was talking, a very disabled woman in a wheelchair pulled on Tammy's sleeve. Tammy squatted down and talked to her for at least ten minutes. I wasn't close enough to hear the conversation, but I could tell that the woman had difficulty even speaking. Tammy stayed very close to her so she could hear. She was very engaged with her and focused entirely on the disabled woman while she was talking to her. It wasn't like the typical campaigning scene where the candidate would be looking around to see who else she should be talking to. She could have shaken 40 more hands in those ten minutes. I was watching this with a Phelps' aide and we were both astounded. You just don't see that kind of warmth and humanity in the heat of a campaign.

A reporter for the *Isthmus* also noted Baldwin's ability to connect with voters, "People joke that even if there's a hurricane or a nuclear war, Baldwin's supporters will make it to the polls on September 8 [the primary date]. That's the level of devotion that she inspires."[16]

Baldwin had considered running for the House even before Klug announced that he would not run in 1998. She attended a Women's Campaign Fund candidate training session early in 1996. The three-day event covered the main aspects of running for Congress and were aimed at recruiting women candidates. Baldwin also made a trip to Washington early in 1996 to meet with various women's groups such as Emily's list, the National Organization of Women, and the National Women's Caucus to sound out the possibility of a future House race.

Musser had seventeen years of experience in the health care field before becoming the insurance commissioner in the Thompson administration in 1993. She started her career as a nurse and served in several managerial positions in the 1980s and early 1990s (with the biodynamic laboratory at the University of Wisconsin, Madison, and the General Cardiac Rehabilitation Program in Madison). Musser is intelligent, confident, and ambitious. Welch said, "When Jo interviewed me for the position we talked for two hours. She impressed the hell out me. She has so many good traits. She is very enthusiastic and very competent."

In many ways, Musser was probably the ideal candidate for the Republicans in the general election. She had a mix of issue positions that was very similar to Klug's: conservative on fiscal issues (low taxes, reduced role for government, pro free market) but liberal on issues that are important in the district (she favors campaign finance reform, protecting the environment, gay rights, and is strongly pro choice—she even said she would have voted to support President Clinton's veto of the ban on partial birth abortions, which places her to the left of Klug and the rest of the Wisconsin House delegation, which voted to override the veto). She neutralized the gender advantage that Baldwin would have had against any of the men. And she had strong ties to the state Republican Party, which is dominated by Tommy Thompson. In fact, both the Cook Political Report and the Rothenberg Political Report changed their assessment of the Second District from "leans Democrat" before the primary to "pure toss-up" when the Musser-Baldwin match-up emerged.

However, two of Musser's characteristics contributed to her undoing: her inexperience in political campaigns and her aggressive personal style. One Republican Party insider said that the campaign was in chaos because it was not clear who was in charge. Welch concurred, saying, "We had too many conflicting messages. Jo listened to a lot of people, including her circle of advisers, the party people, me, Ruth, and Linda DiVall. The problem was that this created a lot of dissension and friction, and nobody was making decisions. It was a day-to-day struggle to maintain a semblance of a campaign. This is less likely to happen when the candidate has been through it all before." In a refreshing display of candidness, which is rarely evident in postelection analysis of what went wrong, Musser said, "My inexperience definitely played a role in the loss. I made three or four major screw-ups that the campaign did quite well in recovering from." Musser also took some responsibility for the difficulty in unifying the party. She said, "I could have made better use of the other Republican candidates. I am sure that Sharpless and Fuhrman would have done anything that I asked them. They were available, but I didn't ask them. They didn't offer, but if I had been more experienced at this, I would have had a better sense of how to use the party." All first-time candidates make mistakes, and there is no single incident that one can point to as pivotal. However, the cumulative effect of several decisions that were rooted, at least in part, in inexperience helped bring down the campaign.

The second characteristic, Musser's personality, is more difficult to assess because it is hard to sort out postelection finger pointing from something that was real and may have mattered a great deal. David Welch summarized the problem when he said, "Jo was extremely difficult to work with. She could be very unpleasant. She would ignore advice that she didn't like. She blew up at people when they made mistakes. Sometimes it seemed like she enjoyed the fights." If this was simply a losing campaign consultant's attempt to shift blame to the candidate, it would not be worth mentioning. However, many different sources mentioned Musser's temper, and all but one said that it played a role in the disarray of the campaign.[17] There are two consequences of Musser's personality: first, it contributed to instability on the campaign team.[18] Musser went through five campaign managers, and at least one was fired because he stood up to Musser and told her what he thought about the way she treated people. Second, it contributed to the inability to recruit and maintain a cadre of committed volunteers. In this regard, Musser and Baldwin were polar opposites, and this was a critical difference between a losing and winning campaign. As Welch said, "Human warmth matters. Musser didn't have the committed core of people who wanted to see her win because she was so mean to people. She always complained about not having enough volunteers, but she was the biggest problem in that regard." It is impossible to say how big a role personal factors play in the outcome of a campaign. It is one of many things to throw into the hopper.

The Consultants

Baldwin first interviewed Will Robinson two days before Klug announced that he would not run for a fifth term. Baldwin had previously decided that she did not want to challenge Klug (she had been approached to run against Klug in 1996) because he was firmly entrenched in the district and had committed to serve no more than six terms, so the seat would be open by 2002 at the latest. Thus, the initial interview with Robinson was not with an eye on 1998 as much as laying the groundwork for a campaign at some point in the near future. The future arrived much more quickly than Baldwin anticipated.

After it became clear that Baldwin was going run for the open seat, the calls from consultants began to pour in. "For a while there," Baldwin said, "I was getting three calls and two tapes a day [from consultants who wanted her to hire them]. It felt like the vultures were circling." But

Robinson was different. In the first interview, before Baldwin knew she was running in 1998, Robinson was very low key. Baldwin said:

> I thought that he was going to give me a big sales pitch, but he just talked about his experience as a campaign manager and a field director. He talked for about an hour and told me things I needed to do to win a campaign. He gave advice as a friend, even though we had just met. After all the rest of the calls started to come in, Will kept on calling, but he didn't ever lay on the hard sell. Will was just sort of there. He would say, "Just keep your feet on the ground. Just get through this legislative session." It was basic stuff, but it was so refreshing. By that point I was sold, but it was a decision based on trust in a person who had run campaigns rather than a sales pitch.

Before Baldwin's final decision to hire Robinson he asked if he could conduct a "life story interview. "He said, 'Just in case you do hire me, I want to be ready to go,'" Baldwin related. This two-hour taped interview was to discover the candidate's core beliefs. "By the time I hired Will, he knew me and why I was running," Baldwin said, "My guess is that most candidates don't get that kind of personal attention. As the campaign wore on, I also recognized that it was personally important to him to win this race. That kind of personal stake in a campaign matters."

Robinson has extensive background in state and national campaigns, including Brian Baird's (D-Wash.) successful House campaign in 1998 and the recent Idaho antigay initiative. As Baldwin put it, "Will is not one of the superstar consultants yet, but he will be soon. . . . Robinson has a very liberal political outlook. Will and I used to have arguments about which one of us was more progressive." Another thing that Baldwin liked about Robinson is that he recommended tactics for the campaign that were not in his own financial interest. For example, the media consultant could be expected to push television ads, given that their compensation depends on media buys. However, Robinson pushed the field and get-out-the-vote (GOTV) effort, recognizing that it was pivotal to this campaign.

Musser's selection of Welch was a much easier and more informal process. "She just called me out of the blue," Welch said, "I wasn't even looking for the job." Her first choices for a consultant and pollster were John Roach and Lisa Nelson, however, they had been snapped up by Don

Carrig. Brandon Shultze, Republican Party insider and consultant, told Musser to call Welch. Welch had been active in Wisconsin politics, serving as the consultant for the three special elections in the state senate in 1993. The Republicans swept these elections to regain control of the senate. He also worked for state senator George Petak in his recall election, state senator Alberta Darling, and U.S. Representative James Sensenbrenner. Welch says, "Musser called me and we talked for about two hours. This is what is known in the business as an 'easy pitch.'" Welch was the main impetus behind much of the early strategy, but he lost control of the campaign in its closing weeks as dissatisfaction with the direction of the campaign grew among party leaders. One party insider said, "Welch was just spread too thin. He was involved in seventeen different campaigns in the 1998 cycle. There is no way you can do an adequate job when you have your fingers in that many pies."

Once again, the Baldwin and Musser campaigns were at opposite ends of the scale. Baldwin was extremely happy with her general consultant and the attention she received. She had a close working relationship with her consultant, and they were on the same page on most important decisions. As will be discussed in more detail below, differences were easily resolved and the campaign stayed on track. Musser and Welch had a much more adversarial relationship. There were frequent and sharp differences in campaign strategy, and disputes were not easily resolved.

The Campaign Managers

The differences were not as great between the two campaigns when it came to the campaign managers. Both had competent, dedicated managers who handled the day-to-day activities with great skill. Equally important, both candidates had good working relationships with their managers. Musser said of her manager Ruth DeWitt, "Ruth was head and shoulders above any of the other managers I interviewed or worked with. She was incredibly dedicated to the campaign; she was putting in 20 hour days much of the time." When the relationship between Musser and Welch turned sour, DeWitt served as the intermediary to keep the communication lines open. The only person who raised any questions about DeWitt was one Republican Party insider who wondered whether she had enough political experience. He said, "The campaign was in perpetual chaos. There are a lot of reasons for this, but the infrastructure was never in place and that is partly the campaign manager's job." While it is true that DeWitt did not have extensive experience (she had managed two state representative races and a court of common pleas race in Pennsylvania), she made the best of a very difficult set of circumstances. She was especially effective in dealing with the media.

Paul Devlin, Baldwin's campaign manager, had extensive political experience. "I came from a very political family," Devlin said:

> I have been involved in politics since I could walk, starting with doing lit[erature] drops for George McGovern in 1972. My first paid position was on the Dukakis campaign in Boston in 1988. I ran a state representative campaign in Massachusetts in 1990, was field director for Clinton in Maryland in 1992, and in the Boston mayor's race in 1994. I also worked for a governor's race in Maryland and four or five other races in the Boston area, doing everything from political telemarketing, to voter ID and GOTV. It had been about four years since I had worked full time for a campaign, so I was looking around early in 1998. A friend who was with EMILY's List recruited me for the Baldwin campaign. Tammy and I talked on the phone and I was out there two and a half weeks later running the campaign.

Devlin played a crucial role in keeping the finely tuned Baldwin machine running. He likened the experience to running and then dissolving a $1.4 million start-up company over a ten-month period.

The major difference between the two campaigns was the stability provided by Devlin, who was with the campaign from the beginning, compared with DeWitt, who joined the Musser campaign (which had already been through four other managers) only four weeks before the primary. However, the stability in the Baldwin staff can be overstated. Like many campaigns, there was a substantial shake-up after the primary. They went from a full-time staff of nine before the primary, down to three after the primary. The staff was quickly built back to eight for the general election. Several people had indicated that they would only work through the primary when they started, and a few others were fired. The turnover on the Musser campaign was similar, with only three of the seven full-time staffers in the general election carrying over from the primary (and one of those three was DeWitt, who had not been there long). However, continuity at the top is important because the campaign manager position is the most visible position on a campaign to the outside world.

Laying the Groundwork: Opposition Research and Polling

Opposition research was nonexistent in the primary campaign because of the large number of candidates. It would have been too costly to research the opposing-party candidates because any one of six Republicans or three Democrats could have won. Research on the other candidate within one's own party also was of limited value because negative campaigning is more likely to help others in the race than one's own campaign. The exception is when a clear front-runner in a multicandidate primary may become the target of an attack (as happened when Carrig took on Musser). Once the general election was under way, there was not much time for opposition research. Both campaigns had assistance from the state party organization. Rob McDonald did some research for the Musser campaign, but he was also responsible for advance work and communication, so he was spread pretty thin. Musser noted that general research (both opposition and more positive research for her own positions) was lacking on her campaign. She said, "My team just forgot about the fundamentals. There were many interviews with media people, joint meetings and debates where I walked in with just my wits. We didn't have position papers, we didn't have enough intelligence on what the other candidate was doing. There was a real lack of packaging and research. No fundamentals." There were no comparable complaints on the Baldwin side, and the author's observation of her campaign was that she was always well prepared.

Both candidates conducted three polls in the general election (Baldwin also did a baseline poll in 1997). Interviews with the candidates and their staff revealed that polls played an important part in the campaign decisionmaking process (table 7-2). Perhaps the most important one for the Musser campaign was a poll late in September that showed Musser down by a 40 percent to 48 percent margin. A poll just two weeks earlier showed Musser up by a single point (41 percent to 40 percent). The poll showed Musser underperforming in the rural areas, which were her strength, and Baldwin's favorable ratings were up and unfavorable ratings were down. DeWitt said:

> Baldwin's health care message was working. She had a simple solution and a simple argument: single payer health care and Jo is in the pocket of the insurance industry. It was a good package and a dynamic message. The most disturbing part about the poll was that

Table 7-2. *Polling in the General Election Campaign*

Percent

Source and date of poll	*Baldwin*	*Musser*	*Undecided*
Linda DiVall, September 15 and 16, 1998	40	41	19
Linda DiVall, September 28 and 29, 1998	48	40	12
Linda DiVall, October 25 and 26, 1998	42	40	18
Diane Feldman, September 17 and 18, 1998	46	37	17
Diane Feldman, September 17 and 18, 1998, with leaners	51	39	10
Diane Feldman, October 14 and 15, 1998	48	38	14
Diane Feldman, October 14 and 15, 1998, with leaners	51	43	6
Diane Feldman, October 25 and 26, 1998	51	37	12
Diane Feldman, October 25 and 26, 1998, with leaners	53	39	8

> it showed that the health care message was bleeding over into other issues. The real eye-opener was when Jo was down 11 points on taxes in the rural area. When I saw that, I was, like, "Oh my god!" This was our wake-up call. All of Tammy's negatives were sticking and her message was on course.

Apparently there were some internal differences on how to react to this poll. Welch said that he viewed the bad poll as a midmonth blip. "Everybody started freaking," Welch said, "but it wasn't a real number. It was just a blip. We had just been beaten up on the Neumann thing and Hillary [Clinton] had just been in town. We overreacted." However, the poll led Musser to get more aggressive in her media campaign. Within a few weeks the margin had closed back to 40 percent for Musser to 42 percent for Baldwin (but an 18 percent undecided loomed large with only one week until the election).

Musser said that she primarily looked to Linda DiVall and the polling to confirm her patterns of thinking. But she also indicated that polls played a more dominant role than she would have liked. She said, "Most campaigns today, and probably more Republicans than Democrats, rely too heavily on polling. This was true in our campaign as well. We strayed too far from the basics [by which she meant GOTV and field work]."

Devlin said that their polling "confirmed what we were doing," and the Baldwin campaign did not seem as prone to midstream corrections as the Musser campaign. Of course, it is easier to stay the course when one is ahead. Diane Feldman, Baldwin's consultant on polling, pointed out that a baseline poll conducted in 1997 contributed to the campaign's emphasis on field work. Feldman said, "Field is message. We made an enormous investment in field activity because we knew it was important to mobilize our base but it also was a way of conveying the message that Tammy was a different kind of candidate—a grassroots candidate." Other polling also revealed that Baldwin's status as a lesbian actually was a positive in the Madison area, and it had no impact in the rest of the district (Feldman conducted a split-sample survey where half of the sample respondents were asked how they felt about a candidate who was an "out lesbian and active on gay issues" versus a candidate who was "active on gay issues"). Polling for the Baldwin campaign was also important for showing that Baldwin could withstand most attacks; Feldman said that support for Baldwin surged among young voters when various attacks were tested. Despite the aggressive campaign on both sides, the last poll showed that respondents did not think the Second District race was negative. "This was important for us," Feldman said, "because you can't mobilize voters with a negative campaign." The integral link between polling, field work, and mobilization is indicative of the central role of the grassroots effort in Baldwin's campaign.

Fund-raising

Baldwin broke the all-time spending record in the Second District (the previous high was the $1.26 million spent by Klug in 1996). She had raised $1,523,444 and spent $1.34 million by election day. The Center for Responsive Politics shows that 81.6 percent of her contributions came from individuals and 18.6 percent from PACs; 53.6 percent of the money from her individual contributions of more than $200 came from out of state, a figure that is quite high for a nonincumbent. The biggest sector of contributions, by far, for Baldwin were "single-issue-ideological" groups and individuals who contributed $136,312 as of October 14, 1998 (reflecting her strength with women's and gay rights groups); next on the list was the health sector at $21,216. Baldwin spent twenty hours a week (ten two-hour sessions) "dialing for dollars." Nearly all candidates hate this process, and Baldwin was no exception. "It was awful, just awful," Baldwin said, "It was the worst part of the campaign." Devlin said, "I know she hated it. She just forced herself to do it. We gave her the call sheets with the appropriate amounts of money to ask for, but it didn't make it any easier."

There was a distinct difference between the primary and general elections in Musser's campaign. In the primary, her campaign was mostly self-funded ($284,026 from personal loans, compared with less than $100,000 from individuals and PACs for the primary). She said it was extremely difficult to raise money in the primary. "We would call people and they would say, 'Get back to us if you win,'" reported DeWitt. The money was easier to come by in the general election, but Musser was outspent by nearly a half a million dollars. Some of the problems, as with the rest of Musser's campaign, were organizational. Dave Roberts, who had been in charge of fund-raising in the first part of the general election campaign, had no experience in this area. Amy McGee Polaski was recruited in the middle of October, but by then they were playing catch-up. McGee Polaski had extensive experience in state and local politics, including fund-raising for David Prosser, the former speaker of the state assembly, and U.S. Representative Toby Roth. She ended up raising about 75 percent of the money during her tenure as finance director and contracted out the remaining 25 percent to a D.C. firm, the Townsend Group, and Lisa Nelson. McGee Polaski said that Musser was "better than most candidates at making phone calls and spent about two hours a day working from the call sheets." More than a third of money for the campaign came from a personal loan from Musser. Of the remaining money raised, about half came from individuals and half from PACs. According to the Center for Responsive Politics, 15.8 percent of Musser's money came from out of state and her top sector of contributions was finance-insurance-real estate, with about $16,000 in contributions.

Campaign Conduct: Decisionmaking in the Trenches

One of the key goals of this study is to identify key junctures in the campaign and how the decisionmaking process worked, both in general and on those important decisions. In the Baldwin campaign, there was a clear locus of decisionmaking that revolved around Will Robinson, Diane Feldman, Paul Devlin, and the candidate. Baldwin signed off on all key decisions, such as the text of polls and ads, but typically this approval was perfunctory (she said that she typically spent no more than five minutes on the task, but there were some exceptions that will be discussed below). The impetus for most of the key decisions on the media campaign came from the consultants, but there was general discussion on other campaign issues, with the impetus coming from Baldwin (such as the focus on the field campaign). Devlin says that Baldwin rarely said no and that the decisionmaking process was fairly consensual. Feldman said, "Tammy was the ultimate decisionmaker on everything. Some candidates abdicate responsibility and say, 'Do what you have to do.' She didn't do that. She didn't micro-manage, but she was always there in the decisionmaking process."

In contrast, the Musser campaign evolved with no clear lines of authority. Klug noted, "There was no real organization. Before the primary they made some good decisions, like linking Musser to Thompson. But after the primary there was no infrastructure in place. There was nobody making the key decisions." Welch was far less charitable and much more blunt, "It was often chaotic. The candidate never ordained anyone to be in charge and she listened to too many people. She listened to all her liberal Republican friends and at the end of the day she would be all conflicted and pablum would come out. Our job was to take the pablum and pretend it was a campaign. There was no definitive decisionmaking process."

Campaign Theme, Message, and Strategy

The campaign theme for the Baldwin campaign was one of its real strengths, while Musser's message never seemed to get on track. Baldwin developed a "message triangle" that she stuck with throughout the primary and general election. The three legs of the triangle were "a different kind of candidate," health carc, and a "visionary, future orientation." The "different candidate" leg was "malleable," according to Baldwin, depending on the audience. For students, she might emphasize that she was the youngest candidate with the strongest grassroots campaign. For a women's group, she would emphasize that she was the only woman candidate (in the Democratic primary). To business groups she would note her commitment to bipartisan cooperation in getting things done. This "malleable difference" could be seen as a cynical attempt to tell voters what they want to hear, but instead it was an astute way to run a campaign by building on the candidate's range of strengths.

The "visionary" message was the part that seemed to come from the candidate's heart. In Baldwin's standard stump speech, she talked about linking the past and future. She personalized this connection by talking about her grandmother and her two-year-old cousin, Jennifer. One of Baldwin's direct mail pieces said, "Raised by her 92-year-old grandmother, Tammy has a unique understanding of issues affecting our seniors. Caring for those who raised us should be made easier through compassionate policies that recognize the contributions our parents and grandparents made to this country." This focus on the past was then linked to the candidate's vision for the future: the mailer noted Baldwin's commitment to protecting Social Security and Medicare, and several television ads mentioned Baldwin's experience in helping take care of her grandmother as one of the reasons she was so committed to improving health care coverage. The direct mail piece also had a picture of a little girl waving an American flag, with the caption on the opposing page, "What kind of future should we build for our children?" On the front of the mailer was a picture of the candidate and this message, "Dear Friend, This election is about our future. My vision for the next generation is stronger schools, safer communities and quality health care for everyone. Working together, there is nothing Americans can't accomplish. I'd appreciate your vote on Tuesday, November 3," signed "Tammy." These themes were reinforced in Baldwin's stump speech in which she emphasized the need to protect Social Security by noting a personal concern that the program would still be strong when her cousin Jennifer would retire in the year 2062. This deft linking of past and future worked well with Baldwin's emphasis on her idealism and optimism, which she contrasted to her opponent's "politics of cynicism." When Baldwin talked about her vision of the future, she spoke with passion. Her standard stump speech usually included a quote from Margaret Mead that "small groups of committed people can change the world."

The final leg of the three-part message triangle was the focus on health care. To some extent this was a poll-driven position that would not have been as central in the campaign if it did not appear toward the top of most of the district voters' "most important problem" list. In the primary election, Wineke, Phelps, and Baldwin all emphasized health care to some extent. Baldwin distinguished herself from the others (the "different kind of candidate" theme) by advocating a comprehensive, single-payer health care system, whereas her opponents, both in the primary and general election, favored more incremental reforms such as the HMO legislation that was being considered in Congress. On one hand, this seemed like an odd choice given the demise of comprehensive health care reform in 1993 and the clear rejection of a single-payer plan as being too radical. On the other hand, the position squared nicely with Baldwin's message of optimism and idealism. Recognizing that this idealistic position could be criticized as naive, in her stump speech Baldwin argued that we need to fight for what we believe is best. Baldwin also emphasized her reputation in the state assembly as someone who was willing to work with Republicans to get things done. By linking the health care theme to the other legs of the message triangle—the different kind of candidate and the vision for the future—Baldwin was able to make the unlikely position on health care work.

The health care position became even more important in the general election. The dynamics of how this issue played out is a good example of how campaign themes and strategies interact to influence the outcome of an election. Musser had some real strengths on health care: she was a former nurse and had been the state insurance commissioner in the Thompson administration. Therefore, the Baldwin campaign was worried that the health care theme could be preempted, or at least weakened, by Musser's relative strengths on this issue. Consequently, Baldwin's campaign moved quickly to define Musser before she could define herself as a champion of health care reform. The strategy was simple and effective: Baldwin would take Musser's potential advantage, her experience as insurance commissioner, and turn it into a liability. Baldwin ran a series of ads that portrayed Musser as a tool of the insurance industry. Ads detailed the PAC contributions that Musser received from the insurance industry and argued that she "supported the insurance industry over the consumer in 97 percent of the complaints brought to her department." In contrast, the ads pointed out that Baldwin supported comprehensive health care reform and an expansion of the Family Leave Act (which Musser approved of but did not want to expand).

At the same time Baldwin was defining Musser as a pawn of the insurance industry, she continued to expand the policy leg of the message triangle by changing health care into a cluster of issues, including pay equity, education, and crime. Baldwin said, "We wanted to make sure that we weren't viewed as a single-issue campaign." The themes were still consistent with the candidate's background, but they allowed her to expand her base.

Musser's campaign started with a very general strategy rooted in an analysis of the various constituencies in the Second District and a specific campaign plan. The general strategy was rooted in Klug's formula that got him elected four times: win big in the rural areas (at least 60 percent to 40 percent), avoid getting clobbered in Madison (no worse than 35 percent to 65 percent), and win the battleground of the suburbs (by

55 percent to 45 percent).[19] Clearly these were the absolute minimums, because no campaign wants to win by less than 1 percent of the vote. But this was the baseline with which to work. The campaign came very close to hitting these targets, but as will be discussed, it did not anticipate the heavy turnout in the Madison area.

The campaign plan had four phases that would each last about ten days in the forty days leading up to the general election. The first phase would reintroduce Musser to get past the clutter of the six-candidate primary. "We didn't know anything about Baldwin," said DeWitt, Also we couldn't do any contrast ads. Also, 79 percent of the Republicans in the primary hadn't voted for Jo, so we needed to establish our base." This phase of the campaign was executed according to plan with little disagreement among the key decisionmakers on the campaign.

The second phase provided a stark contrast between Baldwin and Musser. DeWitt said that the campaign believed that Baldwin would try to win by appealing to the "Klug middle." "They were going to try to make her like Jo, so we had to draw a contrast based on Tammy's voting record that would portray her as the liberal that she was, rather than a moderate," said DeWitt. Unlike phase one, there was some disagreement on the focus of the contrast ads. While DeWitt, Welch, and Musser agreed that Tammy's record on crime and taxes would be part of the equation, Musser wanted to push health care while Welch wanted to stick to taxes and crime. Welch said, "Tammy's record on fiscal issues was enough to take her down. We should have stuck to that, stressing how Jo would protect your pocketbook. We even had the polling showing that Tammy's position on health care didn't hurt her at all. We asked, 'Would you be more or less likely to vote for Baldwin if you knew she favored a Canadian-style, single-pay health plan?' It was a wash. It just wasn't there. In general, if you have a Democrat and a Republican on health care, the Democrat is going to win. It just isn't a good Republican issue. Taxes and crime are our meat and potatoes."

Welch largely won this debate, and the contrast ad mentioned taxes, the balanced budget, and crime on the negative side and Musser's record as insurance commissioner, protecting Social Security, and taxes on the positive side. However, a tougher version of this ad, advocated by Welch, was vetoed by Musser. The ad had a visual with a sex offender and ominous music in the background. DeWitt said, "We had the ad ready to go, but we blinked. We lost a couple of crucial days as we toned down the ad." Ironically, by the end of the campaign, Musser was wishing that the campaign had gone negative earlier and with more punch.

The third phase of the campaign plan was to go back to positive themes with testimonials from Sue Ann Thompson (the governor's wife) and Klug. The theme of these ads was going to be "hire Jo" and would focus on her experience and "ability to get things done." However, this phase coincided with what came to be known on the campaign as the "implosion week" with the Neumann/partial birth abortion controversy and the debate over the "mud" ad. Needless to say, phase three "got junked." "We needed to get back on message," said DeWitt.

The campaign was scheduled to close with a strong contrast ad that would force a choice. It would have portrayed Baldwin as soft on crime and taxes and Musser as the responsible alternative. However, with the campaign struggling to regain its footing, its managers decided to go negative instead. This was the point at which the "coup" took place, Welch was fired, and Klug essentially took over the campaign.

Through this shifting terrain, Musser's message was never firmly established. The roots of a strong message were there: Musser was an experienced, moderate, competent leader, who would protect your pocketbook while fighting to protect Social Security and improve health care. However, Baldwin was able to define Musser as a tool of the insurance industry before Musser was able to establish this message. Thus, much of Musser's time was spent on the defensive.

There was one issue concerning the campaign message that everyone on Musser's team agreed upon: she would not raise the fact that Baldwin was a lesbian. This was even put in writing in the campaign plan. However, there was an implicit message in many ads that seemed to be aimed at the issue. DeWitt argues that Musser's frequent mentioning of her status as a "nurse, wife and mother" who "understood Wisconsin families," while "Tammy Baldwin just doesn't understand how we live," did not have undertones that were intended to bring attention to Baldwin's sexual status. "We would have had the same message if Tammy had been straight," DeWitt said. However, Welch said (without me even asking about it), "Was there some subtlety on the gay issue behind the 'I understand how you live,' line? Sure, it was there." As an unscientific test, the author showed two of Musser's direct mail pieces that raised the "understanding how we live" message to people who had no knowledge of the Second District race to see if they detected an underlying message.

None of them picked up any antigay sentiments. However, the "understanding how we live" message may have been obvious enough to nudge toward Musser some voters who had concerns about Baldwin's status as a lesbian.

Earned and Paid Media and the Internet

According to candidates and campaign managers, "earned media" coverage is always hard to come by. Despite these claims, the print media coverage of the Second District race was intense, and the broadcast media coverage was heavier than usual. The primary election was a very low-key affair until Ron Greer entered the campaign, and then the race was front-page news for weeks. The national attention brought by Greer was only a small taste of the media circus that would have ensued had there been a Greer-Baldwin match-up (in Feldman's words, "It would have been ugly"). Even in the primary, it was relatively easy to get good information on where the candidates stood. A series of one-hour interviews with each of the candidates, with questions from listeners, on Wisconsin Public Radio was especially useful. There were numerous candidate forums, which were not very useful when they attempted to include all ten candidates. Even when they split them up by party, there were too many candidates in the Republican primary to have reasonable exchanges. However, such forums still played a very useful role.

The candidate's television spots in the primary election were informative and positive. One advantage of multicandidate fields is that they cut down on the incentive to go negative. Baldwin ran six ads in the primary, and all of them were positive, developing her focus on health care, pay equity, and education. One humorous spot on "drive-by deliveries" showed a young couple pulling up to "Baby Quik," a fast-food version of delivering a baby. After the ad explains that Baldwin fought for allowing mothers to stay in the hospital for at least two days after delivering a baby, the camera closes to the "Baby Quik" drive-up where the voice asks, "Would you like fries with that, dude?" The only Baldwin ad that had even a hint of contrast was the wording of her last ad that said, "Tammy Baldwin will be willing to take on the issues that congress*men* won't," a very subtle shot at her male opponents. Devlin and Feldman noted that this wording was poll tested.

In the general election, the intense media coverage continued. A Nexis search revealed ninety-five articles in the *Capital Times* (46), *Wisconsin State Journal* (38), *and Milwaukee Journal Sentinel* (11) in the fifty-six days between the primary and general election. There were several general profile articles, specific "truth in advertising" pieces that dissected ads, and articles covering specific events and issues. There were so many candidate debates and joint appearances that the media stopped covering most of those, but there were at least three televised debates during the general election campaign. Other events that generated media coverage were appearances by Donna Shalala, Dick Gephardt, Candace Gingrich (the former Speaker's sister), Robert Redford, Hillary Clinton, and Ann Richards at fund-raisers for Baldwin and appearances by Bob Dole, John Linder (the NRCC chair), and Dick Armey at fund-raisers for Musser. As noted, the story about Musser's reuniting with her son received television and print coverage for a couple of days. In general, the television coverage was not as intense as the newspaper coverage, but it was well above average.

I have already discussed the paid media campaigns to some extent in the section on theme and message. Baldwin went on the attack first with contrast ads that portrayed Musser as an agent of the insurance industry while arguing that Baldwin would fight for real reform. At the same time she ran a positive ad that talked about Social Security, education, and health care. She continued this pattern throughout the campaign, alternating contrast, negative, and positive ads. Overall, she ran three positive ads, four contrast ads, and one negative ad in the general election campaign. Two of the positive ads ran relatively late in the campaign. One that started on October 16 raised many of the same themes that Baldwin used in the primary. She mentioned her grandmother and her commitment to health care. Devlin said, "It was important for us to get away from the negative ads. We thought this might help us break through all the clutter on TV." The other positive ad was an ad labeled "Bucky," which was brought back from the primary campaign and was targeted again at University of Wisconsin students.

The decisionmaking process concerning the media campaign was fairly consensual on the Baldwin campaign. The only moment of doubt came with the first hard-hitting contrast ad that portrayed Musser as in the insurance industry's pocket. When she first saw that ad, Baldwin remembered thinking, "Oh my goodness. This is much stronger than I thought it would be. Will emphasized the importance of making a contrast on health care because it was so central to our campaign. I said to him, 'Explain to me again the difference between a negative ad and a contrast ad.' Running that ad was the toughest decision I had to make during the campaign." One thing that Baldwin insisted on was having documentation for all of the assertions in an ad.

The only purely negative ad that Baldwin ran was actually much lighter than some of the contrast ads. It did not have the jarring black and white photos with big red xs through them and the "death march music" in the background (as Baldwin called it). Rather it featured a woman folding the laundry and talking about Musser's comment on a Wisconsin Public TV interview that many young men neither needed nor wanted health insurance. The woman says, "My son needs health insurance. Why take a chance?" The ad briefly mentions Baldwin's support for universal health care, so it could be considered a contrast ad, but it was about 90 percent attacking Musser and 10 percent pro Baldwin, whereas most of the contrast ads in the campaign had a 50-50 balance.

Musser ran five ads in the general election campaign, one positive, one contrast, one inoculation-defensive, and two negative. The controversy over the inoculation ad was briefly mentioned above (the one with the elderly couple getting covered with mud). An article in the conservative-leaning *Wisconsin State Journal* asked, "But are Baldwin's ads really mud-slinging? This is open to debate. Mud-slinging more often refers to personal attacks on someone's character or family. Musser doesn't have a voting record, so her record as insurance commissioner is fair game. Musser, however, feels her reputation as a regulator is being questioned, which could be taken as a swipe at her character. Still, if this is all the mud-slinging we see in this race, we're lucky."[20]

The biggest debate over Musser's media strategy came in the last two weeks of the campaign. Welch argued for keeping the Klug ad on television, which attacked Baldwin for "never meeting a tax she didn't hike," through the end of the campaign and then complementing it with an ad where Jo would talk directly to the voters.[21] Welch wanted that ad to include a statement from Musser along the lines of, "I know there has been a lot of negative advertising in this campaign. But now it is time to cut through all the clatter and realize what is at stake in this election. Tammy Baldwin simply doesn't understand how Wisconsin families live. She is in favor of big-government programs like government-run health care and she would raise your taxes to pay for it. I would protect your paycheck, while working for the programs that are important to you like Social Security and education. Please vote for me on November 3." Nichols concurred that this strategy may have been more effective, saying that the biggest mistake that the Musser campaign made was not putting her on camera. She never spoke in a single ad, which is odd because she is a very effective speaker. In contrast, Baldwin spoke in four of her six primary election ads and two of the eight general election ads.

However, Musser rejected this approach, and Klug was brought in to rescue the campaign. A party insider said that there was not much of a choice in the last ten days. The campaign knew that a strong negative ad was a risk, but Musser felt they had to do something dramatic. The ad they ran in the last week of the campaign shows a man talking about Baldwin's position on several crime bills and concludes, "It seems Tammy Baldwin thinks that social workers are more important than jail time. Do you? I would vote for Tammy on November 3, but (then the jail bars slam shut and the music turns ominous, showing the mug shots of the person who has been talking to the camera) I have a prior engagement."

Many voters viewed the "Convicts for Baldwin" ad as too extreme in the way it was framed for the message to be believed. Even if several of the points in the ad were correct (and one was somewhat misleading), the context of the ad negated that message. It is true that Baldwin took a "softer" approach on crime than Musser. Baldwin favors more prevention and treatment programs as opposed to stiffer sentencing, more prisons, and "three strikes and you're out" provisions. Nobody wants sex offenders running around our communities; the question is how best to protect us? However, this more nuanced debate is difficult to present in the competitive atmosphere of a campaign. Campaigns do not lend themselves to subtle shadings of differences. Consultants and candidates have an incentive to paint differences as starkly as possible, even if that means having a "convict" sing praises of one's opponent.

It is hard to say whether the ad backfired. Musser polls show the gap between Baldwin and Musser went from two points before the ad ran to six points on election day, but Baldwin's polls showed that she stayed at 53 percent while Musser picked up all 8 percent of the undecideds. Other factors clearly played a role in the last week of the campaign, but the perception of most of the political observers interviewed for this study is that the ad was a sign of desperation and probably did more harm than good for Musser. Musser, however, does not second guess the decision to go negative. She said, "I wish to god that we would have thought of bringing in Klug sooner. It's just what needed to be done."

One relatively minor point that struck me as interesting was an offhand remark by Paul Devlin when we were going through the campaign ads. He said, "You know, Jo Musser's ads never directly asked people for their vote. We thought it was important to have Tammy ask." This remark reminded me of a story that former House speaker Tip O'Neill was fond of telling. The line that is always quoted from Tip O'Neill's memoirs is the memorable adage "All politics is local." On the same page of his book relating that bit of wisdom, O'Neill offers this advice:

> The second political lesson I learned from my first campaign came from Mrs. O'Brien, our elocution and drama teacher in high school, who lived across the street. The night before the election, she said to me, "Tom, I'm going to vote for you even though you didn't ask me to." I was shocked. "Why, Mrs. O'Brien," I said, "I've lived across the street from you for eighteen years. I cut your grass in the summer. I shovel your walk in the winter. I didn't think I had to ask for your vote." "Tom," she replied, "Let me tell you something: people like to be asked." She gave me the lesson of my life, which is why I have been telling that story for fifty years.[22]

In modern House campaigns in districts with 550,000 residents, it is obviously impossible for candidates to personally ask for everyone's vote. However, the tag line, "Please vote for me on November 3," is today's equivalent of this basic political courtesy.

A new technique for reaching voters burst onto the scene a few years ago and is rapidly becoming an indispensable tool of modern campaigning—the Internet. The tool is so new that nobody knows how many voters it influences (however, the same could be said of older tools, such as the ubiquitous yard signs and bumper stickers). However, the potential is there. The *Washington Post* website reported that one-third of all adults now use the Internet; 82 percent of them are registered to vote, and 55 percent voted in the last election.[23] A historical first happened this year when Ted Mondale, the former vice president's son and gubernatorial candidate in Minnesota, took out an ad for $100 a month on the "Checks and Balances" website that covers Minnesota politics. Many of the best sites in 1998 provided video clips of the candidates' thirty-second spots, rebuttals of their opponents' attacks, and links to other political sites. While the precise value of web communication is not known, at a minimum this tool provides a relatively low-cost way for candidates to disseminate information, recruit volunteers, and even solicit contributions.

Musser and Baldwin both had excellent websites. Baldwin's was updated more frequently than Musser's and contained more information about the campaign. A review of all the Wisconsin candidates' websites said that Baldwin's was "the most specific" of the four candidates in the First and Second Congressional Districts.[24] Both sites provided basic information about the candidates' positions, press releases, text of some ads, scanned versions of the direct mail pieces, lists of opportunities for participating in the campaign (including contributions), and ways to contact the campaign. Baldwin employed a creative use of the web when she mentioned a site in one of her ads (nohealthcare.com) that provided evidence to back up some of the charges that she made against Musser in the ad. Devlin said that the site had 45,000 hits during the campaign.

Field Work, Volunteers, and Get Out the Vote

An editorial in the *New York Times* two weeks after the 1998 midterms argued that the surprising success of the Democratic Party could be attributed to the massive "ground war" aimed at turning out Democratic voters.[25] A targeted GOTV campaign enlisted thousands of volunteers to register voters, make phone calls, distribute leaflets, and personally urge voters to go the polls. This was a combined effort that was primarily driven by labor unions but also included black community groups, gay activists, women's groups, and seniors. In 1996 the AFL-CIO spent millions of dollars on negative ads to attempt to elect a few dozen Democrats in targeted races. Not only did this effort largely fail but it drew the wrath of the Republican-controlled Congress and state legislatures around the nation that attempted to curtail the political power of unions. The 1998 shift in strategy appeared to have a huge payoff. Although voter turnout was down substantially from 1994, reaching the lowest level since 1942 (though only marginally lower than 1978, 1982, 1986, and 1990), Democratic turnout was down only 2.1 percent from the previous midterm compared with a precipitous 19 percent drop for Republican voters. The GOTV campaign helped produce a gain in House seats for the president's party for only the second time since the Civil War (the only other time was in 1934 in the middle of the partisan realignment of the 1930s).[26]

This national GOTV campaign was evident in the Second Congressional District, but the larger story was the parallel effort by the Baldwin campaign. Baldwin's field organization was very impressive. Baldwin said that very early in the campaign she made it known that "one of the legacies that I wanted to leave, win or lose, was to build a grassroots organization. This was a goal of mine. I had no idea how to do it. I'm not a field person. But we did it!" The field consultant, Joe Kowie, directed the effort, but Paul Devlin and Pam Porter played the key role in handling the day-to-day problems and organization (Robinson and Feldman also have extensive field experience). Throughout the campaign, Baldwin had 3,000 volunteers who put in from two to sixty hours a week. Most of the 3,000 did a literature drop or two, or worked the phones for an evening, but a smaller group put in substantial time. Devlin estimates that there were 20 full-time volunteers during the primary and 35 during the general election. The field organization had a regular meeting on Sunday night. On the night before the election, there were 51 people working on the GOTV efforts. Baldwin described the weekly field meeting as "rejuvenating." She said, "I would go to these meetings just to listen to the discussion and to get fired up. Joe would be on the speaker phone in the middle of the room barking out questions, 'OK, how many building and floor captains do we have in the dorms?' Someone would answer, 'We have 87 of the 150 positions." How many more can we get by next week?' he would ask. . . . Everyone was energized by these meetings. In many ways, our campaign was an old-fashioned, person-to-person effort. It really came together in the last week of the campaign."

One important part of Baldwin's field campaign was reaching students. The 40,000 students on the University of Wisconsin campus constitute about 10 percent of the potential electorate in the district, but students are notorious for not voting. Baldwin attempted to break this pattern by conducting a coordinated "ground war" and "air war." "I hate military metaphors," she said somewhat apologetically, "But we knew that the grassroots effort would be more effective if we would run ads to back it up—provide air support for the effort on the ground." The field effort was incredibly efficient with 1,700 student volunteers, building captains and floor captains in every dorm, and a targeted registration and GOTV effort on campus. There was one ad that was targeted specifically at students and ran on MTV and during shows like *Ally McBeal*. The ad said that "there is one candidate who understands *our* issues." It ended with a pitch (with phone number) to get out and vote and even mentioned that one can register at the polls. The ad also contained a reference to Baldwin's website. Devlin said that every time the ad ran, all ten phone lines in the headquarters would light up. The person handling the phones would yell out "Bucky," which was their unofficial name for the ad (after the University of Wisconsin mascot "Bucky Badger," so that others in the office would pick up a line.

On election day, a coordinated Democratic effort, which was staffed primarily by Feingold and Baldwin volunteers, contacted identified supporters, urged them to vote, and offered to drive them to the polls. Poll workers checked names off lists as people entered the polls, and people who had not shown up yet toward the end of the day were contacted again by volunteers.[27] The coordinated effort clearly paid off. In the six wards with the highest concentrations of students, Baldwin carried 70.1 percent of the vote (3,899 to 1,662). Several of the downtown precincts, which also have high concentrations of students, went 90 percent to 10 percent for Baldwin.

Volunteers provided a tremendous boost for the day-to-day activities in the Baldwin campaign. Devlin coordinated the volunteers into a smoothly oiled machine. With the large group of volunteers, there was always somebody there to do the work. Devlin cited one example of a mailing of 2,000 letters that went out in fifteen and one half hours, from the reproduction, to addressing the envelopes, and getting them to the post office. "At first we designated Tuesday night as volunteer night. Then it was Tuesday and Thursday," Devlin said, "Then Tuesday, Thursday, and Saturday. Finally, people were coming in all the time. They manned the phones, photocopied checks, did the daily deposit, thank-you letters, data entry, mail merges, and many other things. We emphasized to the interns and volunteers that they were part of the chain. If any link of the chain was broken, the task wouldn't get done. The thousands of hours of volunteer time that we had freed up the staff to do other things. We were always able to get the continual flow of small things done very quickly."

In contrast the Musser campaign only had 350 to 400 volunteers who put in a few hours on a literature drop or working the phones, and a group of 20 to 30 "hard core" volunteers according to Pete Kammer, the field coordinator. Musser said, "We didn't ever have any tough discussions about getting out the vote. We didn't talk about how to counter Baldwin's efforts, or how we were going to make a dent in the Madison vote. When I heard about Baldwin's targeting of the campus, I asked several people what I should do, including Klug and Brandon Schultze. They both said, 'Don't worry about it, students don't vote.' The lack of a strong field effort killed us." Welch was even more blunt, "Our field campaign was virtually nonexistent. We didn't have any *people*. There was never anybody around. We even had to pay people to walk with Jo in small-town parades during the primary. At the end of the day, it's the people you put on the street that make a difference. They're the ones who make it happen." This was clearly a campaign that was won and lost in the trenches.

Outside Forces

The Wisconsin and national party organizations heavily invested in the Second District race. The Republican Party spent nearly $500,000 on media buys in the district and the Democratic Party a relatively small fraction of that amount. However, this research has not been able to sort out how much of that money was for the House race (both parties spent heavily in the U.S. Senate race, and some of the state party money may have been directed at a competitive state senate election in the district). The one expenditure that is clearly identified with the House campaign was the $63,000 that the NRCC spent on Musser in coordinated spending. Strategically, the most important role played by the parties is when they stepped in to keep both campaigns on the air when they ran out of money after the primary (they ran two weeks of ads for Musser and for Baldwin on all four network stations).

The party ads were typical issue advocacy ads that hammered the opponents record. The NRCC ads criticized Baldwin's vote against W2, the Wisconsin welfare reform program, and her votes to raise sales and property taxes as a Dane County supervisor. A national Republican Party insider said, "Advocacy ads are a call to action. Contrast ads can't do that. One of the primary jobs of an ad is to make people aware of a candidate's record. We need to talk about the things that the candidates are unwilling to talk about themselves. It is incumbent upon organizations to have a free and open debate. To do that, you need to know what the candidate's record is."

The only controversy in the campaign surrounding a party ad came when WMTV, the NBC affiliate in Madison, refused to run a state party ad that suggested that Musser was too friendly with the insurance industry. In the ad, a hand is seen removing wads of $100 bills from a briefcase that is stuffed with money. Dave Trabert, the general manager of WMTV, said that they decided not to run the ad because it left the impression that Musser was accepting large cash contributions, which is illegal under federal law.[28] The party changed the opening scene of the ad to show a man walking down a marble hallway in an expensive pair of shoes, as the voiceover explains that Musser has taken contributions from the industry that she used to regulate.

Another important outside group, Americans for Limited Terms, spent $200,000 against Baldwin. They spent most of the money on direct mail (I received three pieces of mail from the group in the weeks leading up to the election). One of the direct mail pieces had the words in huge type "Abuse . . . Corruption . . . Neglect" on the outside; the glossy mailer unfolds to reveal a picture of the U.S. Capitol with the words scrolling down the page, "Million dollar pensions, midnight pay raises, secret deals, partisan bickering, gridlock, hidden tax hikes." Then across the top of the inside, "We deserve better. We can have better" and went on to say:

> Josephine Musser has agreed to limit her own terms. She has taken a stand in favor of real reform in Washington, D.C. . . . Tammy Baldwin still refuses to limit herself. She refuses to sign the U.S. Term Limits Declaration [which would limit candidates to three terms]. . . Please contact Tammy Baldwin and demand that she sign the U.S. Term Limits Declaration to limit her own terms. Demand that she side with the People of Wisconsin and not the Washington, D.C., elite. And please thank Josephine Musser for her stand.

The term limits group also ran more than $60,000 worth of thirty-second spots in the last week of the campaign, including a spot during a Green Bay Packers' football game, which is the most expensive slot that can be purchased in the Madison media market ($12,000 for a thirty-second ad; in contrast, a spot during the local 6 o'clock news was $300). Incidentally, the other candidate in Wisconsin who was targeted by the term limits group, Paul Ryan, the Republican running in the First District, also won handily over Lydia Spottswood. Two races do not prove anything, but it does seem that the term limits movement has lost its power to sway voters.

There were several other groups that did some direct mail and television ads, such as Wisconsin Citizen's Action and the Sierra Club, which invested in several districtwide direct mail pieces. However, their participation was on a relatively small scale.

Conclusion and Broader Lessons

David Welch summed up his frustration with the Musser campaign when he said, "We could have won this race. We lost it more than Baldwin won it, but I give them credit for running a great campaign." While this race could not be characterized as an upset, given its underlying Democratic leanings, it is clearly an example of how campaign organization, grassroots effort, and a good campaign theme and message can make the difference in a campaign.

But turnout was the key. Pundits typically argue that turnout is crucial in midterm elections, and in this case the pundits were right. The author made a prediction the day before the election that if turnout was greater than 45 percent Baldwin would win, if it was less than 40 percent, Musser would win, and if it was between 40 and 45 percent it would be a toss-up. The 48 percent turnout far exceeded expectations and certainly contributed to Baldwin's victory.[29] But the gross turnout was not as important as the differential turnout in parts of the district. More than half of Madison voters turned out (52.9 percent), compared with 49.6 percent of the suburban voters, and only 43.9 percent of the rural voters. Given the relative strengths of the candidates in the city and rural areas, it is easy to see why turnout was so critical. Baldwin carried 65.9 percent of the Madison vote, 48.2 percent of the suburban vote, and only 43.5 percent of the rural vote. If one recalls Musser's original electoral strategy, these numbers were not far from the Musser campaign's goals. They fell less than 1 percent short of the Madison goal, 3.2 percent short of the suburban goal, and 3.5 percent short of the rural goal. Thus, turnout was key, but Baldwin also ran somewhat stronger in the suburban and rural areas than projected. She actually carried a few of the suburbs, such as Middleton (Feingold's coattails helped here; it is his home town), Monona, and Oregon (which she carried by two votes). She even won a few rural towns, such as Stoughton, Mount Horeb, Black Earth, and Mazomanie (table 7-3).

One Republican Party insider pointed out that Musser was hurt by a confluence of five elections that turned out Democratic voters in Madison: Feingold (U.S. Senate), Joe Erpenbach (state senate), Ed Garvey (governor), James Doyle (attorney general), and Baldwin. The first two were especially important because they were running against Republicans whom Democrats were especially wary of (Mark Neumann and Nancy Mistele). Musser's problem was that her campaign did not anticipate the Democratic field effort and do anything to counter it.

There are several broader lessons from this campaign for campaign conduct and strategies. First, conventional wisdom holds that in competitive districts such as the Second Congressional District in Wisconsin, moderate candidates are better positioned than either liberals or conser-

Table 7-3. *Vote Totals and Turnout, Second District General Election*

Region	*Voting age population*	*Percent turnout*	*Baldwin vote*	*Musser vote*
Madison	163,952	52.9	57,158 (65.9%)	29,597 (34.1%)
Suburbs	69,992	49.6	16,726 (48.2%)	17,989 (51.8%)
Rural (non-Madison, suburb)	224,090	43.9	42,880 (43.5%)	55,609 (56.5%)
Total	458,034	48	116,764 (53.1%)	103,201 (46.9%)

Note: See note 1 for a description of the towns included in the Madison, suburban, and rural categories. The voting age populations were supplied by the Dane County clerk and the state of Wisconsin Department of Administration, Demographic Service Center. The voting age population is based on the January 1, 1998, Census estimate of persons over eighteen years old. This proportion (77.03%) was then applied to the total population for each of the geographic subregions (Madison, suburbs, and rural). This method assumes a constant proportion across the three regions and therefore probably understates the turnout in the suburbs and Madison and overstates the turnout in the rural areas (the proportion of residents under eighteen is higher in Madison and the suburbs than in the rural areas, thus the voting age population in the city and suburbs is slightly overstated (which would underestimate the turnout).

vatives. This should have been especially true in 1998, which has been dubbed "the year of the moderate." Anthony Downs's famous spatial model asserts that candidates in a two-way race should converge to the median voter in the district.[30] This bit of common wisdom was clearly rejected in the Second District. Musser had the perfect mix of social liberalism and fiscal conservatism in the tradition of the popular incumbent, Klug. She was closer to the median voter than Baldwin, who was probably the most liberal candidate in the nation running in a competitive district; yet Baldwin won.

The second bit of wisdom comes from Baldwin: don't watch TV if you are running for office. Baldwin said that she knew at the start of the campaign that there were going to be negative ads, and that she would be able to maintain a better frame of mind if she did not see them. Nichols thought this was an important decision, "You could just see in the debates how personally Jo took the ads, whereas they didn't bother Tammy. They didn't bother her because she hadn't seen them! When Jo complained about the ads during debates, the audience saw this as a continuation of the tit-for-tat battle that they were sick of, while Tammy was able to stay emotionally above the fray. If I were a political consultant, I would put this one in the playbook."

Third, it is essential to have clear lines of authority and communication among the candidate, campaign consultants, and campaign manager. The breakdown in the Musser campaign and the smoothly running

Baldwin campaign provide vivid testimony on this point. The differences between the two cannot be dismissed because a winning campaign has an easier time maintaining harmony than a losing campaign. Throughout the entire campaign, internal polls in Musser's campaign showed this race to be a toss-up.

Fourth, while it is difficult to generalize from two candidates, the strategies, tactics, and major decisions of this campaign were not dominated by the consultants. In Musser's campaign, the candidate made most of the key decisions, but the lack of an organizational hierarchy harmed the effectiveness of the campaign. Indeed, if Musser had listened to Welch's advice to develop a campaign theme rooted in economic issues and taxes, rather than bringing in health care, it is possible that Musser could have won. Musser also resisted going negative for longer than her consultants counseled. This decision too may have cost her the elections (while such counterfactuals are impossible to prove, many Republican insiders held this view, including Musser). Firing Welch in the last weeks of the campaign is conclusive evidence that this campaign was not dominated by the consultant.

Baldwin's campaign is a good example of successful collective decisionmaking. The candidate, the campaign manager, and the media, polling, and field consultants engaged in a consensual decisionmaking process that produced a coherent campaign strategy. While Baldwin was at the center of the process and exercised ultimate veto power, the consultants, especially Will Robinson, played an important role in shaping the campaign's media strategy. Baldwin balked at running the toughest ad of the campaign but ended up listening to her consultant. The ability to work through differences, listen to a variety of positions, and treat staffers and volunteers with respect contributed to the success of Baldwin's campaign. The skills that it takes to keep a campaign humming along smoothly are not unlike those needed to make any personal relationship work. Having an active, involved candidate like Baldwin, paired with a consultant like Robinson who personally cares about his clients and gives them personal attention, is a winning combination.

Finally, and most important, this campaign demonstrates the hazards of ignoring grassroots organization and GOTV efforts. In an era in which campaigns are increasingly waged on the airwaves, it is refreshing to note that an old-fashioned focus on "people power" can make a difference. This does not imply that it is possible to return to the William Proxmire era of politics.[31] However, the lesson of the 1998 midterms may be that the pendulum had swung too far in the direction of television-based campaigns, and it is time to put more effort into field organization and getting people to the polls. Musser made precisely this point in assessing why she lost, "We forgot about the fundamentals. We have to get away from the formula-based, media campaigns and back to the grassroots." Perhaps a national trend in this direction could help arrest the slide in voter turnout and simultaneously restore confidence in our democratic process.

Notes

1. This argument concerns the relative positions of the rural, urban, and suburban areas. In absolute terms, the population in all three areas has grown since 1970, but the suburban areas have grown the fastest and the rural areas the slowest.

2. A fourth Democrat, Patrick O'Brien, was a relatively late entrant and was not a serious candidate. He spent only $300 on the election and "neither solicited nor accepted campaign contributions." Melanie Conklin, "Pick One," *Isthmus*, August 28, 1998, p.12.

3. Jeff Mayers, "Democratic Campaign Strikes Sour Note with Phelps Mailing," *Wisconsin State Journal*, September 5, 1998, p. 3B; and John Nichols, "Unity Pledge Doesn't Stop Dem Bickering," *Capital Times*, September 8, 1998, p. 8A.

4. Nichols, "Unity Pledge."

5. Voters in Wisconsin vote in an open primary, which means that they can vote in either the Democratic or Republican primary but not for candidates in both parties (as is true for Washington's "blanket primary"). For example, in Washington a voter could vote for a Republican candidate for the Senate and a Democratic candidate for the House. In Wisconsin the voter must vote for all Democratic candidates or all Republican candidates. In a closed primary state, only registered voters in a given party may vote in that primary.

6. All quotations that do not include a reference are from personal interviews.

7. Jeff Mayers, "Quit Whining and Get to Work, Klug Tells GOP," *Wisconsin State Journal*, May 3, 1998, p. 2E.

8. The author's personal experience is illustrative. Before Greer entered, the author had only received a few phone calls from television, radio, and print reporters asking about the House race. After Greer was in, the author was getting two to three phone calls a day.

9. Jeff Mayers, "Two GOP Hopefuls Scoff at Signing Tolerance Pledge," *Wisconsin State Journal,* July 16, 1998, p. 3.

10. All turnout statistics presented in this chapter are the percentage of all registered voters who actually voted.

11. Paul Alongi, "Musser Gets Unity, Not Unanimity; All but Greer Rally for Her," *Capital Times*, September 21, 1998, p. 2A.

12. Aaron Nathans, "Dems Fall in Behind Baldwin; Say Clinton Won't Be Factor," *Wisconsin State Journal*, September 11, 1998, p. 6A.

13. Chris Murphy, "Abortion Stand Assailed; GOP Pledges Support Amid Call for Fund Cut," *Capital Times*, October 16, 1998, p. 1A.

14. Murphy, "Abortion Stand Assailed."

15. Jeff Mayers, "29 Years Later, He Calls Musser Mom," *Wisconsin State Journal*, October 20, 1998, p. 1A.

16. Conklin, "Pick One," p. 11.

17. The one party insider who said it did not have much of an impact said, "There are lots of difficult people in politics. The problems in the campaign were much more systemic than any personality characteristics."

18. This assessment is based on many interviews with people who had contact with the campaign. The author did not personally observe any of these incidents. Indeed, the author's contacts with Jo Musser were extremely pleasant. Apparently, it was only in the heat of campaign battles that her temper became a problem.

19. Based on the distribution of population in these three areas, this formula would produce a winning margin of just over 50 percent ($.6 \times .491 + .35 \times .359 + .55 \times .153 = .5044$).

20. Jeff Mayers, "Musser Tactics Widely Used," *Wisconsin State Journal*, October 18, 1998, p. 5B.

21. One aspect of the Klug ad drew some negative press. In the ad, Klug points out that Baldwin opposes the balanced budget amendment. However, Musser also opposed the balanced budget amendment. Chris Murphy, "Musser Ad Rips Baldwin for Mutual Stance," *Capital Times*, October 27, 1998, p. 6A.

22. Thomas P. O'Neill, *Man of the House: The Life and Political Memoirs of Speaker Tip O'Neill* (with William Novak) (Random House, 1987), p. 26.

23. John P. Martin, "Nationwide, Candidates Spin the Web," *Washingtonpost.com*, August 3, 1998.

24. John Lepinski, "Internet Powerful Tool for Candidates, Voters," *Wisconsin State Journal*, November 1, 1998, p. 2I.

25. Steven R. Weisman, "A Democratic 'Ground War' Slips by the Radar," *New York Times,* November 11, 1998, p. A24.

26. Ibid.

27. Amy Rinard, "Dane County Voters Made the Difference: Get-Out-the-Vote Efforts Helped Push Democrats to Victory in Key Races," *Milwaukee Journal Sentinel,* November 5, 1998, p. A1.

28. Rinard, "Dane County Voters Made the Difference"; and Chris Murphy, "TV Station Reject Dems' Attack Ad on Musser," *Capital Times,* October 21, 1998, p. 2A.

29. Baldwin still would have won the election if districtwide turnout would have been 43.9 percent, as it was in the rural areas. However, the victory margin would have shrunk to 9,054 votes.

30. Anthony Downs, *An Economic Theory of Democracy* (Harper and Row, 1957), pp. 117–18.

31. The only money the popular Wisconsin senator ever spent to get reelected was to pay for the filing fee; clearly Proxmire was a throwback to an earlier time—he left office in 1989.

APPENDIX

Case Study Framework and Methodology

JAMES A. THURBER

BEFORE CONDUCTING FIELDWORK, the researchers in this volume met several times to formulate a common framework for investigating the congressional races. Together we identified the central research questions, primary units of analysis, case selection criteria, and variables to be collected. Establishing the same key components for each of the respective studies ensured that fruitful comparisons could be made between and across analytic objects in each case. However, we chose not to develop a "checklist" so restrictive that investigators could not pursue other, more inductive, types of inquiry.

We also agreed that multiple measures of data collection would bolster the conclusions of each case and allow us to confidently answer any concerns about validity of observation.[1] Investigators differed in the relative emphasis they placed on each form of data collection, but each utilized participant observation, in-depth interviews with candidates, staff, and consultants, and content analysis of primary source documents from the campaigns. Outside materials, especially media coverage of the campaign, were also reviewed. In several cases the investigators had complete access to campaign surveys, campaign budgets, and candidate time analyses. The combination of all these forms of data collection allowed for a unique view of congressional campaigns.

During the course of the 1998 election we stayed in close contact. This did two things. First, it ensured that each investigator remained focused on the main topics of inquiry we initially set forth. Second, as field researchers, contact with other political scientists helped us resist any temptation to get so involved in the excitement of a campaign that we lost analytic focus, or critical distance, from the campaign.[2] We also remained in close contact while writing the case studies.

Central Research Question of the Case Studies

The primary purpose of the study was to understand the role of political consultants in competitive U.S. House election campaigns. As a group we agreed that consultants are key actors in modern campaigns but that there had been little empirical inquiry, especially qualitative fieldwork, examining their role in the electoral process and relationship with candidates. These observations drove us to a central research question: what is the impact of political consultants on congressional candidates and their election campaigns (and ultimately on our governing institutions)? To answer this question, we focused on the behavior of congressional candidates and political consultants—especially on their interactions and perceptions of one another. Consultants' role in decisionmaking during the campaign, and their overall influence in the election campaign, also received attention. These considerations served as our primary units of analysis.

Case Study Selection Criteria

Individually, each piece in this volume is a single, revelatory, case study. Research designs of this sort are favored when "an investigator has the opportunity to analyze a phenomenon previously inaccessible to scientific investigation."[3] Given our interest in the relationship between consultants and candidates, and the dearth of fieldwork examining this relationship, the revelatory case study design was most appropriate.

With the research design in place, we next considered case study selection issues. Because competitive races are most likely to have large campaign staffs, and hire consultants with more frequency, we chose to only select competitive races.[4] This decision ensured that the consultants would be present in the race and made it more likely their work would influence the electoral outcome. To ensure that we had a fairly representative mix of competitive House races the following criteria for case study selection were also used:

—Regional variation (California, Washington, Wisconsin, Kansas, Connecticut, and Georgia);

—A sample of an open seat, quality challenger, quality incumbent;

—Balance among races that were toss-ups and leaning Democratic and leaning Republican;

—Sample of at least one complex (multiple) and simple media markets (one market);

—Balance among urban, suburban, and rural districts; and

—Primary and nonprimary states:

Mixed system: Connecticut, Wisconsin, and Georgia
Caucus system: Kansas
Primary: California and Washington.

Data Collection

Methods of data collection included content analysis, archival work, participant observation, elite interviews, and statistical analysis. Using these methods, we examined several key analytic considerations hypothesized to influence consultants' role in political campaigns. By including the same variables in each case, readers gain an understanding of the context that each campaign operated in. Further, because similar data were collected across cases, the volume as a whole allows readers to make analytic conclusions about consultants by systematically comparing across individual cases.

Standard background characteristics (political experiences, education, occupation) were taken into account for all of the candidates, as was a short history of the opposition (if any) in the primary and general election. Indicators of the legal, political, economic, and social context of each district and campaign setting were also included. Data from Washington's Third Congressional District provide an example:

Population: 540,745

Race: white (95 percent), black (1 percent), other (4 percent), Hispanic (3 percent)

Age: 18 and over (73 percent), 62 and over (15 percent), median age, 34.

Normal turnout presidential and off-year elections

Competitiveness of general elections:

1996: Linda Smith (R) (50 percent), 123,117; Brian Baird (D) (50 percent), 122,230

1994: Linda Smith (R) (52 percent); Jolene Unsoeld (D) (45 percent); Caitlin Davis Carlson (Independent) (3 percent)

Third District vote for president:
1996: D: 49 percent, R: 38 percent, I: 10 percent
1994: D: 42 percent, R: 33 percent, I: 25 percent

Investigators also reviewed relevant past and present Federal Election Campaign finance data. Again, an example from Washington's Third Congressional District is illustrative:

	Receipts	*Receipts from PACs*	*Expenditures*
1996			
Smith	$1,222,302	$ 26,375 (2 percent)	$1,216,368
Baird	719,798	246,589 (34 percent)	718,322
1994			
Smith	522,896	115,766 (22 percent)	515,316
Unsoeld	973,401	424,827 (44 percent)	987,242

When data were available from reliable sources, the investigators also collected information about the following: campaign receipts (when and how much), source of receipts (PACs, individuals, party organization), campaign funds from outside the district versus inside the district, the campaign budget, how the budget was actually spent, consultant costs, media expenditures, field and grassroots spending, cost of polling, and opposition research.

Campaign Organization and Structure

Each investigator described the formal and informal organizational structure of the campaign throughout the entire campaign cycle. We wanted to know what the power structure looked like in the campaign organization and the relationship among candidates, consultants, campaign managers, volunteers, and political party officials. Reasons for stability and change in the campaign structure were also of interest. Interviews with the candidates, staff, consultants, volunteers, party leaders, and interest group representatives were done in almost all of the cases to support this portion of the case studies.

Strategy, Theme, and Message of the Campaign

Political professionals and students of politics both report that the electoral fate of a campaign is determined, to a large degree, by its ability to develop, and maintain, a strategy, theme, and message that resonates with voters.[5] Given the importance of these considerations, investigators focused on the strategy, theme, and message of the campaigns and described the following factors: the primary themes and issues (national and local) in the campaign and the major plans and tactics used to convey theme. The role of political consultants in developing and projecting these considerations was of particular interest.

Campaign Schedule

To obtain an unobtrusive measure of campaign priorities, each investigator obtained a detailed schedule of the candidate's time from the campaign staff. Beyond the analysis of campaign priorities, we also asked: who does the candidate's scheduling? What was the role of the candidate and staff in scheduling? What was the amount of time spent campaigning, fund-raising, and other activities? Where was the candidate scheduled and with whom?

Campaign Manager

Following our planning meetings, each case study investigator agreed to consider the role of the campaign manager and to answer the following questions about these important actors: what is the experience and background of the campaign manager and what was her or his authority, responsibility, and influence? How was she or he selected? What was the relationship between the campaign manager, the consultants, and the candidate? What were the background characteristics of the campaign manager?

Political Consultants

The primary question we wanted to consider in each of the case studies was the role of campaign consultants. To help address this issue, most investigators administered a standard consultant questionnaire used in a study of campaign consultants.[6] The questionnaire asked the following:

—Who are they (background characteristics)? Professionals versus amateurs?

—Size of firm? Local or national?

—Criteria for selecting consultants?

—What is their activity in the campaign?

—How much do they cost?

—Level of use in the campaign?

—What are their attitudes (see baseline attitudinal data from survey) over the course of the election campaign?

—When do they enter into the campaign and what do they do?

—How influential are the consultants in the campaign?

—How do they resolve disputes and "ethical dilemmas" in the campaign?

—What is the relationship between the candidate and the consultants?

Pollsters, Opposition Research, and Field Operation

The cases attempted to describe who the pollsters were and what their role was in the campaign. Given concern that polls, not in-depth issue considerations, dictate candidate behavior, we considered the impact that survey data had on each campaign's strategy, theme, message, and tactics. The way candidates responded to survey results was also of interest.

The case studies also addressed the following questions about opposition research: what was the role of opposition research, who did it, and what was its influence on the campaign? The impact of candidate field organizations was also addressed—especially the impact of party organization and professional get-out-the-vote operations.

Media Staff and Paid Campaign Advertising

Previous research indicated that media consultants are integral in electoral campaigns.[7] Because of this relationship, each investigator focused on the role of the media staff and campaign advertising by focusing on the following questions:

—Who were the media staff/consultants?

—What was the media strategy, theme and message?

—Did they go "negative" in television, radio, or pamphlets?

—How much money and time were spent on the media campaign?

—What was the authority of the media professionals?

—How much time and space was purchased in the media?

—What was the impact of the direct mail, collateral media such as "door hangers," pamphlets, videos, buttons, posters, and bumper stickers in the campaign?

Earned (Free) Media Coverage of the Campaign

Rarely does a political campaign succeed without garnering media attention. Because of this, each author analyzed the television, radio, and print media coverage of the campaigns. Investigators also recorded ad watch activities in the electronic and print media. Questions about the role of candidate debates were asked such as, were debates and candidate forums held? How did the campaign prepare for these events? Who was involved in the preparation of the candidates for the debates? All investigators collected an extensive file of national and local news articles about the campaign for their analysis.

External Factors

Major external factors influencing the candidate organization were considered. They included party involvement in the campaign (local, state, and national); involvement by interest groups in the campaign; visits by outside political leaders to the district (such as the president and party leaders); issue advocacy advertising; expenditure of soft money by national and local party organizations; volunteer activities by outside groups (such as the AFL-CIO, religious groups, the National Rifle Organization); and outside contributions to the campaign (information, money, people).

Impact of the Campaign

In the final section, investigators used the data collected, and their general impressions from spending time with the respective campaigns, to assess the impact of the campaign consultants, candidates, campaign staff, political parties, and campaign finance on the citizens of each district. We also considered the normative implications of each campaign, and especially the political consultants, on candidates' ability to govern and the vitality of representative democracy.

Notes

1. Gary King, Robert Keohane, and Sidney Verba, *Designing Social Inquiry: Scientific Research in Qualitative Research* (Princeton University Press, 1994).

2. Richard Fenno, *House Members in Their Districts* (Scott Foresman, 1978); Danny Jorgensen, *Participant Observation: A Methodology for Human Studies* (Sage Publications, 1989); and Robert Yin, *Case Study Research: Design and Methods* (Sage Publications, 1994).

3. Yin, *Case Study Research*, p. 40.

4. Paul Hernsson, *Congressional Elections: Campaigning at Home and in Washington* (CQ Press, 2000); and Stephen K. Medvic, "Professionalization in

Congressional Campaigns," in James Thurber and Candice J. Nelson, eds., *Campaign Warriors: Political Consultants in Elections* (Brookings, 2000), pp. 91–109.

5. James Thurber and Candice J. Nelson, eds., *Campaigns and Elections American Style* (Westview Press, 1995).

6. See the consultant questionnaire in Thurber and Nelson, *Campaign Warriors*, pp. 175–201.

7. Robert Friedenberg, *Communication Consultants in Political Campaigns: Ballot Box Warriors* (Praeger Press, 1997).

Contributors

Charles S. Bullock III is Richard B. Russell Professor of Political Science at the University of Georgia.

David T. Canon is professor of political science at the University of Wisconsin, Madison.

Diana Evans is professor of political science at Trinity College.

Jeff Gill is assistant professor of political science at the University of Florida.

Carolyn Long is assistant professor in the Department of Political Science at Washington State University and director of the master's program in public affairs.

Burdett A. Loomis is professor of political science at the University of Kansas.

James A. Thurber is professor and director of the Center for Congressional and Presidential Studies at American University.

Index